MELANIE KLEIN

MELANIE KLEIN

Her Work in Context

Meira Likierman

CONTINUUM
London and New York

CONTINUUM
The Tower Building, 11 York Road, London SE1 7NX
370 Lexington Avenue, New York, NY 10017-6503

First published 2001

British Library Cataloguing-in-Publication Data
A catalogue record for this book is available from the British Library.

ISBN 0-8264-5194-2 (Hardback)

Typeset by BookEns Ltd, Royston, Herts.
Printed and bound in Great Britain

Contents

To Andrew

CHAPTER 1

'Her writing gave me a shock' – Introduction

I n the early autumn of 1926 Melanie Klein left her home in Berlin for good and moved to live in England. She was 44 years old, yet her most creative years lay ahead. Moreover, the vision that was to emerge from her work and writing in England was to prove impressive in its theoretical scope and originality, and to contribute a unique dimension to our thinking on the human condition. A retrospective assessment of Klein's overall achievement marks it out as substantial by any standard. She founded a new theoretical school, pioneered a psychoanalytic treatment for children, influenced her most creative British colleagues and inspired the first psychoanalytic work with individuals suffering from psychotic and borderline conditions.

Beyond this distinguished list of achievements, there is a more profound if less blatant aspect of Klein's influence; although her thinking is not widely familiar it has left a lasting mark on twentieth-century psychoanalysis and on our broader cultural canvas. Even those unfamiliar with Klein's contribution now think in terms of object relations when approaching subjects such as childhood, psychological development or adult mental health. Much of what is taken for granted in relation to these was anticipated by Klein, including, for example, the beliefs that infants are sensitive to their human environment, especially the maternal emotional attitude which they encounter, and that a loving, qualitative parental attention during infancy and early childhood provides a crucial foundation for adult mental health. Such beliefs may seem like commonplaces rather than profound discoveries, but they were not, in fact, fully articulated or even properly considered in relation to early infancy before Melanie Klein published her findings. Klein was the founder of an object-relations theory of the mind and the first to provide a fully interpersonal model of early psychical life.

This is not to suggest that theories on the nature of childhood did not exist before Klein, since one version of it or another came into being in most adult societies throughout history. Not surprisingly, strands of earlier thinking survived into twentieth-century psychoanalysis and also found their way into Klein's work. For example, the great significance attributed by her to the state of childhood was anticipated by some of the writers, philosophers and poets who represented the flowering of romanticism in Europe. Klein's thinking is at one with the romantic emphasis on, rather than idealization of childhood, but even the latter would have been regarded by her as a great advance on earlier thinking. Like the romantics Klein would have objected to former depictions of the child as, at worst, an agent of original sin, and, at best, a deficient version of the adult – a kind of inferior being with no distinct existential locus in the life cycle. However, from the Kleinian perspective the enthusiasts of romanticism erred in the opposite direction, idealizing childhood and turning it into a domain of innocence and perfection which was equally difficult for the real child to inhabit.

Klein, who produced her major work between 1921 and 1957, was able to build on the foundation laid by Freud, and dispel the myth of innocence which shrouded the raw realities of childhood and perpetuated an illusion that children are exempt from instinctual turmoil and suffering. Klein resolutely insisted on the opposite: to be immature is to be acutely at the mercy of impulsive fluctuations which can swamp the mind with anxieties, rages and passions. Children are therefore emotionally dependent on adults for the regulation of their states, and not, as previously believed, dependent in a purely material and educational sense.

By rejecting the notion of childhood innocence, Klein did not, as might be feared, jeopardize the position of the child in adult thinking. On the contrary, her suggestions prised open a genuine space in social awareness, enabling an increasing recognition of the child's vulnerable predicament. This awareness was further strengthened by Klein's elaboration of the infant's mental development in the context of its human milieu. She was ultimately able to mark out the fundamental needs of the growing individual in a way that pinpointed the onerous obligation of society towards its young.

Yet this was not all that Klein offered. While she did begin her professional development with a focus on early mental life, her explorations of this terrain pointed to far-reaching implications almost immediately. Her initial encounters with child patients drew her awareness to a powerful, primitive phantasy life which underpinned their mental activity, shaping their sense of self, their relation to others and their overall ability to tolerate life, process its impact and make sense of the world. While Klein explored these processes in children, she began to suspect that she had chanced on some of the archaic underpinnings of adult mental functioning.

Her further research into the area of primitive psychical activity was of an extraordinarily intuitive depth and range. She was ultimately able to offer a vision of human experience which accounted for a range of mental states, from normality and health all the way to the severe mental illnesses of schizophrenia and manic-depressive psychosis. As part of this process Klein addressed the common human miseries of depression, envy, jealousy, obsessional behaviour, anxiety, suspiciousness, loneliness and other emotions which crucially affect the fluctuations of our everyday existence. Thus as well as articulating the power of human emotionality, Klein's theory has illuminated in a unique way the many poignant personal scenarios hidden in our daily moods.

With such an ambitious agenda, it is not altogether surprising that instead of being received with enthusiasm, or at the very least interest, Klein's work provoked reservations and hostility from the psychoanalytic establishment. Her fraught career was repeatedly shaken by confrontational struggles, which, at one point, nearly cost her the professional membership on which her psychoanalytic practice depended.

The fact that groundbreaking work causes controversy is not altogether remarkable. Original thinking tends to thrive in a climate of intellectual exchange and interaction, and the history of ideas owes much to passionate debates which helped to shape individual thinking. In the case of Melanie Klein, it is none the less necessary to wonder at the intense and extreme reactions typically provoked by her thinking, right from her early days in Berlin. While undoubtedly some critiques of her work have been thoughtful and appropriate, it must also be noted that her work can stir intensely personal responses tinged with intolerance and hostility.

Such reactions can partly be traced to difficulties which were of Klein's own making, and this included the poor presentation of her ideas and what it appeared to indicate about her mode of approach to constructing a theory of the mind. This approach was closely bound up with a personality which was teeming with enthusiasm, intuitions and insights, but which was correspondingly impatient to communicate findings and careless in formulating and expressing them. Klein made the error of phrasing some of her initial insights as bold convictions, and this was compounded when ample substantiation failed to follow.

However, it is necessary to bear in mind that the task with which she was confronted when she first decided to explore the mental life of children was far from simple. The psychoanalytic model available to Klein, though revolutionary in her terms, was none the less itself at a rudimentary stage, as were indeed other social sciences and academic disciplines which might have facilitated her efforts. The only 'laboratory' conditions to which Klein could resort had to be devised by her as well as somehow being fitted into the clinical imperatives of her working day. Her solution to these difficulties was to use her clinical work as an ongoing research project, as was already the norm with psychoanalysts working with adult patients.

Klein had already begun to treat several children psychoanalytically when she started to make use of the session framework as a psychoanalytic research process. A mere handful of psychoanalytic sessions with children had been attempted before her by other practitioners, but these did not seem sufficiently rigorous to Klein. Freud and his adherent Ferenczi had each published single accounts of little boys which had been provided indirectly by parents and observers. More direct work was undertaken by Hermine von Hug-Hellmuth, a psychoanalyst senior to Klein who worked with a few children and published some of her results in 1920. The work was both casual and tentative, consisting of Hug-Hellmuth's attempt to draw randomly on psychoanalytic knowledge during ordinary interactions with children. While such work aspired to curative results, it shied away from the kind of formal rigour that would set it apart as a methodology distinctly adapted to children.

Klein aspired to far greater rigour and to conditions which would isolate as much as possible her object of study. Her radical solution to this was to adopt the structure of the adult psychoanalytic session in her work with children. This culminated in a session framework which focused on individual, confidential work from which parents were kept away, and in which ordinary educative judgements were suspended. At the same time, the children were offered a range of play materials without the usual exhortations, suggestions or guidance that they normally expect from adults. This framework partly recreated the natural conditions of playing alone. Klein encouraged the revelations that might emerge from this freedom by remaining a neutral, nonjudgemental presence who was prepared to discuss normally forbidden subjects in plain nursery language.

In retrospect it became clear that these rudimentary measures yielded impressive results. The children with whom Klein worked grasped the significance of the conditions offered to them and revealed to her a great deal of their inner selves. Klein was able to record their communications and build her theories on this basis. The most valuable aspect of her child patients' communications during this initial period was undoubtedly their strikingly uninhibited content, which gave Klein crucial insights into the most archaic phantasies and processes in the human mind.

These first Kleinian insights, like many of the subsequent ones were, and remain, highly idiosyncratic. To Klein's supporters they appeared to capture brilliantly the unusual idiom of early psychical life. To her critics they confirmed her anarchic reasoning process. And since Klein did not undertake quantitative research to substantiate her beliefs, they remained for the duration of her life and beyond an enigma which could arouse deep fascination or deep suspicion.

When all these factors are taken into account it is not surprising that they created for Klein's work a poor reputation in the growing psychoanalytic community. Now, as in her lifetime, this reputation typically precedes a knowledge of her work. Her critics feel that she is speculative, unrealistic in the degree of mental sophistication that she attributes to infants, and that her vision is inappropriately negative and pessimistic about human nature. Other objections hinge on areas which her theory has not addressed well. While Klein explored pre-verbal experience, she showed little interest in, and even awareness of, the relation between language and the unconscious, and so left a substantial gap in her account of human development. There have been those who have wholly rejected Klein's basic premises, and therefore the entire theoretical edifice that is built on them. Her supporters point to the typically personal, subjective responses to Klein's work as evidence that her ideas tap into deep, nameless dreads and rages in the human heart. They point out that if Klein was blunt, she also possessed great intellectual courage, and like other original thinkers before her, was rejected partly for being the bearer of an unwelcome message. Her theory, like many before it, appears to present an affront to the civilized self and an assault on its cherished image as an integrated, autonomous and civilized entity.

Klein's work did not achieve rapid or easy popularity. It remained mostly ignored for the larger part of the twentieth century, and only a small number of Kleinian psychoanalysts continued to develop its basic concepts through clinical application. Their papers, written late in Melanie Klein's life and after her death, formed the indirect route through which her thinking began to gain a wider circulation.[1] This happened in a rather piecemeal fashion at first, with single concepts, such as 'projective identification' finding their way into a more general professional vocabulary. Ironically though, these concepts have tended to figure disproportionately in international professional recognition in relation to the position which they occupy in Klein's *oeuvre*. While she herself dedicated relatively little space to projective identification, there are countless clinical papers devoted to exploring its clinical ramifications.

In one sense this may seem positive, in that it does underscore the value which became apparent when the concept came into clinical use; projective identification turned out to be highly applicable, as well as filling a crucial gap in theoretical understanding. However, from another point of view the emphasis on it has kept attention focused away from large areas of Klein's thinking to which she herself devoted ample space.

Other issues are raised by this. The fact that Klein's thinking has tended to reach a broader readership via other parties means that those of her concepts which have become familiar are known mostly through secondary sources; this might well exacerbate the neglect of the not easily approachable primary texts. A selective use of individual concepts, especially as circulated by others through clinical papers, may be felt to provide an adequate substitute for bothering with Klein's vision in its entirety. Yet this is likely to perpetuate a vicious cycle of prejudice which becomes entrenched by default; when texts are only partly known, their author may remain only partly trusted. To this day, Kleinian theory is likely to engender a response of wholesale acceptance or rejection, as if it should be assessed as being either 'right' or 'wrong', rather than thought of as offering a model with which to approach the endeavour of understanding human experience.

The aim of this book is to address some of these obstacles and facilitate a fresh approach to Klein's texts. However, it is not intended to be a retrospective critique of what she ought to have done, more an elucidation of her theory in its own terms and from her own perspective as manifest in the texts. By offering an exploration of the themes that gradually gain momentum in her early papers, and placing these in the broader context of professional debates which spurred her thinking, it is hoped to show how her ideas come together in her key papers, and the kind of vision that she conjures for us.

Nothing can replace a direct engagement with primary texts, and an awareness of this is particularly important with a thinker such as Klein. Her impatience can still communicate itself via her rushed prose, tempting both writer and reader to hasten the learning process by skipping over demanding areas of text. In any case, these often appear to be expendable in that they do not seem to clarify very much. However, an understandable temptation to avoid difficult Kleinian passages is likely, if anything, to increase frustration. It not only cheats the reader of the ability to develop a more discerning knowledge of the texts, but also conceals conceptual details which, by their singularity, defy an easy transcribing.

Bearing such factors in mind, this book will engage where necessary with textual difficulties, so as to facilitate a growing awareness of the author's distinct voice within a text that does indeed, at times, generate an overwhelming theoretical cacophony. As part of this process, some of the inevitable imperfections, contradictions and ambiguities in Klein's papers will be noted, so that a clearer progress with her main argument is facilitated. But, like all secondary accounts, this book would not have covered all that can be derived from the texts.

An evaluation of Klein's contribution is not possible without attention to some of its areas of lack. It is therefore also worthwhile to take account of ways in which her theory falls short, whether in terms of its own internal logic, or in terms of expectations articulated in the psychoanalytic critiques of her immediate colleagues. The scope of this examination is restricted to those critiques with which Klein herself was immediately concerned. Other, later critiques of Kleinian thinking are outside the scope of this book. Because of the particular context in which Klein's thinking reached maturation, she had, as suggested, no complex awareness of the role of language in mental life. She also made no attempt to offer a comprehensive account of cognitive development. While she did have revolutionary and original ideas on different stages of cognitive awareness and on the primitive roots of cognition, the actual factor that propels mental growth, or what was, in her terms, the drive towards integration, remains a mysterious process and a secret of nature. As far as she was concerned, her insights were intended not to account for this process, but to illuminate how it is either impeded by anxiety and aggression, or aided by the instincts of life, curiosity and love.

Indeed, it is necessary to bear in mind that Klein did not regard herself as offering an all-encompassing theory of the mind, a new epistemology or a wholesale alternative to Freudian metapsychology. She thought of herself as adding some dimensions to the Freudian theory of her day, and as responding to the ideas and challenges of other colleagues who were also trying to do so. All her research was propelled by clinical imperatives, and it is these that delineate the scope of her theoretical reach. Examining some of the reservations which Klein encountered in her immediate circle therefore goes some way to create a sense of the intellectual context in which she was operating, with both its limitations and its unique advantages. It also enables a fuller reflection on how Klein handled direct charges levelled against her, including two of the most persistent ones – that she wrongly attributed too much sophistication to infantile mental processes, and that her view of human nature is inappropriately negative and pessimistic.

A fresh approach to Klein's contribution is timely. Her extraordinary life, personality and ideas can be re-examined with the more dispassionate stance that more than half a century's distance now makes possible. The historical and professional context in which she functioned is an essential part of understanding her developing thinking, especially as this shows her to have been deeply inspired by the collegial group which at times proved to be so troublesome to her. Perhaps the best place to start is with some salient biographical and historical details which clarify essential features of her early professional development, and which take us back to the point of her 1926 departure from Berlin.

MOVING AND SETTLING: BUDAPEST, BERLIN, LONDON

There is no doubt that Klein felt under pressure to leave Berlin in 1926, as a difficult period, both personal and professional preceded her decision to do so. In her personal life a divorce from her husband Arthur was finalized a year earlier in 1925, bringing to a close the only period of her life that was devoted to marriage and a full family life. Out of her three children Klein took with her to England only one – her youngest, Erich, who was twelve years old. Klein's eldest daughter Melitta was already married, while her older, fifteen-year-old son Hans remained with his father.

These personal circumstances were understandably painful, but they are unlikely to have been sufficient in themselves to uproot Klein, were it not for the fact that they compounded a severe blow in her professional life. Klein's psychoanalyst of at least fifteen months' duration, Karl Abraham, died on Christmas Day in 1925. In him Klein lost a mentor who commanded high respect in the Berlin Psychoanalytical Society, having been its founder. At the time of Abraham's death Klein was not securely established in the Berlin Society. She was still a beginner, struggling to put across the significance of her pioneering child psychoanalytic work. For as long as Karl Abraham had been alive her efforts were protected by his good opinion of her ability. Now with Abraham gone, the weakness of Klein's position became apparent. She found her professional progress blocked by Sándor Radó, the new Berlin Society secretary who was also Freud's appointee to the editorship of the two major psychoanalytic journals. Radó turned down the highly innovative papers that Klein was submitting for publication and even became abusive to her at meetings. But his outspoken hostility was only symptomatic of the increasing qualms about her work that existed in the Berlin Society more generally. The aftermath of Abraham's death brought to the surface opposition which gave Klein a foretaste of what she was to encounter repeatedly in her unusually agitated career.

What was it that mobilized such objections? A mix of personal and professional factors can certainly be identified, because, for a start, Klein was an outsider and not originally from Berlin. The Berlin psychoanalysts, who formed a particularly gifted, energetic group of individuals, are unlikely to have regarded as exceptional

Klein's high degree of commitment to the discipline, nor her unusual perseverance with its taxing requirements. But they are also unlikely to have been fully aware of the extent of Klein's personal growth. Her spirited efforts to lift herself out of what had been unpromising circumstances in her adolescence and young womanhood, remained a mostly lonely, unknown struggle.

Klein was born in Vienna in 1882, and moved to Berlin in 1921 after a number of other moves in central Europe and a longer spell of eleven years in Budapest which began in 1910. It was in Budapest that Klein first went into psychoanalysis for her own difficulties and in the process discovered Freud's works. Klein's Hungarian and first psychoanalyst, Sandor Ferenczi, inspired and cultivated her growing interest in the discipline. She wrote her first ever psychoanalytic paper in Budapest in 1919, and on its basis was able to gain admittance to the small Hungarian Psychoanalytic Society. Regrettably this membership could not last for very long. Political tensions in Hungary made the climate inhospitable for members of the Hungarian Psychoanalytic Society, and many were driven to seek professional affiliations further afield. This was the context for Klein's decision to move to Berlin which had a thriving psychoanalytic society.

Klein's passage to Berlin was negotiated with the help of Ferenczi. He recommended her warmly to Karl Abraham, the eminent founder of the Berlin Psychoanalytic Society, who was well liked by Freud. Three years later, after becoming a full member of the Berlin Society, Klein embarked on her second psychoanalysis with Abraham. But in spite of his strong support, Klein's position remained precarious. She was not only newly arrived from a somewhat marginal psychoanalytic outpost, but also seemed like something of an upstart, since she lacked both a university education and a medical training.

There is a painful irony in this, because in her youth, well before discovering psychoanalysis, Klein yearned to study medicine. Sadly, her family circumstances did not leave much room for personal aspirations. Its potential breadwinners, her father and brother, died when Klein was in her teens, and marriage, with its secure prospects, seemed like the most realistic option for a young woman of this period who was left to cope with a widowed mother and impoverished sisters. Klein did get along well with Arthur initially, and was enthusiastic about the prospects of marriage. However, this decision soon took its toll. As generally tended to be the case at the beginning of the last century, marriage ushered in heavy domestic and childrearing responsibilities for a woman, exacerbated in the case of Melanie Klein because Arthur, not yet established professionally, needed to move his family several times in central Europe for the sake of job security and promotion.

For the duration of her early married life Klein struggled with a rootless, socially isolated existence. Her low spirits and isolation were intensified by the burdensome plight of her emotionally needy, widowed mother, and by an increasing realization that her marriage was not developing into the kind of intimate bond which could become emotionally sustaining. These circumstances also meant that Klein's uneducated but powerful intellect remained starved until a move to settle in Budapest brought her into contact with psychoanalysis. There is no information on how Klein came to learn about the possibility of psychoanalysis for herself, but she does appear to have had an immediate response to the experience. It offered not only emotional relief, but also an intellectual satisfaction and enrichment the like of which she had not previously known.

Several years later Klein was in Berlin, breaking new ground with her application of psychoanalytic work to young children and with her original theoretical formulations on this work. The intense enthusiasm stirred in Klein by this initial work left its mark on her early papers which were presented to her Berlin colleagues from shortly after her arrival in 1921. These papers are characterized by intense outpourings, both of the little patients' imaginative life, and of the author's ideas, intuitions and bold assertions. The papers may still come across as simultaneously brilliant and ridiculous. Klein wrote without inhibition, and, for example, thought nothing of resorting to the language of the nursery when spelling out details of infantile mental life. Regrettably, this did not reflect the kind of scientific decorum which the formal Berliners expected. Nor did her style appear to be furthering the cause of a learned society eager for scientific respectability.

However, content and not only style was at issue. To the uneasy group of Berlin psychoanalysts Klein introduced a new kind of human child, drawn from clinical data that covered the age spectrum from the first years of life all the way to adolescence. This clinical work was not only experimental, it also seemed subversive, challenging some of Freud's beliefs on the timing of psychosexual development. It therefore required a cautious, politically tactful introduction to colleagues, something that Klein, whose passionate approach was now fuelled by her intensely exciting discoveries, found difficult. Her depictions of the child's inner life were thus raw and unsparing, as were her interpretations of the savagery of oral, anal and Oedipal impulses which her little patients expressed in their sessions of play.

Taking detailed note of the verbal and symbolic expressions of her patients, Klein chronicled the many states of instinctual turmoil, sadistic cruelty and acute anxiety which she witnessed when allowing the child free expression in a confidential setting. This data opened a door into the child's inner life and led Klein to conclude that young children suffer from extremes – their cruelty is uncontrollably sadistic and the corresponding anxiety generated by it is, in turn, fierce and terror-laden.

The Berlin psychoanalysts were taken aback partly because such accounts were the first of their kind, and the handful of earlier accounts of direct work with small children were docile by comparison. The most famous of the earlier accounts was Freud's paper on 'Little Hans', which focused on a five-year-old boy who developed a horse phobia during his mother's pregnancy and the subsequent birth of his baby sister. Freud explored Hans's Oedipus complex with its attendant hostile and incestuous impulses, but he did not work directly with the child and only dealt with what was reported to him by the father. Freud's paper thus offers an account of a child's mental life as filtered through the composure of a once-removed, adult perspective. As well as this, it does not provide a record of the child's free expressions. All of Hans's communications were observed and noted by his parents at home, and hence in the modifying context of their parental and educative functioning. There is no doubt that the account is revolutionary in its own terms, as well as revealing something of the reality of the sway of irrational childish fears. But the anxiety is reported as observed from without, and does not contain the kind of raw, subjective detail as experienced by the child from within, something that was to become the hallmark of Klein's accounts.

However, it is not simply that Klein's very different accounts disturbed the preconceived notions of her colleagues. Her very manner of constructing a theory seemed to them to play havoc with the method and order which Freud had been striving to impose on the endeavour of building a theory of the mind since he first began to do so, as far back as 1889. True, Freud had also caused controversy with his own thinking, but his theory was respectful of scientific and scholarly conventions. Its starting position was tenable within its historical context and relied on a background of existing scientific research and literature. Everything that was built on this basis was argued closely. Freud's professional colleagues were unlikely, for example, to quarrel with his view of the human infant as starting its mental life in a state of minimal awareness, or a foetal-like, primary narcissism which Freud saw as governed by the pleasure principle. It also seemed reasonable for Freud to insist that the move towards developing a mind is a gradual one, depending on stages of mental expansion that enable an increasing accommodation of the reality principle and hence a greater recognition of the world.

All the complex processes of childhood development which Freud explored were felt by him to depend on this prior mental expansion. As far as he was concerned, by the time the child engages in his first significant relationships and undergoes the stormy emotional conflicts of the Oedipus complex, he is able to organize his impressions coherently, is in command of language and motility and is therefore able to think and act, even though he is often not reasonable. The child depicted by Freud was undoubtedly primitive, but his primitivism lay chiefly in his inability to control urges and impulses, specifically those which belong to the realm of infantile sexuality. And while it is sometimes mistakenly assumed that Freud's theory of infantile sexuality was controversial, this was not in fact the case in the scientific circles of his time, where the notion of an infantile sexuality already existed.

Klein's thinking, though ostensibly building on Freud's, seemed to do no more than subvert its method and reason. It led her right back to early life, where she hypothesized sophisticated and highly complex mental operations in very young children, as well as highlighting an infantile intentionality that seemed stupefying in its complexity and bizarre nature. Klein's colleagues were also to complain that she seemed to be confusing descriptions of subjective experience with the objective designation of mental phenomena, as if mere descriptions of mental contents were automatically explanatory. Not surprisingly, the Berliners rejected her fiercely.

However, rather confusingly, responses to Klein's work were already resisting the kind of predictability and consensus that could give some indication of how they might fit into the broader developments in psychoanalysis. This becomes apparent when the opposition of the Berlin psychoanalysts is juxtaposed with the accolades which Klein's work received in London during the very same period. Her first lecture visit to the British Psychoanalytical Society in 1925 was nothing short of a great success, as was indeed reported to Freud by the British Society president, Ernest Jones: 'Melanie Klein has just given a course of six lectures in English before our society . . . She made an extraordinarily deep impression on all of us and won the highest praise.'[2] Nor could this British enthusiasm, so strangely at odds with the view of Klein's work in Berlin, be attributed to a misjudged first impression or a temporary intoxication with new ideas. Although some initial impressions were negatives, and James Strachey, for example, complained that 'her writing gave me a shock', this kind of response did not prevail. The British psychoanalysts seemed to have understood very well the significance of what they heard. As was to become amply evident, they would find Klein's thinking playing a key role in the future of their Society, affecting it both as an institution of learning and also as a theoretically distinctive, British school of thought. In the short term the British reaction gave Klein a much needed morale boost. When it was followed some months later with an invitation to spend more time in London, Klein accepted eagerly, delighted with the options which now seemed open to her: 'I am going to London in August where I shall find lots of work with favourable material, scientific and personal prospects.'[3] Klein was not disappointed, and a share of the anticipated opportunities did indeed materialize, at least for the first fourteen years of her life in London. During this time Klein enjoyed a sense of creative freedom in a congenial professional environment. She extended her clinical research and presented her evolving theoretical ideas to a receptive group of gifted psychoanalysts.

An enthusiastic British reception and facilitating work climate released Klein's inhibitions. Initially this resulted in a torrent of excess that almost rages through aspects of her early London papers, written between 1926 and 1930. In them the child's psyche is etched harshly and rather defiantly, as if the author needs to prove that she has freed herself from the petty criticisms and constrictions of the Berlin psychoanalysts. The human child in these writings is exposed as ruthlessly acquisitive in its thrust for survival, and as fiercely propelled by its bodily life and oral impulses to extract from the mother all the life-giving energy and sustenance of which she is capable. The child's basic instinctual propensities manifest in a primitive psychical life characterized by unconscious cannibalistic attacks on the child's most proximate human presence – the maternal body.

The legacy of these early Kleinian descriptions lingers on in some contemporary beliefs, including, for example, the occasionally encountered, but mistaken, assumption that they represent Melanie Klein's only and final verdict on the human child. As well as this, the impact of Klein's harshness during this period is such that it can still arrest attention at the expense of deeper and more subtle shifts in her outlook that were beginning to manifest in the texts at the same time.

The tolerant climate of the British Psychoanalytical Society was working its spell on Klein, gradually softening her stance and transforming her initially grim outlook into a more fair-minded, empathic and sustained scholarly fascination with primitive psychical dimensions of experience. As a result, she began to intersperse her clinical papers with publications of a rather different nature, linking her vision of infancy with a host of social and cultural phenomena. She wrote about creativity, painting, opera and symbol formation. From around 1930, her thinking on early infantile development begins to go in tandem with her thought on adult mental life, and is best understood as her exploration not of one-off childhood events, but of the simultaneous primitive processes which function in the adult mind and form an underpinning to adult rationality. The detail of this picture remains fine-grained and rich, negotiating the depths of pre-verbal existence with the help of a particularly ingenious conceptual repertoire.

During this period a greater balance is evident in Klein's thinking, and indeed it led to significant shifts in it. The infant was no longer described as unilaterally aggressive in its survival behaviour. It was shown instead to be a far more sophisticated being who relates in complex ways to its human environment and structures a world of meaning around its mother's body, especially through experiences of gratification and frustration at the mother's nurturing breast. Klein was now explicitly departing from Freud. Unlike him, she suggested that the infant can relate to its mother from birth, even though it possesses only a rudimentary capacity to apprehend aspects of her nurturing. These are none the less qualitatively distinguished as good or bad by the infant, and furthermore, are absorbed into its psyche.

Klein reasoned that all of the infant's experiences leave traces in its psyche, and that such traces accumulate to the point at which they gather substance and assume more stable, identifiable forms. Since experiences are necessarily transmitted to the infant via the agency of a live human object, they are absorbed by its psyche in a highly anthropomorphic manner. The first constructs in the psyche are not simple representations, ideas, words or even symbols. They precede such sophisticated forms of thinking, and are, in Klein's language, 'internal objects'. The early psyche is thus populated with beings who continue to represent dynamically what the infant has known in its interactions thus far in its life.

These strands of Klein's thinking are but a sample of the theoretical multifariousness which gradually paved the way to her three most important papers, written in 1935, 1940 and 1946. In these papers Klein linked her understanding of infantile mental life to a new understanding of human suffering. She mapped out two basic configurations of human anxiety, showing how these confront our species from the beginning of life, and how an initial negotiation of them is crucial in shaping character and determining destiny. Klein also showed how the severe mental illnesses of schizophrenia and manic-depressive psychosis were subject to predictable unconscious patterns which could be traced back to early anxiety situations and their impact on the partially formed, fragile psychic apparatus of the infant.

With these complex depictions Klein's papers get the furthest away from

Freud's idea of building a model of the mind. For Klein's critics they are no more than a confirmation of her always dubious thinking. Her enthusiasts are accepting of the fact that what changes in her prose is the very mode of representing the human mind. Her representation gradually shifts towards the 1940s from an originally realist, to a far more abstract, representational vision, and one that is not far from other modernist modes of expression typical of the period. Many modernist representations no longer aspired to a status of equivalence with the object of contemplation, whether on the canvas, on the page or in the score sheet. But their dissonance, fragmentation and high degree of abstraction could not be further from the clear order and the diagrammatic, explanatory topographies so beloved by Freud. Klein's key chapters express, far more than they explain, the unruly, highly complicated processes of mental life. They also show them to be exquisitely, if also precariously, attuned to housing and nurturing a self through the harsh conditions of living.

It is an irony that around the time of writing her key papers, Klein's peaceful professional existence in London came to an end, and was, for the second time in her life, disrupted by professional confrontations. These confrontations were to be the last, but the most traumatic in her career. They were to establish her professional entitlement once and for all, and ironically in the process, deeply damage her reputation as a thinker.

The fierce controversies were also highly explosive because Klein found herself pitched against Freud's daughter Anna, who was regarded as Freud's intellectual heiress as well as being his spokeswoman in his frail old age. In what became popularly referred to as the Controversial Discussions, Anna Freud and Melanie Klein confronted each other in a series of Scientific Meetings. What is more, the whole of the British Psychoanalytical Society became engaged in this protracted event and was to change irrevocably as a result of its conclusion. There was a further personal dimension to the controversies which was particularly painful for Klein. Her daughter Melitta, now also a psychoanalyst and living in London, joined the opposing camp of psychoanalysts, objecting openly to her mother's theories. But before tracing the impact of this debate on Klein's late papers, it is necessary to explore the theoretical background and start with some of the important insights that emerge in Klein's first psychoanalytic efforts.

NOTES

1. See Spillius, E. B. (1988) *Melanie Klein Today*, Vols 1 and 2. London: Routledge.
2. Grosskurth, P. (1985) *Melanie Klein*. London: Maresfield Library. p. 138.
3. Letter dated 18 January 1926. Grosskurth, P. (1985) *Melanie Klein*. London: Maresfield Library. p. 147.

CHAPTER 2

'The necessity of noticing the delicate indications of criticism' – Ferenczi, Freud and Klein's Encounter with Psychoanalysis

K lein's first significant publication 'The development of a child' was inspired by her personal experience of psychoanalysis with Sandor Ferenczi, and, as such, owes much of its originality to the psychic shifts and expansions that the analytic process triggered in her. At a later date, and with far more experience behind her, Klein was to complain that Ferenczi had been too kind and so had shied away from interpreting the negative transference, leaving her treatment 'incomplete'. Yet even if this was indeed the case, their psychoanalytic encounter was a particularly animated one, not least because it happened to come about at a time when neither had been involved with psychoanalysis for long enough to feel jaded by its limitations. At 41 years of age and with much of his best work still to come, Ferenczi understandably shared with Klein a sense of psychoanalysis as dazzling adventure and discovery. To both of them the endeavour seemed full of promise, and it was this optimism and vigour that Klein carried over into her own paper.

Klein's psychoanalysis with Ferenczi lasted approximately from 1914–19, and she wrote the first part of 'The development of a child' towards the end of this period, taking five months during 1919 to complete it. This first part presents her first ever psychoanalytic project: a short study of her four-year-old son Erich, which was carried out in her own home. The aim of the study was not merely to observe his behaviour over this brief period. More specifically, Klein describes her own psychoanalytically informed approach as a parent to the emergence of his sexual curiosity. His sudden and repeated demands to know: 'Where was I before I was born?' gradually convinced her to enlighten him along the lines advocated by Freudian psychoanalysis. She had an additional incentive, in that her son appeared to be a slow and inhibited developer, and caused her concern. There was now an opportunity to address issues that preoccupied him, and, furthermore, to do so with a deeper understanding of unconscious factors which psychoanalytic knowledge afforded. Klein did so, proceeding to record her frank responses to his questions, his reactions to her replies and the resulting conversations that developed between them. A year later, Klein presented her findings to the Hungarian Psychoanalytic Society, and on this basis gained admittance to its membership. The paper went down well, and Klein also noted the comments on her presentation and felt encouraged to add a sequel to it in 1921, this time consisting of an analysis of Erich. A period was set aside daily for this, and the child was encouraged to relate his thoughts and phantasies.[1] Erich was much more inclined to communicate as requested if his play was not interrupted, and Klein soon found that she was structuring the 'sessions' around his play, and it was this that removed his inhibitions, gave access to his primitive fantasies and anxieties, and provided the raw material for her interpretive responses. And thus, between mother and child, the revolutionary play technique was first indicated.

Klein was to remain convinced of the theoretical and clinical value of this project, and in time its two parts were published as a single treatise in which the identity of Erich was disguised as 'Fritz'. A letter of 1920 to Ferenczi shows her requesting Ferenczi's comments on the paper, and further correspondence indicates that she felt encouraged by his response.[2]

Because of Ferenczi's obvious impact on this innovative first paper, it is worth considering the kind of context which he was able to provide for Klein during its writing, and this includes some of the sources that informed his own psychoanalytic understanding and practice. Such background factors make it possible to locate Klein's own emergent idom in a paper which was otherwise imbued with a range of influential elements within her psychoanalytic milieu.

Ferenczi's influence was, itself, the complex outcome of three intertwining strands. First was the potent combination of his dual role as Klein's psychoanalyst and professional mentor; second was Ferenczi's own professional development during Klein's treatment period, crucially through his correspondence with Freud; and last was Ferenczi's own theoretical vision, which formed a distinct strand in an otherwise faithfully Freudian input into her therapy. These three aspects made for a complex amalgam that was to leave a lasting mark on Klein's approach. They thus deserve some attention and will be briefly surveyed as a preliminary to examining in more detail 'The development of a child'.

The first aspect, which was Ferenczi's dual role as therapist and mentor, is bound to have amplified his significance at such a formative and early stage in Klein's psychoanalytic development. Not that either of them had anticipated the spontaneous mentorship which was to emerge in the course of the treatment. Melanie Klein began psychoanalysis for purely personal reasons. However, she soon found herself keenly interested in the theories that informed her treatment process and was drawn to exploring them. She began to pursue her interest with further study, first by reading Freud's works. She was also beginning to observe the manifestation of Freudian principles in the behaviour and play of her own young children. The deep impressions gathered through such observations in her daily life would have naturally surfaced in the material brought to her sessions. They became a focus for discussions with Ferenczi, who was himself particularly interested in the psychical life of children. And since Klein was an astute, original observer and Ferenczi was quick to appreciate new thinking, a pioneering psychoanalytic dialogue developed between them, forming a subtext that underpinned Klein's growing understanding of her own psyche.

Their inadvertent broadening of the analytical relationship was also not out of character for the period, when such a brand of therapy-cum-psychoanalytic education was regularly tolerated. Psychoanalytic practitioners had not as yet reached the point of separating therapy proper from other modes of discussion in which their patients sought to involve them. They also saw no reason why some analysands should not use their treatment as a first step towards a professional psychoanalytic career.

Ferenczi was thus not out of line when he accepted Klein's increasing reliance on him for added professional mentoring within the treatment framework. Their theoretical discussions also convinced him that she was gifted and deserving of his support. By 1919, five years into the analysis, he asserted confidently that Klein had been taught by him for several years.[3] It was in the same year that Klein decided, with Ferenczi's encouragement, to present her study of her son to the Hungarian Psychoanalytic Society. By this time both she and Ferenczi were agreed that she should pursue her interest in psychoanalytic work with children. While child psychoanalysis did not as yet exist as a profession, occasional psychoanalytically informed work with children was being attempted by some practitioners. Ferenczi had high hopes for the future of this work, encouraging other female patients besides Klein to pursue it.

Ferenczi's impact as supportive mentor was bound to become amplified for Klein because he was also, simultaneously, an analytic transference figure for her. Like all patients, she would have invested the person of her psychoanalyst with intense emotional significance as part of the treatment process, and this, combined with his mentoring role, would have made for a particularly potent mixture, intensifying Ferenczi's impact as a professional authority figure. The early history of the psychoanalytic movement was characterized by many similarly overdetermined relationships between mentors and novices, and the results were often fraught for both parties.

However, Ferenczi and Klein appear to have been able to retain a balance that neither led to an overinvolvement, nor to explosive hostilities. Klein appears to have largely benefited from the work. Ferenczi's encouraging words imparted a sense of confidence that was to stay with her and to which she turned for comfort several times in the course of her troubled career. As well as this, Ferenczi's approval had a liberating effect on Klein's first attempts as a psychoanalytic thinker, evident in the lively tempo and intellectual confidence that infuse 'The development of a child'. The text gives no evidence of the intellectual unease of a novice, and freely sides with Ferenczi on issues that were still being debated in the broader psychoanalytic community, some of which will be discussed later in this chapter.

However, while Klein was indeed impressed by Ferenczi, it must also be remembered that in due course she felt free to criticize and reject some of his findings. This suggests that his influence, though potent and permeated with transference feelings, none the less enabled her to retain an independent intellectual position. And indeed, Ferenczi's character and behaviour tally with the likelihood that he would have encouraged independence in all his analysands. Even from the days of his youth, Ferenczi instinctively hated power and was fiercely liberal in his views. While still a newly qualified doctor, he poured considerable energies into work with the socially disadvantaged, writing 50 articles based on his work with prostitutes, and, in 1905, campaigning vigorously for the International Humanitarian Committee for the Defence of Homosexuals.[4]

Ferenczi's liberal instincts, first manifest as youthful passions and ideologies, matured with time, and were to emerge again in his psychoanalytic thinking. For example, he could not fail but notice the imbalance of personal power between analyst and patient. This was to lead him down some controversial pathways, culminating in his experiments with a 'mutual analysis', which required the analyst to disclose some of his own struggles to the patient. Understandably, the psychoanalytic establishment was never able to approve this 'wild' measure, but fortunately there was far more to Ferenczi than might be suggested by a single controversial idea. At a deeper level his entire technique was permeated with empathic currents that subverted authoritarian rigidity and conferred dignity on even the most infantile of the patient's needs. In line with this, Ferenczi legitimated the patient's infantile longings for 'maternal friendliness' within the analytic setting: 'We give our patient the parental imago which he has sought from earliest childhood and on which he can emotionally live out his libido.'[5] It is this kind of empathic approach which indicates that Ferenczi is likely to have encouraged freedom of thought in his patients, in spite of the fact that another of his controversial techniques, the 'active technique', appears to suggest the opposite. Both Grosskurth and Petot speculate that Ferenczi might well have used the active technique with Klein,[6] and this seemed somewhat dictatorial – it involved instructions to the patient to abstain from certain activities in the course of analysis so that feelings associated with these actions could become manifest.[7] It may well be that Ferenczi used this with Klein. However, a fuller understanding of his position on technique is to be found in his own distillation of his accumulated thinking two years later in 1922, and this is *The Development of Psychoanalysis* monograph, coauthored with his colleague Otto Rank. In the publication Ferenczi refutes the crude view of his active technique. He explains that it is intended only for extreme cases in which the patient succumbs to obsessive and meaningless repetition in the analytic situation.[8] Even in this situation, his active technique is not aimed at '... overwhelming the patient with commands and prohibitions, which one might characterize as a kind of "wild activity"'.[9]

Thus, however inadequate, the active technique was no more than conventional professional experimentation and an attempt to address a commonplace technical difficulty, rather than the rampant discharge of a personal pathology cloaked as technique. This becomes even more obvious when set in the context of the monograph as a whole. It is most telling when Ferenczi warns against 'the narcissism of the analyst', which can 'create a particularly fruitful source of mistakes',[10] and provoke 'the person being analysed into pushing into the foreground certain things which flatter the analyst and, on the other hand, into suppressing remarks and associations of an unpleasant nature in relation to him'. In this situation patient improvements are only apparent, undertaken in order to please and 'bribe the analyst', who is also spared 'the necessity of noticing the delicate indications of criticism'.[11] Altogether, the monograph repeatedly examines the adequacy of what is provided for the patient, and there is little in it to indicate a power hungry individual at work.

But there was a further factor which would have prevented Ferenczi from assuming an overpowering position in relation to Klein. The two of them were not merely working with a reference to each other, but with a common allegiance to an external framework which set the treatment parameters, and this was Freud's psychoanalytic method. The most awesome authority figure in Klein's psychoanalysis was Freud and not Ferenczi, both because Klein wanted a Freudian psychoanalysis and because Ferenczi himself worked under the powerful impact of Freud.

As Segal points out, Klein undoubtedly considered herself a disciple of Freud, and what she was seeking was a faithfully Freudian psychoanalysis. She must have also been aware that for a disciple she had little contact with Freud himself. Many early enthusiasts of psychoanalysis either sought psychoanalysis directly from Freud, or else attempted to correspond or converse with him. Klein did not avail herself of these options, and might well have experienced them as beyond her reach. She must therefore have felt fortunate to be analysed by a member of Freud's immediate circle, and this highlights the second significant aspect of Ferenczi's influence on Klein, which was his close and deeply instructive dialogue with Freud during the period of her treatment.

Ferenczi first began to discover Freud's work in the years leading up to 1908, by which time Freud had established the main principles of his theory and was no longer working in isolation. However, psychoanalysis did not as yet comprise a complete or stable body of knowledge, and was still an evolving discipline which hinged on Freud's continual elaboration of his framework. A close contact with Freud's thinking was essential to any enthusiast, and a handful of adherents was meeting regularly as part of Freud's Wednesday evening circle in Vienna. This group was already witnessing disagreements, but it none the less comprised the only genuine forum for the development of psychoanalysis. Ferenczi immediately realized that he needed to find some way of participating in it, but was also aware that unlike other members of the group, he was not living in Vienna and so would not be able to attend meetings in person.

Yet this did not deter him. Besides, the geographical obstacle was also not insurmountable. Within the then-integrated Austro-Hungarian Empire, Budapest and Vienna shared easy access and communication, with a reasonably short rail journey enabling their daily exchange of mail and facilitating more general cultural contact. This meant that it was not unusual for members of the Hungarian intelligentsia to speak German and to be well informed on German thinking.[12]

It was thus that after seeking a personal introduction to Freud in 1908,

Ferenczi found it relatively easy to follow the meeting up by initiating a correspondence between the two of them. At the same time he pursued the possibility of an affiliation to Freud's Wednesday evening Circle, eventually proposing himself as a corresponding member of it. His contributions as member were immediately apparent and active. Indeed they heralded his future prominence both in the theoretical exchanges of the group, and also in its gradual establishment as a scientific body and professional association, eventually to become the International Psychoanalytic Association (IPA).

These activities provided for Ferenczi much sought-after knowledge, but his deep hunger for psychoanalytic understanding impelled him to continue his separate correspondence with Freud. The correspondence grew and intensified, gradually becoming a close and significant collaborative relationship. There was an almost daily exchange of letters in which professional experience was shared, patients were referred for diagnosis and impressions of their symptoms analysed. As well as this, theoretical papers were exchanged and discussed and Freud increasingly involved Ferenczi in plans for the expanding psychoanalytic movement. All this was punctuated with meetings at regular intervals, and eventually also with Ferenczi arranging to receive some direct psychoanalysis from Freud during extended visits.

While the relationship was indeed substantial, it was complicated by a multitude of personal factors, as is astutely discussed by Forrester.[13] And indeed, the correspondence reveals that even as Freud's habitual address of 'Dear colleague' changes into 'Dear friend', all sorts of unrealistic expectations emerge in the two correspondents regarding what a 'dear friend' should be and should offer. It seems that a 'dear friend' was expected to be a soulmate, intimate confidant, loyal colleague, political ally, and all this, without ever becoming a rival or an antagonist. Not surprisingly, there were disappointments, and in the 1920s Freud and Ferenczi gradually grew distant and their correspondence began to peter out.

More personal and biographical information is now available on the founding generation of the psychoanalytic movement than ever before. The sheer quantity of material in recently published biographies and correspondences is almost overwhelming. Many contain stories of intrusiveness and control in which Freud figured prominently. The personal histories revealed in these, the complexity of relationships and political affiliations, all understandably lay claim to our attention. And because the subject is psychoanalysis, personal information on its theorists always presents the allure of hidden meanings that might be prised from actual life events which underpinned theory-making. However, taking too much of this into account can become as misleading as it is revealing. The incestuous entanglements to which early psychoanalysts were prone, their overclose, intrusive intimacies, the disappointments and rows which came in their wake, all of these fit into a specific historical context. They are in keeping with the norms of a bygone age in which personal distances were lived out in immediate, intense ways which made them subject to extreme, and sometimes violent fluctuations.

Many of the details revealed in the Freud–Ferenczi correspondence seem raw from our present perspective, but we must allow that like individuals throughout the ages, they were able to sustain some objective distance from their ideas and operate as thinkers who are also able to prioritize their theories. It is therefore important to remember that before the 1920s, the correspondence with Freud provided for Ferenczi the most formative learning experience. The voluminous correspondence shows a depth of collegial intimacy which enabled Ferenczi to follow at close quarters Freud's thought process as it was unfolding, and hence to experience psychoanalytic theory in the making. Ferenczi also never adopted the position of a passive recipient in their dialogue, actively following up issues which Freud raised.

Haynal points out that it is often not appreciated 'how much Ferenczi and Freud did *together*'.[14] Ferenczi even participated in what is arguably Freud's most significant technical exploration, that of the phenomenon of transference. This phenomenon, denoting the patient's deep emotional investment in the psycho-analyst's person, was beginning to seem crucial to the curative process. Freud was struggling to discover its scientific underpinnings, and involved Ferenczi in the exploration. While not everything which Ferenczi contributed to this exploration was strictly practical, it none the less affected Freud's direction. Ferenczi's lifelong interest in telepathy and nonverbal communication, for example, was instrumental to Freud's 1922 paper on 'Psychoanalysis and telepathy'. More significantly, Ferenczi showed a particular sensitivity to the nonverbal elements of the patient–analyst communication. He was able to observe this in exquisite detail, thus underscoring the intensity of human unconscious life and emotionality. This contribution proved significant in helping Freud to appreciate the force and danger of unspoken feelings that are stirred by the analytic encounter.

Ferenczi's substantial interaction with Freud could not but infiltrate his work with Klein, forming a decisive element within his influence on her. The extent and depth of his correspondence with Freud, his active contribution to the development of Freud's thinking, and, crucially, his direct involvement in exploring the transference, all went to ensure that he was able to offer Klein a Freudian psychoanalysis which was informed at source. Indeed, a large share of his clinical interactions with Klein would have taken place under the fresh impact of letters in which Freudian revelations were emerging. However, Ferenczi, who was himself an original and inspired individual, could also not resist the pull of his own prodigious ideas and insights. The third aspect of his influence on Klein consisted precisely of those areas of individuality which represented his own identity as a thinker.

Ferenczi's originality is now recognized to have laid the foundation for a separate and highly influential psychoanalytic school of thought. This is the British object relations school, which counted among its thinkers the gifted persons of Winnicott, Balint and Fairbairn, as well as indirectly inspiring many other eminent thinkers such as Bowlby and Bion.

It was Klein who used Ferenczi's thinking to develop crucial conceptual vocabulary for this new psychoanalytic discourse, but many of its features were germinally present in Ferenczi's thinking. Papers such as 'Stages in the development of a sense of reality' gave Klein a wealth of ideas on which to build her thinking. She was able to formulate thoughts on the complexity of the earliest mother-infant relationship, on the infant's ability to absorb, or introject, the essence of this earliest relationship, and the importance of this event to the formation of a well-functioning ego. It was Ferenczi's thinking that also helped Klein to conceive of the earliest mother-infant relationship as providing a primitive template for the later development of symbolic thinking and hence of a capacity to make sense of the world. But it was not only Ferenczi's explicit theorizing which inspired Klein and left a mark on her. Ferenczi's individual brand of psychoanalytic sensibility, as well as his personality were equally to contribute to Klein's development as a thinker.

In the early years, when Ferenczi was just beginning to discover psychoanalysis, he wanted to publicize its principles through different professional and public forums in Budapest. His papers from this period show a deeply informed and penetrating grasp of Freud's texts, and still offer some of the most lucid introductions to these that can be found. Yet the Freud who speaks through these texts already has a distinctly Ferenczian slant, celebrating the subject with a lively emotion and an easy eloquence which Freud himself would have found difficult. Ferenczi's writing shows little evidence of the Freud who was habitually, and sometimes obsessively, weighed down with concerns about the scientific authentication of his ideas. Freud's pedantic intellectual rigour is played down, and in its place Ferenczi inserts his own and different kind of rigour: an intense emotional rigour with which he probes the qualitative aspects of mental states in order to refine psychoanalytic awareness.

Ferenczi's mode of conveying Freud's thinking captured something essential about his personality. While Freud became increasingly wary of what he regarded as a wild aspect of Ferenczi, Ferenczi's own analysands appreciated his clinical sensitivity, his extraordinary intuitive resource and his genius for human intimacy. Indeed his life's work can be regarded as an extended discourse on human intimacy, which enabled him to shed light on phenomena as diverse as the infant's first moments in its mother's arms and the patient's most intimate bodily language on the couch. Ferenczi's ability to examine raw mental states with ease and compassion, and his exhortations to 'not only feel ourselves into the mind of the infant but think ourselves into it' led him down the path of the earliest relationships in life and hence the importance of object relations to development.[15]

In relation to Klein, Ferenczi's influence was far more complex than a bequest of specific concepts. His mode of listening and his particular quality of reflection helped to usher original Kleinian insights into the world, thus shaping something of their ultimate nature. Ferenczi's ability to handle clinical intimacy and derive crucial knowledge from it would have provided a framework which ultimately helped Klein to examine primitive mental states without flinching. Maybe this also enabled him to give of himself without anxiety, and it is this ability to accommodate rather than fear intimacy which is evident also in Klein's first paper.

In spite of Ferenczi's important influence on Klein, it went unnoticed for almost a whole century.[16] This was partly the result of his predicament as a thinker. Towards his death in 1933, Ferenczi's oeuvre fell into disrepute, thereafter languishing in obscurity for at least another half century. His divergence from Freud and his controversial originality were rejected by a psychoanalytic community which strove, above all, for a cohesive and accepted professional identity. This had implications for Klein. Her actual textual references to Ferenczi petered out early on, and added to this, her increasing professional difficulties obliged her to abandon all but persistent declarations of allegiance to Freud. And while such declarations were in no way false, they did, at times, tend to be forced.

By the early 1940s, when Klein's troubles were at their height, Anna Freud attacked her works as alien to Freudian psychoanalysis and therefore as best excluded from the psychoanalytic canon. At this stage, any remaining links with Ferenczi would have proved merely troublesome to Klein. Given his reputation, he was hardly an authoritative figure whom she could invoke, whether in order to impress her professional opponents, or else in order to reassure herself privately. This set an unfortunate precedent among her adherents. Klein's concern to emphasize her Freudian lineage affected the first and second generation of her followers. Like her, they tended to ignore Ferenczi and look to Freud to legitimate Klein's works.

This underrating of what was, in reality, one of the important associations of twentieth-century psychoanalysis has now begun to be redressed. But its impact lingers in readings which show no awareness of Ferenczi's input, and as the next chapter shows, this represents a loss both general and specific.

NOTES

1. Klein's concept of phantasy was to acquire a particular significance as discussed in Chapter 9. It was to be designated with the spelling of 'ph' in order to distinguish it from ordinary day-dreaming. For the purpose of simplification, the 'ph' spelling is used throughout the book.
2. With kind permission of the Melanie Klein Trust and the Contemporary Medical Archive Centre in the Wellcome Institute.
3. Grosskurth, P. (1985) *Melanie Klein*. London: Maresfield Library. p. 75.
4. Stanton, M. (1990) *Sandor Ferenczi: Reconsidering Active Intervention*. London: Free Association Books.
5. Ferenczi, S. and Rank, O. (1986) *The Development of Psychoanalysis*. Madison, CT: International Universities Press Inc. (First published in 1922.) p. 21. Authorized English translation by Caroline Newton.
6. Petot, J. M. (1990) *Melanie Klein: First Discoveries and First System 1919–1932*, Vol. 1.

Madison, CT: International Universities Press Inc. Translated from the French by Christine Trollope.

7. Ferenczi, S. and Rank, O. (1986) *The Development of Psychoanalysis*. Madison, CT: International Universities Press Inc. (First published in 1922.) p. 11. Authorized English translation by Caroline Newton.

8. ibid., p. 43.

9. ibid., p. 41.

10. ibid., p. 42.

11. ibid., p. 42.

12. Haynal, A. (1993) *The Correspondence of Sigmund Freud and Sándor Ferenczi*. Cambridge, MA: Harvard University Press.

13. Forrester, J. (1997) *Dispatches from the Freud Wars: Psychoanalysis and its Passions*. Cambridge, MA: Harvard University Press.

14. Haynal, A. (1993) *The Corresponence of Sigmund Freud and Sandor Ferenczi*. Cambridge, MA: Harvard University Press.

15. Ferenczi, S. (1952) 'Stages in the development of a sense of reality', in his *First Contributions to Psycho-Analysis*. Authorized translation by Ernest Jones. London: The Hogarth Press. (First published in 1913.) p. 221.

16. Stanton, M. (1990) *Sandor Ferenczi: Reconsidering Active Intervention*. London: Free Association Books.

CHAPTER 3

'How ships get on to the Danube' –
The Development of a Child

Bollas points out that patients use their psychoanalysts 'quite unconsciously' and explains that, 'Through the use of the analyst, the patient can elaborate, or give rise to and articulate, different parts of the self'.[1] In the case of Melanie Klein, there was a conscious use of Ferenczi as psychoanalytic mentor, with a significant outcome for some of her key concepts. However, Klein realized that she had absorbed something more essential from Ferenczi via an unconscious route. His individual psychoanalytic idiom as expressed in 'His strong and direct feeling for the unconscious and for symbolism, and the remarkable rapport he had with the minds of children' were felt by her to 'have had a lasting influence on my understanding of the small child.'[2]

Ferenczi's impact extended well beyond this contribution to an understanding of children. The therapeutic experience which he strove to provide was imbued with his belief that '... affects in order to work convincingly must first be revived, that is, made actually present and ... what has not affected us directly and actually remains ineffective.[3] The affects thus revived in Klein were lasting in a very specific sense, since they were ultimately written into a theory of emotions and object relations. Not surprisingly, Klein used strong terms to describe what she had learnt from Ferenczi overall, suggesting that it amounted to no less than the 'real essence and meaning' of psychoanalysis.[4]

Klein's 'The development of a child' sheds some light on these claims since it captures the germinal moment at which she began to put this knowledge into use. And while her paper has all the expected limitations of a first theoretical work, it is none the less remarkable for including all the important ingredients that were to figure in her future thinking. The style of the paper, with its somewhat rambling narrative and overenthusiastic rhetoric can belie the exactitude that is hidden in its making. Klein's use of Ferenczi's ideas, though still undeveloped, heralded the main themes that were to occupy her lifelong thinking.

However, as suggested, for all of its importance, Ferenczi's influence on Klein was slow to register in the psychoanalytic community and therefore not broadly understood. When it comes to 'The development of a child', his impact might be obscured by a further factor, because Klein drew on a second substantial source in her paper, which was none other than Freud. And since Freud's influence has been more easily recognized, and also, at times, more welcome, it created the conditions for an over-Freudian reading of Klein's first paper – a reading that puts at its heart her continuity with Freud's 1909 'Little Hans' paper. Such a reading is incomplete, and more importantly, takes no account of Klein's very deliberate selections from her two respective influences, her way of bridging their differences and, above all, her view that the theories of Freud and Ferenczi have important compatibilities, a belief that later became one of the hallmarks of her thinking.

This belief has been thrown into question by a number of academics since. For example, Greenberg and Mitchell trace a line of development which leads through Freudian, Kleinian and object relations thinking.[5] They regard Klein's theory as the transitional moment in this development, which is poised between Freud's biological drive model and a full object relations theory that develops thereafter. According to this view, Klein never quite managed the transition to an object relations theory proper, and this was completed instead by other Klein-inspired thinkers such as Winnicott, Fairbairn and Balint. Her theory thus remains a kind of hybrid of incompatible frameworks.

However, many of Klein's papers highlight ways in which her theory can be regarded differently – not as a transitional and incomplete version of an object relations model, but rather, as a genuine theoretical alternative that, while drawing on Freudian drive theory on the one hand, and object relations thinking on the other, fashions a unique view of the psyche. 'The development of a child' is particularly valuable in shedding further light on this, since it offers tangible evidence on how Klein proceeded to select and combine themes from Freudian drive theory and from Ferenczi's embryonic object relations model. It also provides valuable clues on Klein's mode both of negotiating their incompatibilities, and of perceiving their complementarities.

But in order to follow Klein's thinking in this respect, it is necessary first to note how she actually worked the ideas of Ferenczi and Freud into her first paper. Even a cursory overview reveals that her approach to each of them was distinct, and that together they provided for her thinking two different but compatible functions. Klein used Freud in conscious, practical ways, as a provider of models to imitate, and of scientifically credible, biological substantiations of psychoanalysis. Ferenczi, on the other hand, was used in more metaphysical ways, as an inspirer of global visions which encompass social, ethical and philosophical concerns. The more tangible, visible presence in the paper is thus Freud, whereas in the hidden essence is Ferenczi.

Moving on to a more detailed view, it becomes immediately apparent that Klein's use of her sources in this way not only signalled her preferences, but also grew from practical necessity. Her use of Freud's thinking was bound up with the fact that her own paper was based entirely on a project which involved a psychoanalytic intervention with a child, her son Erich. This undertaking would have been unthinkable without some sort of precedent, and indeed Freud provided an admirable one ten years earlier, in his account of the first-ever child analysis. 'Little Hans' had something in common with Erich, in that both were of the same age and preoccupied with similar issues concerning their developing sexual awareness.[6] The 'Little Hans' account was also helpful in highlighting the anxieties and confusions to which this process subjected a young child.

Freud's 'Little Hans' manifested his anxiety in an acute form. As suggested, he was initially brought to Freud's attention because of a horse phobia which gave rise to fearfulness, frequent bouts of crying and an inability to tolerate the town's traffic of horse-drawn carriages. As also mentioned, Freud carried out the psychoanalytic intervention via the father, who reported to him regularly and then communicated Freud's interpretations to his wife. Both parents accepted Freud's view that Hans's phobia was triggered by his Oedipal conflicts and their attendant castration anxiety, all stirred by the events of his mother's pregnancy and the birth of his baby sister. These events activated aggression and fear which were repressed and then displaced on to the symbolic substitute of horses, hence becoming greatly exaggerated and overpowering in Hans's mind. Guided by Freud, the parents discussed Hans's anxieties with him and, in the process, reassured him with a frank account of the realities of sexuality and reproduction. Hans responded to this sexual enlightenment well, with a visible diminution of anxiety.

When Klein considered a psychoanalytic intervention with her own son, she discovered that 'Little Hans' was far more than a precedent which justified her project in principle. This was because it provided a working model which was useful in practice, since it contained information on what she was likely to encounter in the course of her endeavour. Typically Freud had written at length, providing a full background history, and including the minutiae of Hans's interactions with his parents, much of them as reported verbatim to him.

It is not surprising that Klein chose to follow what was set out so clearly in the paper. Freud not only provided an accessible model, but one that was successfully tried and tested, and in this sense, comprised a practical manual which demonstrated how childish questions on sexuality were actually answered. It is thus that Klein's first paper bears so much resemblance to the 'Little Hans' model, both in content and in the style of delivery. Like Freud, Klein's case account includes verbatim reports which adopt the child's spontaneous questioning style and nursery language. Beyond this immediate appearance, however, lies a deeper response to Freud's paper, and it is here that Ferenczi's influence gains momentum in Klein's reflective process. The first sign of this influence is an apparently trivial but telling detail, which is Klein's somewhat mysterious decision to treat her son in the first place.

Unlike Hans, Erich was not phobic, nor indeed obviously symptomatic. On the contrary, Klein describes him as healthy, alert and reasonably cooperative and friendly. The only symptoms which she does list have not seemed persuasive to subsequent commentators. Petot, for example, questions Klein's labelling as 'slow' Erich's language acquisition at the age of two, and wonders if Klein's perception has more to do with her maternal ambition, her anxious monitoring of her children's intellectual development, as well as the grandiose quality of her expectations in general.[7] Grosskurth regards Klein's approach in the paper as a reflection of the early stage of her career which was '... the high point in Klein's own optimistic sense of omnipotence.'[8]

At a later date, Klein herself reflected on her first paper, suggesting retrospectively that Erich's real difficulty did not manifest obviously because it was the hidden, deepseated and unconscious anxiety of infancy and early childhood, now considered by her to be a universal occurrence in children. Yet this understanding of Erich antedated her paper, and while it is indeed possible that she sensed, but could not as yet account for, Erich's anxiety, she did not articulate any of it at the time of writing 'The development of a child'. In fact, the paper is noteworthy for its disregard of the importance of immediate symptoms, at least as far as children are concerned. Unlike Freud, Klein was not setting out to treat a child who had already succumbed to a nervous condition, but to prevent the child's future succumbing to pathology if certain present tendencies in his behaviour were not addressed in good time.

Her preventive scheme, which was so revolutionary for its time, was partly rooted in personal reasons. Klein's son worried her from early in his life because of behaviour that, while not extreme, indicated to her an inhibited and insecure personality. Compared with his older sister and brother, Erich seemed to be a slow, hesitant developer who spoke later than them, struggled to grasp ordinary facts and refrained from the normal boisterous inquisitiveness of childhood. She wondered why he was past the age of four and could still not distinguish different colours, and why, at the age of four-and-a-half, he could not as yet make sense of 'yesterday, today and tomorrow'. The possibility that he was simply less intelligent than his siblings had to be ruled out, since he gave the unmistakable impression '... both in looks and behaviour of an alert and intelligent child'.[9] As well as this, his memory was excellent as was his grasp of detail, once acquired. These facts were at odds with his laborious struggles to comprehend relatively simple things. Concern was exacerbated for Klein by his corresponding intellectual passivity. Something in Erich prevented a healthy curiosity which alone could remedy his situation and yet he only 'asked few questions'. Instead, he coped with childhood ignorance by fleeing into omnipotent phantasies, 'So in spite of all proof to the contrary he was convinced that he could cook, read, write and speak French perfectly.'[10]

Put together, his symptoms appeared to Klein to amount to a condition of intellectual inhibition, and she worried that while this did not matter greatly in a young child, a failure to address it in good time would none the less result in later pathology. Placing such concerns against personal factors in Klein's own history helps to shed further light on them. The act of writing her first paper spelled for Klein the moment of her own intellectual emancipation. Her youth had been marred by thwarted desires for more education and she now found the opportunity to redress this. However, in spite of her own exciting intellectual launch, she found that she was not freed from anxiety. In the manner of a family script, intellectual impediments now reappeared in her life, this time located in her son. Klein had lived with this script since childhood, particularly in relation to the key male figures in her life.

The family culture which dominated Klein's childhood was characterized by a high regard for intellectual development, and at the same time, by difficulties and inhibitions which beset intellectual endeavour. Klein's father came from a rigidly Orthodox Jewish home, and in accordance with his parents' wishes, adopted the restricted lifestyle of a religious Jewish scholar. However, in his thirties he rebelled, undertook a medical training and began to practise medicine. This change of direction was doomed to relative failure and continued to be haunted by the family conflict which occasioned it in the first place. Klein's father was not only rejecting the intellectually restricted life of religion, but also, necessarily, the parents who advocated it and who modelled their own identities on its principles. Their objections were absolute, and they hoped and prayed that he would fail his medical exams. In his choice of medicine, Klein's father found a forceful conceptual weapon against religious dogma, and this was science and scientific rationality. In identification with him, Klein's first career ambitions were also to centre on medicine, and like him, Klein was to reject institutional religion in favour of a scientifically founded belief system, and do so explicitly in her first paper. Like him, Klein was to become intellectually rebellious and balk at narrow traditionalism all her life, in her case, the dogmas of the psychoanalytic establishment.

The difficulties of Klein's father did not end when he became a medical practitioner. His path was fraught with struggles which were sadly not of his making. The many restrictions imposed on Jewish professionals during his working life meant that in practice, his career failed to take off. He struggled to provide for his family, and was even obliged to become a dentist to make ends meet. The poverty that afflicted the family as a result was a decisive factor in the family dynamics for many years, and had a strong impact on Klein, who appears to have been aware of poverty and anxious about it since childhood. This anxiety needs to be understood in its historical context, as being in tune with a world which was pre-state-regulated welfare generally, and indifferent to Jewish welfare in particular. Jewish families who failed to make ends meet were in danger of being reduced, quite literally, to begging and starvation. The failure of Klein's father to provide for his family adequately resonated with all the terror of death. His intellectual rebellion set both an exhilarating example and a dangerous precedent.

Another sadness around the quest for intellectual satisfaction was experienced by the other important male in Klein's life, who was her brother Emanuel, although in this instance, the difficulties had internal rather than external sources. In her childhood Klein idealized her brother for his intellect and his artistic and musical interests, but she never saw these talents flourish. Emanuel was a 'self-willed and rebellious child' who did not get on with his teachers and who tried the patience of his parents.[11] Klein described him as contemptuous of his teachers, a detail that suggests her first intuitive awareness of how omnipotence can interfere with the process of learning. Emanuel's difficulties were exacerbated in his adolescence, when he fell ill with tuberculosis. Learning, which had been such a conflictual process for him in the first place, now seemed barely manageable. Emanuel left the university course which he attended briefly and gave his life over to travelling around Europe, sustaining himself with the notion of becoming a writer. However, his living allowance from a poor home remained meagre, and eventually, a combination of illness and self-neglect led to a pitiful early death at the age of 25.

Yet again Klein witnessed a loved figure who had exciting intellectual promise but failed to bring it to fruition. This painful predicament was undoubtedly exacerbated by the fact that during his travels in his twenties, Emanuel needed to borrow money from Klein repeatedly, and was, in practice, a financial burden to her. Like her father, his choice of intellectual rebelliousness resulted in financial difficulties which affected those around him and increased Klein's anxiety.

A pattern of unfulfilled intellectual and professional promise was the inescapable family background which Klein had inherited, and which necessarily accompanied her to the moment of her own professional launch. Placed in this context, her anxieties about Erich's slow developmental tempo become more comprehensible. A telling example is her undue emphasis on Erich's difficulty, at the age of four, to comprehend the difference between receiving a gift and needing to pay for an item in a shop. The fact that this harmless childish phantasy of having free access to all that is displayed in shops was not dismissed as such, makes more sense in the light of how it must have resonated for Klein with years of witnessing a father and a brother who, in different ways, ignored financial realities at their peril. Against this background, it is also possible to make sense of Klein's urgent need to create a preventive, and not simply curative, use for psychoanalysis, and so to free her son of his apparent learning inhibitions before they became too entrenched, as had been the case with Emanuel.

And yet, however strong the personal factors which converged in Klein's thinking, 'The development of a child' went beyond the personal, and Klein went further than making an individual case for treating her own son. Freud had been content to address the difficulties of one little boy. Klein, on the other hand, took the important step of generalizing her conclusions to all children. The maternal chords struck in her by reading about 'Little Hans' who so invited identification with her own son, elicited also a regretful awareness of the impoverishment of conventional upbringing. Many children suffered from nervous difficulties, but unlike Hans, few could enjoy the freedom to question their parents and receive frank answers. The intellectual confidence that was inculcated in Hans was sadly a rarity, and yet children were in particular need of adult help. They were often at the mercy of their raw impulses without the means to understand or master them. The adult world tended to add to the child's load by instilling moral guilt in him rather than offering helpful knowledge. It seemed to Klein unfair not to enable many more children to benefit from the kind of openness and trust demonstrated in 'Little Hans'. And even those children who did not show obvious neurotic traits, such as her own son, might well be stifling their impulses in countless small ways which adults were simply not accustomed to noticing.

This generalizing of individual conclusions into a global social vision bore the hallmark of Ferenczi's intense interest in the potential of psychoanalysis for children. It enabled Klein to generalize what had begun as a purely personal situation of mothering and so do what Freud had not done with 'Little Hans' – consider the individual child both in his own right, and as a representative of the therapeutic needs of the rest of young humanity. This dual view of the child opens two paths of inquiry in Klein's paper, one that leads outwards to the child's social environment, and one which moves inwards into the child's unconscious life.

The external, social dimension of the paper, while using Freud's 'Little Hans' as its starting point, carries the unmistakable stamp of Ferenczi's liberal leanings throughout. In the numerous details of her son's communication and play, Klein glimpses a vast potential for Freud's model, both for therapeutic, educational and social applications. The reflective content of her paper thus scans an ambitious spectrum which encompasses everything from revolutionizing childrearing and nursery education, to defining the child's rights in society.

While admiring the open familial communication that is illustrated in 'Little Hans', Klein asserted that it could be used to do more than treat children occasionally. If it were adopted throughout society as a permanent feature of childrearing, it could revolutionize family culture: 'Honesty towards children, frank answering of all their questions, and the inner freedom which this brings about, influence mental development profoundly and beneficially'.[12]

Parents could learn to respond to the natural sexual curiosity of their child and to provide a gradual enlightenment attuned to the child's rate of development. This would 'safeguard thought from the tendency to repression' and so prevent a further 'withdrawal of instinctual energy' followed by yet more damaging repressions, since all the rich associative links to the forbidden thought are also stifled. Such a downward repressive spiral can be avoided when sexuality is freed from its 'dense veils of secrecy', so that the natural 'wishes, thoughts and feelings' of the child are neither stifled, nor become a 'burden of false shame and nervous suffering'.

Klein felt that her suggestions had other advantages besides the averting of sexual repression. In 'Little Hans' Freud repeated his belief that sexual curiosity is the origin of, and first step towards, a general thirst for knowledge. Klein greatly enlarged on this idea. She suggested that the child who is freed to ask about sexuality is better able to reach out to the world with a lively curiosity, and that this has 'a decisive influence upon the development of intellectual powers'. It is this freeing of intellectual powers, this significant educational gain that lent the case for universalizing openness with children its decisive weight.

The idea of universalizing psychoanalysis by bringing it to every child in every home was bold enough. But Klein wished to go further. As a parent she was aware that some of the child's crucial moments of development took place away from the parents and in her nursery school. She saw no reason why psychoanalytic knowledge could not spread to this environment as well, with analytically trained women available in nursery schools to detect and address developmental difficulties. And if these measures were to be accepted widely, adult society would recognize an important but largely overlooked human right – the right of the child to develop her mind through her own endeavour, by using her innate psychic tool of curiosity and urge for knowledge, rather than remaining a passive receptacle of foregone adult conclusions. Most importantly, forcing intellectual acquiescence on the child was a dangerous practice, and could lead to an 'intellectual injury' which would haunt the child for life.

The vision proposed in 'The development of a child' was radical because it suggested that psychoanalysis could be used routinely with children and that society should begin to think in terms of preventing neurosis from the early years via a different kind of upbringing. This upbringing needed to give the child a sense of intellectual potency and prevent adults from using their authority by forcing a mindless acquiescence on the child.

All these conclusions are redolent with Ferenczi's most cherished values – his liberal instincts, his qualms about all manner of inequality in human relations, and his psychoanalytic empathy for the childish psyche. They also reflect some of Ferenczi's specific views on the education of children. From as early as 1908, he believed that the conventional education of his day had harmful aspects, especially if it proceeded through 'the repression of emotions and ideas', or worse, through cultivating 'the negation of emotions and ideas'. In fact, it seemed inevitable to him that a '... moralizing education based on repression calls forth a modicum of neurosis even in the healthy.'[13]

Ferenczi felt that the main instrument of tyrannical intellectual suppression used by adults was religion. Institutional religion did not tolerate the child's natural sexuality and ultimately prevented the child from finding 'unselfconscious pleasure in the natural joys of life'.[14] Ferenczi's thinking was in keeping with other progressive currents in European intellectual life, but he was also most likely attacking the educational establishment of his day in Budapest and parts of eastern and central Europe, where religion and superstition still held sway, intolerance was rife and upbringing was stifling and cruel. He cited for comparison progressive countries like France which had removed the catechism from the school curriculum, and instead introduced the child to an intellectually sound civic value system via 'an elementary book which gives the child his first instruction in his position as a citizen'. He considered that this progressive measure would be complete if sexual enlightenment was added to the child's store of knowledge.

Such powerful sentiments are clearly echoed and endorsed in Klein's first paper. Like Ferenczi, she accords the liberating of sexual curiosity a large role in development and the move towards intellectual independence, and like him, she counts religion and moral pressure as obstacles in this path. When considering the damage caused by religious irrationality, sexual enlightenment is seen to have a further advantage in her eyes: it introduces scientific rationality to the most formative and intimate area of the child's quest for knowledge, where she is most apt to fall prey to the anxieties stirred by her powerful sexual urges. In learning to understand these as scientifically natural, the child's mind can adopt sound intellectual habits from the start, choosing reason and science rather than distortion and superstition.

It is easy to be dismissive of such ideas in retrospect. They may seem to be both glaringly obvious and at the same time, impossibly inflated. However, this is to miss some of their historical significance. It was Klein who at this early stage articulated the need for a universal application of psychoanalytic principles to childrearing, something which was not at all obvious at the time. She was thus, at the very least, right in principle. In spite of this, there are those who continue to feel critical of her, suspecting that she must have been so carried away by lofty ideas as to give insufficient consideration to the son on whom she tried them out. If this were indeed the case, it would throw into question the full validity of Klein's procedure, showing that while she may have been right in principle, she was mistaken in practice, with possible implications to her overall conclusions.

However, there is every evidence to suggest that Klein did not use her son as an experimental object, and that, in fact, her practical mistakes emerged for the opposite reason, that is, from her subjective involvement in the case. The highly charged situation of treating her own son exercised a powerful restraint on Klein's actions. While enthusiastic to apply Freud's model in principle, she was hesitant and cautious about it in practice. It is thus that Klein observed her 'slow' son with a growing concern, and yet did nothing until, at the age of four-and-three-quarters, he suddenly began to display a persistent sexual curiosity with questions such as 'Where was I before I was born?', and, 'How is a person made?'

These questions provided an essential rationale for Klein to embark on her task, since she was resolved to support Erich's emergent curiosity with frank answers. And yet her paper shows that any actual moves to enlighten Erich on sexuality fall well behind her rhetoric, and are continually subject to prevarication and concern. Her doubt is not surprising when viewed in context. Enlightenment had worked well for Little Hans, but this did not provide conclusive proof that it was always desirable. Klein must have worried that in the particular case of Erich who was not neurotic but only inhibited, enlightenment would prove inappropriate and overwhelming. Hence her decision to proceed with great caution, offering information piecemeal and avoiding irrevocable moves.

Such details are not significant for what they can contribute towards an apologia on Klein's mothering, but because they impacted on Klein's interactions with her son in unexpected ways, and so complicated Klein's project. For example, in order to proceed as safely as possible, she decided to offer only one item of information at a time, starting with aspects of sexuality which seemed to her to constitute a more harmless and uncontroversial kind of information. She thus told Erich that babies come from the maternal body, but kept from him the full realities of adult sexual intercourse. Klein reasoned that this was a way of offering knowledge safely, so that Erich could respond to one piece of information at a time, presumably so that she could gauge any adverse reactions in good time.

Thus her first answers were factual and yet resounding with a deep omission, culminating in a nongenital, nonsexual account of origins which focused on only mother and baby. Klein was to realize later that this account was unsatisfactory. In spite of this, it opened up a dialogue with her son which brought a great deal to the surface and gave her much to reflect on.

The most surprising fact to emerge from the first piece of information that she offered was that, far from feeling freed, Erich was, quite the contrary, most resistant to it. He immediately and shrewdly went in search of alternative versions of the truth by questioning other adults in the household, and so came back to challenge his mother with the opinion of his governess, who told him that babies were brought by storks. Klein's assertions that baby-bearing storks were 'only a story' unleashed a torrent of objections from Erich. What about other magical animals and beings, was the Easter hare also only a story, and was Father Christmas similarly so? And what about angels?

Klein discovered that before sexual enlightenment could proceed any further, she needed to negotiate a confrontation with her son who was disinclined to give up a world of mythic beings and angels. What is more, her sessions of information did not elicit the undivided interest which she had expected. She noted 'a certain "pain", an unwillingness to accept', which led Erich to repeat questions endlessly and show an 'absent-minded, somewhat embarrassed behaviour' with a 'visible endeavour to be quit of the subject he himself had begun'.[15] Erich was obviously too young to disagree openly with adult opinions, but he showed objections in a number of ways. He repeated questions tirelessly when he did not like the answers, and when Klein stuck to her answers none the less, he asked to leave home and move to live with the neighbours. And yet in spite of this, he was continually drawn back to a further questioning of his mother, and even appeared to begin to accept some of what he was told. His overall attitude, however, betrayed his lingering reservations towards the version of reality offered by Klein, and the two of them soon found themselves mired in a particularly intractable argument. Erich reasoned that while his mother denied the existence of angels, she would need to account for the extraordinary world around him by conceding the existence of at least one magical being, a supreme creator. So he questioned her directly on the existence of God, something that must have been anathema to Klein's progressive educational programme. For good measure, Erich enlisted his father, who did believe in God, for support with this part of the debate.

Klein thus arrived at a hazardous juncture in her work with Erich, realizing that out of the two possible routes open to her, neither seemed straightforward. Encouraging Erich's belief in God would amount to a denial of her own convictions, and worse, a collusion in precisely the kind of magical primitivism and omnipotence which her educational programme was seeking to counter. And yet to discourage Erich's belief in God seemed equally complicated. For a start, she would be seen to disagree with his father and so create doubt on the status of adult judgement in general, an issue which was not within the intellectual range of a small child. This latter consideration would have also obliged Klein to reflect on the significance of transmitting to a child beliefs which were not subject to scientific verification and still a matter for adult debate. Telling a child about the facts of sexuality was one thing, making assertions on the nature of God and existence was quite another. And yet it was not possible to shirk some of Erich's questions while answering others with sincerity. Klein realized that the knowledge which children require from adults is not conveniently restricted to what the adults know already, and may well spread to inaccessible areas. Parents who embark on a programme of enlightening their child therefore need to cope with both the child's, and their own, intellectual limitations in the process of doing so.

In spite of discovering this challenge, Klein was not deterred. She managed to navigate her way in such deep waters by following, yet again, the guiding light of Freud and Ferenczi. From Ferenczi she drew the confidence to challenge religion with science, and so told her son that some people, his father among them, chose to believe in God, although no one had visible proof of His existence. And from Freud Klein drew the background knowledge which helped her to see that in spite of the conflicts raised by Erich's questioning pattern, it none the less represented progress.

In a manner anticipated by Freud, Erich's pattern of questioning followed a distinct thread which led from sexual to general curiosity. Once a question concerning sexuality was answered for him, it broadened the field of inquiry and gave rise to questions that emerged by implication and that were concerned with general meaning. Erich's discovery that babies grow inside their mothers thus led him to question a whole range of implicated beliefs, such as tales of magical origins, storks and various magical and omnipotent beings, among them the Easter hare, Father Christmas and angels. These questions led in turn to a further broadening of the field of inquiry, with questions on the existence of God. When the latter was thrown into doubt, Erich logically wondered how, without God, things become created in the first place, and 'how does anything grow at all'?

Klein realized that his sexual question 'How is a person made?' led all the way to 'an enquiry concerning existence in general'. She found herself responding to a wealth of questions which began to emerge, including 'how teeth grow', 'whether the stalk of the cherry grows with it from the beginning', 'whether picked flowers can be replanted', 'how a river is made' and 'how ships get on to the Danube'.[16] Erich also explored the reality status of visible worldly objects. He reasoned that, unlike angels and baby-carrying storks, electric cars were visible to him, and so demanded to know if this qualified them as real, and if so, whether only visible, tangible objects were real.

Klein immediately noticed the significance of such questions, because by asking about his tangible environment, Erich was also reaching after more intangible aspects of his world so that '... he had found, to begin with, in tangible things the standard by which to measure also the vague unreliable things that his feeling for the truth made him reject.'[17]

In spite of these comprehensive explorations, Klein did not as yet feel surefooted with Erich. Her answers were not liberating in a simple, cause-and-effect manner, and even after Erich began to overcome his initial resistance and accommodate doubts about the existence of God, his loss of belief left an intellectual vacuum rather than a sense of freedom. It was this which led him to more difficult philosophical questioning on the differences between 'the actuality of what is seen' and 'the actuality of what is thought'. The absence of God now called into question other intangible dimensions of reality, and left Erich more with troublesome enigma than with freedom.

The history of psychoanalysis is strewn with examples of significant moments of discovery that were initiated as much by the patient as by the psychoanalyst, and Erich's questioning pattern is a case in point. It helped Klein to see that the unknowable realm of religion was required by the child because it represented another unknowable realm, later to be understood by her as the inner world of the unconscious mind. She was to discover that like religion, this unconscious realm contains powerful mythical beings or primitive internal imagos which hold immense power over the self.

Without the individual situation of Erich's questioning, Klein's thinking in 'The development of a child' might have not gone very far, and possibly amounted to little more than a Ferenczi-inspired manifesto on the psychoanalytic entitlement of children. The way in which her enlightenment project met with resistance, however, led her beyond this relatively simple project and its endorsement for all children. This is important because in order to qualify as a psychoanalytic paper in the first place, 'The development of a child' would require an intrapsychic dimension which goes beyond what is purely social and interpersonal.

As suggested, Klein accepted Freud's view of infantile sexual curiosity as the forerunner to general intellectual inquiry, and also agreed with Ferenczi's resulting objections to the moralizing of religious education. Yet Freud's ideas on the child's intellectual development were general, and as Klein discovered through her particular interactions with Erich, sexual enlightenment is not significant for providing the child with facts, but for something much more fundamental. It promotes intellectual development because of an important underlying intrapsychic process which can only be understood with the help of psychoanalysis, and this is the developmentally crucial, reality-oriented decrease in infantile omnipotence.

In elaborating this further, Klein was able to make use of Ferenczi yet again, but this time not for his social visions and views on education. Instead, she drew on one of his distinctively psychoanalytic contributions to the understanding of psychical development. This contribution was expounded in his 1913 paper 'Stages in the development of a sense of reality'. Taking Freud's loosely formulated concept of infantile omnipotence, Ferenczi not only fleshed it out, but conceived of the way in which it declines with growth to make way for a developing reality sense.

FERENCZI'S 'STAGES IN THE DEVELOPMENT OF A SENSE OF REALITY'

Ferenczi outlined intellectual growth as a process of increasing recognition of the world as it actually is – separate from the infant and not subject to his omnipotent control. In this vision, the dawning of recognition is inevitable and prompted by life necessities. The human infant initially relies on his environment for a fulfilment of urgent bodily needs, both of survival and of pleasure. The infant is only able to communicate his needs in direct physical ways; his body deals with accumulated tension by discharging it and simultaneously using discharge mechanisms – crying, for example – as communication gestures. Initially these gestures are felt to be magical in that their very force is imagined to have conjured up the desired satisfaction. When the infant encounters actual frustrations or delays, his mind fends them off through the use of omnipotence, described by Ferenczi as 'the feeling of having everything that one needs and wants'.[18] The mother complements this natural state because she instinctively wishes to shield the infant from the full force of his helplessness. She thus simulates for the infant some of the conditions of his lost intrauterine perfection, such as reliable warmth and nourishment.

Time and growth bring a greater recognition in their wake, and the infant begins to make use of a more evolved communication repertoire. Uncontrolled bodily discharges of tension are gradually abandoned in favour of gestures and sounds which are orchestrated in increasingly evolved ways to convey meaning. Ferenczi regarded the culmination of this line of development as the acquisition of language, which necessarily also carries the acknowledgement of a separate world. Development in thinking can therefore be described as an expedient shift in the site of the infant's expressive life from the body to language.

Although in her own paper Klein referred to Ferenczi's paper only once, she none the less made extensive use of the thinking in it, concluding that the decline of Erich's omnipotence feeling was 'intimately associated with the important development of his reality sense'. She thereby bridged Freud's generalized idea of sexual curiosity as the basis of intellectual development with Ferenczi's idea that the ultimate destination of this development is not an arbitrary accumulation of facts, but a crucial psychic shift from omnipotence to reality.

Erich's questioning pattern shows this clearly. Once he understands that the baby is not brought magically by a stork but grows slowly inside the mother, he naturally begins to wonder 'How does one grow at all?', and, 'How is a person made ?' The origins of existence lead directly to the issue of omnipotence, both his own, and that of authority figures. After realizing that there is no final proof of God's existence, he begins to doubt omnipotence altogether, and this extends to the omnipotence which he has been attributing to his parents. He follows this with questions on the nature of parental power and authority. He wonders, for example, if his mother would prohibit, without apparent reason, activities which he enjoys, such as singing to himself.

Klein welcomed such a challenging to her own parental omnipotence, because it seemed to her entirely in line with the desired outcome of a child's questioning, that is, his healthy acquisition of intellectual independence. Were the child to fail in this respect, the result would manifest in a submissive attitude towards the parents and in a further 'permanent submission to the authority principle' and a lifelong intellectual dependency. Klein felt that there was an intimate relationship in the child's mind between parental and divine authority, and that parents could easily invoke religion to bolster their own power so that, '... by this authoritative introduction of the idea, at a time when the child is intellectually unprepared for, and powerless against, authority, his attitude in this matter is so much influenced that he can never again, or only at the cost of great struggles and expense of energy, free himself from it.'[19]

In this way, Freud's generalized ideas about the child's curiosity become specific in Klein's thinking, and are seen to lead to an increasing recognition of reality, a corresponding diminution of omnipotence and an ultimate ability to appraise authority figures, now divested of their omnipotence. It is significant that in this bridging of the ideas of Freud and Ferenczi, Klein did more than superficially tack on one theory to another and needed to work at their integration. This resulted from the fact that she both appreciated their theories, but also perceived important lacks in them. Freud's insights on the development of curiosity were not sufficiently detailed, and Ferenczi's were not complete.

As far as Ferenczi was concerned, the child's increasing recognition of the world evolved naturally – all that the environment was supposed to do was wait for development to take its gradual course. Ferenczi did not specify a psychic instigator for development, but Klein reasoned that without some kind of psychic trigger the infant might never want to leave the bliss of his omnipotent, self-sufficient paradise. She was also not content with the thought that the best which adults hoped to do when helping a child was wait passively for the process of recognition to take its course. This latter, facilitating permutation of Ferenczi's paper was to filter down, in due course, to Winnicott's writings, but Klein never lost sight of the instinctual motivational forces that drive human nature, aptly designated by Freud as drives. Ferenczi's paper did not conceive of a drive or an urge towards greater knowledge. On the other hand, Freud had supplied the possible root of such an urge, precisely in his suggestion that intellectual interest begins its life as infantile sexual curiosity, itself a function of the infant's position as ignorant outsider in the world of adult sexuality. It was the infant's libidinal instincts which remorselessly pushed its sexual life and also its sexual curiosity onwards.

Klein thus traced a path from Freud's libido theory to Ferenczi's embryonic object relations view of development as emotional separation from loved objects. In doing so, the personal situation of treating her own son became the emotionally-charged testing-ground for linking their two theories. Furthermore, the insights which emerged in the process took root in Klein's thinking, and were to develop through her life's work, reverberating in all her key concepts. Her later formulations on infantile psychic positions, the complex array of defences that these trigger, and the other major idea of a primary envy that preys destructively on the developing individual, are all, in important ways, versions of the infant's move towards a reality sense and away from omnipotence. As will be shown in later chapters, this reality sense would be portrayed by Klein as an almost literal recognition of the world and of the mother as she really is, in all her ordinary, good and bad, humanity. Essential elements in Klein's ultimate vision are thus in direct continuity with Ferenczi's original 1913 sense of reality, described by him as the recognition of a mother who is separate rather than magically manipulated by infantile urges, and who, as a result, is only fully reached via language.

Lastly, a very crucial part of Klein's paper emerged by default in the course of applying her theoretically complex hypothesis to a live situation. Erich's resistance presented her with not only practical obstacles, but also with theoretical ones, for she now needed to account for the fact that sexual frankness did not lead to immediate liberation and that Erich continued to cling to omnipotent solutions and a belief in omnipotent beings. Klein also needed to consider why, when Erich's omnipotence did begin to decline, his cheerfulness declined along with it. The first part of 'The development of a child' was written up and presented to the Hungarian Psychoanalytic Society, and Erich, who was now older, was still not as carefree as he should have been. On the contrary, Klein noticed with some dismay that the period of his lively questioning abated, leaving him listless and apathetic.

It was not what Klein had expected. Realism appeared to have brought with it a degree of misery which had not been anticipated. It was because of such disappointing results that Klein undertook further work with Erich, this time treating him psychoanalytically at a set time every day in his room. As suggested, this second phase of her project was also recorded by her, and in 1921 annexed as a second part to her original 1919 account of Erich's enlightenment and finally published as a single paper.

ERICH'S ANALYSIS

The second phase of work provided an opportunity to reflect on what had been missing from Erich's first opportunity at enlightenment, that is, Klein's omission of the father's role in reproduction. By now Klein was not surprised that her attempts to rectify this led to further strong resistance in her son. She continued to work with his resistance as she had done previously, but this time it put her on the trail of an idea that was to become crucial to her thinking. She hypothesized the existence of innate factors which determine the child's capacity to withstand reality. At the same time, and in spite of this pessimistic-sounding conclusion, her work with Erich took a definite turn for the better, and this coincided with the increased use of his play in their communication. Play helped to release Erich's inhibitions, and at long last he was able to communicate his most disturbing thoughts to his mother. His Oedipal phantasies erupted in his play, and Klein found herself interpreting the elaborate games which he showed her in a manner that would come to characterize her technique with children, and that would set her on the trail of her most important discoveries.

She followed Erich's play closely as a mode of symbolic communication, exploring his elaborate games and phantasies in detail and depth, taking up their unconscious significance and thus finding her way to the most primitive Oedipal phantasies. The symbolizations of such phantasies in Erich's play gave Klein her first glimpse of the importance of the mother, and she began to conceive of the maternal body as the first site of the infant's most intense psychical activity. The symbolized maternal body that emerged in Erich's play was a richly populated centre of unconscious psychical activity which reflected the infant's earliest apprehension of his human environment. In these archaic perceptions the mother's body comprised a kind of totality which was experienced as the whole of existence.

The material which emerged in the course of Klein's work with her son was profusely observed and recorded. It was deeply infused with an intuitive, maternal accuracy which took Klein into the nebulous realm of infantile phantasy life. As well as this, it had far-reaching implications for her work in another important sense, because she would eventually decide to separate child psychoanalysis from moral education, and indeed from all educative pressures. The germ of this significant separation, which was another distinctly Kleinian characteristic, began in the 'The development of a child', lurking in a curious and controversial detail, which was Klein's decision to disguise Erich's identity in her final version of the paper.

ERICH AND 'FRITZ'

It might seem ironic that child psychoanalysis was launched with a procedure which would now be deemed so inappropriate for a child, that is, his analytic treatment by his own mother. What is more, two years after writing the first part, Klein disguised this fact, substituting 'Fritz' for Erich. When this detail was unearthed at a much later date it raised misgivings in Kleinian psychoanalytic circles, not least because Klein's decision to disguise her son's identity appeared to confirm her guilt, as if she regarded her behaviour as professionally inadequate.[20]

And yet, as suggested already, what Klein was doing was broadly accepted in her professional milieu, practised by other psychoanalysts, and even felt to be a correct procedure with regard to children. And since the basic model from which Klein proceeded permitted the idea of a parent working with her own child, she had no need to disguise this fact. Indeed a year after her first presentation of the paper, she drew on its contents for another paper published in 1920 where she was still open about Erich's identity. It was only in 1921, by which time Klein was already an accepted member of a psychoanalytic society, that Erich became 'Fritz', and was described as the son of neighbours.

Klein's disguise of Erich's identity is thus unlikely to signify a guilt-induced attempt to hide an episode of malpractice. This is worth considering because of the light which it helps to shed on Klein's view of her paper. In the course of time she came to regard its contents as the proper beginnings of her psychoanalytic play technique rather than a mere 'study', or an episode of psychoanalytically informed parenting.

Some clues to this significance lie precisely in the extent of Klein's communications with Ferenczi regarding her study of 'Fritz', as well as the influence on her thinking of another of Ferenczi's fundamental beliefs – that the psychoanalysis of children could, and should be separated from other forms of interactions with them, especially various forms of direct moral, educative guidance. This was in keeping with Ferenczi's views on adult psychoanalysis and his conviction that there was no place within the treatment setting for patient 'guidance' of whatever kind.

In deciding to follow this view, Klein's paper on 'Fritz' advocated a radical departure from the 'Little Hans' model. In a case controlled by parents, some educative, moral pressure was bound to seep into child psychoanalytic technique, something that later seemed persuasive to Anna Freud. By comparison, Melanie Klein came to believe that like the adult, the child patient required a thinking space in which moral judgement and educative pressures were suspended.

Twenty years after treating her son, all this seemed self-evident to Klein, as is clear from her 1941 correspondence with the mother of 'Richard', a ten-year-old boy whom Klein treated while she was evacuated to Pitlochry during the Blitz. The analysis ended prematurely when Klein needed to return to London, but Richard's mother continued to need support and Klein tried to offer this through correspondence. The letters show that even under these difficult conditions and in spite of the mother's anxieties and desire for advice, Klein was clear that she should not try to work with Richard via his mother, nor should the mother engage analytically with her son: 'I cannot handle the case from a distance, and the help I can give you through advice is extremely limited.'[21] When the mother complained in writing that Richard worried her by behaving dictatorially, Klein's response consisted in commonsense reassurance rather than encouragement for the mother to try out psychoanalytic interventions: 'It is not at all an uncommon thing for a child particularly in times like these when the fears of dictators are so rampant, to try to play the dictator himself.'[22]

As this excerpt shows, a decisive shift took place between 1919 and 1941, enabling Klein to mark out firm boundaries around the child's clinical privacy, and thus initiate an important advance in psychoanalytic awareness. There were substantial implications regarding the domain of parental power. Klein's vision outlined responsibility for children as the subject of a shared democratic dialogue between the home and society, and by implication, placed some of the child's mental welfare squarely with society and its institutions. It is clear in retrospect how such thinking, though not unique in its time, none the less anticipated the broad move of the twentieth century to make the home answerable to society, and to provide mental health safeguards outside the home.

This important shift began the second part of her 1921, second paper on 'Fritz', where she was beginning to advocate the separation of child analysis from parental and educative measures. Indeed, she concludes the second part of her paper with the suggestion that child psychoanalysis could have a distinct role alongside nursery education, and thus be offered to the child outside the home environment:

> There is no doubt that a woman analyst who has under her a few nurses trained by her can observe a whole crowd of children so as to recognise the suitability of analytical intervention and carry it out forthwith. It may of course be objected amongst other things that in this way the child would at a very early age be to some extent withdrawn psychically from its mother. I think however that the child has so much to gain in this way that the mother ultimately would win back in other directions what she has perhaps lost in this one.[23]

Klein's contemporaries are unlikely to have objected to the idea of introducing child analysis into a partnership with ordinary schooling. But they would have been more alarmed at her demarcation of a territory of analytical intervention which excludes the mother. From their point of view, this measure was counter-intuitive and appeared dangerous. Klein did not share this concern. She saw no reason why an analytically trained adult could not contain the child's impulses without the mother's presence, and furthermore do so via the elucidation of meaning rather than educative exhortations. The mother might initially worry about losing her child's attachment, but she ultimately stood to gain, presumably because she would feel relieved to see her child developing well.

Klein's decision to present Erich as 'Fritz' in 1921 thus signifies the beginning of her departure from the 'Little Hans' parenting-analysis model, and her dawning conviction that the two roles should be separated. In this Klein was taking into account not only Freud's 'Little Hans' case, but the work of another practitioner who set important precedents for psychoanalytic interventions with children. This was the respected, and older, Berlin psychoanalyst, Hermine Hug-Hellmuth, who also adhered to the contemporary belief that child psychoanalysis should be educative in essence. Her work did not impress everyone. Klein's British colleague, Alix Strachey, derided it as a 'mess of sentimentality' and sided solidly with Klein's approach: 'Thank God Melanie is absolutely firm on the subject. She absolutely insists on keeping parental and educative influence apart from analysis.'[24]

The roots of this ultimate differentiation begin in 'The development of a child', aptly expressed in the overlaying of one version, in which a mother works with her own son, Erich, with another version, in which a psychoanalyst works with an unrelated child-patient, 'Fritz'. In this layering of alternative versions, Klein presents a dual viewpoint – herself as a mother annexing to her parenting territory the new procedure of child psychoanalysis, and herself as an analytical expert engaged separately with someone else's child. This latter, professional version contains also the idea of a mother who is able to hand over her child to an expert, and who thus accepts that the future of child development might not lie entirely in the province of parental power.

Klein's internal attempt to resolve the conflicting status of the two roles resulted in the mother in her handing over responsibility to her analyst self. It was also manifest in an almost literal manner – at the time when Klein was writing about separating the roles, she was already working with Erich in a more formal psychoanalytic way, and this distancing was manifest in another significant move. Erich was now no longer the sole object of her psychoanalytic scrutiny but shared this with another, older, child, an actual patient called Felix. The analysis of Felix mirrored many of the issues which Klein discovered with her son, and was, in fact, remarkably similar in content. Klein was thus transferring her psychoanalytic focus and moving from working as a mother, to working with the child of another.

NOTES

1. Bollas, Christopher (1997) 'Christopher Bollas' in A. Molino (ed.) *Freely Associated: Encounters in Psychoanalysis*. London/New York: Free Association Books, p. 23.
2. Klein, M. (1975) Preface, 1st edn, *The Psychoanalysis of Children*. London: The Hogarth Press and the Institute of Psycho-Analysis. (First published 1932.)
3. Ferenczi, S. and Rank, O. (1986) in *The Development of Psychoanalysis*. Classics in Psychoanalysis, Madison, CT: International Universities Press, Inc. (First published 1922.) 4, p. 38.
4. Klein, M. (1975) Preface to *The Psychoanalysis of Children*. London: The Hogarth Press and the Institute of Psycho-Analysis. (First published 1932.)
5. Greenberg, J. R. and Mitchell, S. A. (1983) *Object Relations and Psychoanalytic Theory*. Cambridge, MA: Harvard University Press.
6. Freud, S. (1909) 'Analysis of a phobia in a five-year-old boy', *Standard Edition*, 10, pp. 5–149. London: The Hogarth Press and the Institute of Psycho-Analysis.
7. Petot, J. M. (1990) *Melanie Klein Vol. 1, First Discoveries and First System 1919–1932*. Madison, CT: International Universities Press, p. 18.
8. Grosskurth, P. (1985) *Melanie Klein*. London: Maresfield Library. p. 77.
9. Klein, M. (1975) 'The development of a child', in *Love, Guilt and Reparation*. London: The Hogarth Press and the Institute of Psycho-Analysis. (First published in 1921.) p. 2.
10. ibid., p. 3.
11. From Melanie Klein's unpublished autobiography. See Grosskurth, P. (1985) *Melanie Klein*. London: Maresfield Library.
12. Klein, M. (1975) 'The development of a child', in *Love, Guilt and Reparation*. London: The Hogarth Press and the Institute of Psycho-Analysis. (First published 1921.) p. 19.
13. Ferenczi, S. (1908), in Petot, J. M. (1990) *Melanie Klein Vol. 1, First Discoveries and First System 1919–1932*. Madison, CT: International Universities Press. p. 21.
14. ibid., p. 22.
15. Klein, M. (1975) 'The development of a child', in *Love, Guilt and Reparation*. London: The Hogarth Press and the Institute of Psyscho-Analysis. (First published in 1921.) p. 4.

16. ibid., p. 8.

17. ibid., p. 11.

18. Ferenczi, S. (1913) 'Stages in the development of a sense of reality', in *Sandor Ferenczi: First Contributions to Psycho-Analysis*. London: Maresfield Reprints. (First published in 1913.) p. 219.

19. Klein, M. (1975) 'The development of a child', in *Love, Guilt and Reparation*. London: The Hogarth Press and the Institute of Psycho-Analysis. (First published 1921.) p. 25.

20. Grosskurth, P. (1985) *Melanie Klein*. London: Maresfield Library.

21. Letter dated October 1941. By courtesy of the Melanie Klein Trust Archive and the Wellcome Trustees.

22. ibid.

23. Klein, (1975) 'The development of a child', in *Love, Guilt and Reparation*. London: The Hogarth Press and the Institute of Psycho-Analysis. (First published in 1921.) p. 53.

24. Strachey, A. Letter dated 11 February 1925. In P. Meisel and W. Kendrick (eds) *The Letters of James and Alix Strachey 1924–1925*. Bloomsbury/Freud, London: Chatto & Windus, p. 201.

CHAPTER 4

'Not simply a case of uninhibited gratification' – The First Child Patients

K lein's clinical work with children began to expand as soon as she moved to Berlin in 1921. Her overall professional progress was such that within two years, in 1923, she was a Full Member of the Berlin Psychoanalytic Society. By this time she had not only managed to analyse several children, but also fitted in the substantial analytic period of 370 sessions with the thirteen-year-old Felix.[1] She was also soon to begin the even more impressive analytic period of 575 sessions with the six-year-old Erna.[2] Before, during and after obtaining her Membership in the Berlin Society, Klein's psychoanalysis of children continued apace, and records indicate that she treated at least 22 children and adolescents.[3] It was during this period that she decided, in the light of her evolving experience, to stop visiting her child patients in their homes, move the work setting to her consulting room and provide play materials as part of the sessions. The separate child-analytic space and the play technique came into being.

A reader who wishes to discover more about Klein's first child patients is likely to look for fully documented case studies, which, like Freud's 'Little Hans', 'Dora', the 'Rat Man' and the 'Wolf Man' provide distinctive narratives with striking protagonists. By comparison, Klein's published writings do not provide such clarity. There is, for a start, only a vague sense of the chronology and structure of her caseload during the Berlin years. It is also difficult, through the ordinary process of reading, to gain distinct individual impressions of the Berlin child patients, and this becomes more complicated because of Klein's move, not long afterwards in 1926, to London, where she was asked to see more children immediately.[4]

The disorganized element in Klein's first records of her child patients is related partly to her circumstances as a beginner, not yet aware of the full extent of her life's project. She presented her clinical findings piecemeal, sometimes to her immediate colleagues and sometimes to the broader psychoanalytic community in international congresses. The publications based on these early presentations appeared in various psychoanalytic journals such as *Imago* and the *Internationale*

Zeitschrift für Psychoanalyse (*International Journal of Psychoanalysis*). There was also a more systematic presentation of her work to the British Psychoanalytic Society a little later in 1925, but many of the translated clinical vignettes chosen to illustrate her ideas in this London presentation were drawn from material she had already published in earlier journal articles. It is further disorientating to discover that the 1925 London presentations only found their way into print seven years later, in the 1932 book *The Psychoanalysis of Children*, by which time the rest of Klein's theory had evolved considerably.

Klein's first child patients thus make their appearance variously in early 1920s journals, in the later *Psychoanalysis of Children*, and added to this, in illustrations of her thinking late into her writing career. The reader is initially introduced to the children through vignettes that are pressed into service for an overarching theoretical purpose – that of providing a foundation for the principles of child analysis. The vignettes are therefore delivered with an emphasis on technical and theoretical issues. They are there to support an argument rather than elaborate biographical narratives of the kind that Freud favoured. While the adult patient in psychoanalytic literature was normally described following Freud's example, the child patient in Klein's writings rarely occupies the position of a protagonist at the centre of an ordered narrative. Typically, external details of the child's family history, developmental record and schooling appear in sketchy fashion and often related hurriedly to the unconscious phantasy significance of the child's symbolic play in the sessions.

Only two out of the seventeen children whose published treatments were recorded in the early years are the subjects of full narrative case studies: the thirteen-year-old Felix whose treatment was written up in 'A contribution to the psychogenesis of tics'[5] and the highly disturbed six-year-old Erna who provided the material for the most fully documented case study of the early period, 'An obsessional neurosis in a six-year-old girl'.[6] Yet even Erna and Felix do not remain as easily memorable as the significant Freudian patients, and a second reading is often required for a better acquaintance with them. This may be because Klein continued to disperse vignettes from her work with these two children through many of her later papers. Moreover, her emphasis throughout is on the child's inner life, and vignettes from various patients which provide evidence for it can seem almost interchangeable. The result is a paradoxical sense of a text that is vividly populated and bustling with child patients, and yet of children who do not remain sufficiently distinct, dissolving instead into a single collective impression of a childhood psyche.

This is not to suggest that the vignettes lack authenticity, nor that the children fail to come across as real enough. Quite the contrary, they inhabit the texts with a palpable presence that is all too convincing. We meet the three-year-old Peter, a friendless child who fluctuates between excessive timidity and a sneering aggressiveness, the nine-year-old Grete who stammers helplessly, the two-year-old Rita who is moody, clingy and suffers from night terrors, the thirteen-year-old Felix who suffers from a nervous tic, is obsessed with sports and poor at his studies, and the three-and-a-half-year-old Trude who wets her bed and runs into her parents' bedroom at night without being able to explain what she wants. We meet others whose presenting symptoms and difficulties are equally redolent with the typical anxieties and confusions of childhood.

In the room with Melanie Klein the children are both distressed and, in turn, distressing, subjecting her to outpourings of aggression and terror. They are rough with the furniture, push the divan, shake the rug, throw the cushions on the floor, pretend to defecate under the sofa cover, hide behind furniture, cover themselves in cushions, suck their fingers and urinate. They try to attack their analyst in more direct ways, attempting to tie her up, hit her in the stomach, bite her nose, force her to throw away flowers from her vase and repeatedly dictate to her humiliating roles in their play.

When Melanie Klein had set out to provide for her child patients a confidential space that would be free of educative pressures, she may not have imagined some of the unbridled ways in which they would use their freedom. After all, her only previous experience had been with her own son, where the analytical endeavour coincided with normal maternal restraints. Not surprisingly, she had found Erich relatively mild-mannered, and this initial experience would have been echoed for her in the existing but very minimal clinical literature on children. In fact, Klein was the first to witness and record in detail the instinctual riot that is unleashed when a distressed child is allowed free expression.

However, it would also be misleading to represent Klein's child patients as purely troublesome, in spite of being brought to her by obviously overwhelmed parents. It becomes equally clear that their troubled behaviour and strange play are more than random destructiveness, since they fit into a context of symbolic communication in which they struggle to engage their analyst. The six-year-old Ernst helps himself to cushions from the therapy room divan, piles them up and then sits on top. From this lofty position he plays at being a clergyman in a pulpit, who uses mysterious gestures and hand-rubbing as part of his intriguing sermon. Klein is fully taxed by his urgent need to be understood; she is not only required to be his audience, but must struggle to make sense of the sermon's secret significance. Rita plays a game in which a doll is tightly tucked in bed and an elephant made to prevent the doll from getting up. The game is accompanied by obvious anxiety, as Rita worries that if the doll is allowed to get up, she would 'steal into the parents' bedroom and do them some harm or take something away from them'. Klein is subjected, through Rita's mounting panic, not only to the full anxiety, but also the perplexity of this problem.[7] This also happens when Trude plays that it is night, that she steals next to the sleeping Melanie Klein and makes threats that 'she would stab me in the throat, throw me into the courtyard, burn me up, or give me to a policeman'.[8] After such attacks on her analyst, Trude hides herself with the cushions in the corner, crouches with 'vehement signs of fear', sucks her thumb and wets herself. Yet again Klein feels urged to make sense of this behaviour, recognizing it as an essential piece of communication which holds the key to the unconscious, subjective determinants of the child's anxiety.

Such states of childhood misery, both incomprehensible and uncomprehending, are amplified in the most detailed case study of the early years, which is of the six-year-old Erna. Klein's stated aim in presenting this case is to address issues of technique with latency children, but the case account is more noteworthy for exposing in an extreme, blatant form the primitive psychical life already discovered in the work with other children. Erna's play provides a particularly good vehicle for conveying the essence of childhood disturbance because of its frenzied, obsessive quality, and its unremitting exposure of agitated childish emotions. Out of all the child patients in the early period her referring symptoms are probably the most distressing. She suffers from sleepless nights because of compulsive head-banging, body-rocking and masturbation. These activities are carried out incessantly also in the daytime, in front of family and strangers alike. Not surprisingly Erna cannot make either friends or progress at school, thus further disabling and isolating herself, and understandably also upsetting her parents and teachers.

In the therapy room she immediately engages in play of unrelenting sadism. The toys are used to represent people who constantly maltreat each other, who bite, kill, roast and then eat others. Melanie Klein is made to play the child who is continually punished and humiliated, deprived of good food and beaten for being dirty. At the same time, Erna takes the part of a cruel, tormenting mother who uses her authority to promote herself as a superior, royal person. Much of the play reveals grim anal preoccupations, with Erna pretending to sit on the lavatory, eat what she produces there and oblige her analyst to do so as well. All the play materials are subjected to a similarly sadistic use. The drawing paper which Klein provides is cut to pieces and said to be minced meat that is bleeding profusely, or else 'eye salad', or 'fringes' cut into Melanie Klein's nose. Erna shudders and explains that it all makes her feel quite sick.

In the context of such details of the child's private phantasy life, exposed so fully for the first time, Klein's startling interpretations are anything but reassuring. Quite the contrary, she seems to be taking the reader in a completely counter-intuitive direction. Instead of mitigating the impact of Erna's raw sadism with a reassuring adult rationality, Melanie Klein seems to underscore its significance. The sadistic games become even more disturbing when Klein reveals that, far from representing harmless, childish nonsense, they carry the specific meaning of Erna's hatred towards her parental objects, imagined by her to exclude her deliberately and sadistically from all relationship satisfactions. Thus instead of diminishing the importance of disturbing play phantasies, Melanie Klein confers on them the imposing status of a reality, albeit that it is an inner or psychical reality. This approach is not reserved for the work with Erna alone, but typifies Klein's choice of interpretations with all her child patients.

When Trude throws a toy man out of a little cart, heaps abuse on him and shows a preference for a man with a high hat in a picture book, Klein's immediate interpretation is that Trude wants to 'do away with her father's penis'. When Ruth draws a tumbler filled with small balls and tightly shut, having just shut her sister's bag so that nothing should fall out of it, Klein tells her that the balls in the tumbler and the coins in her sister's purse are children in her mother's inside. She explains that Ruth wants to shut them away in order not to have more brothers and sisters. In a later session, the culmination of a play sequence in which Ruth objects to the use of a large adult sponge to wash a baby doll elicits from Klein the astounding response: 'I showed her in every detail how she envied and hated her mother because the latter incorporated her father's penis during coitus, and how she wanted to steal his penis and the children out of her mother's inside and kill her mother'.[9]

When it comes to Erna's particularly disturbed play, Klein's interpretations are similarly disconcerting. In Erna's games, obsessive attempts are made to cure a child of its love of dirt. In a particularly unsettling play sequence, a magician knocks the child on the anus and head with a magic wand which has yellowish liquid pouring out of it. The child is then given red and white powder to swallow. Klein interprets that:

> The magician stood for the penis, and knocking with the stick meant coitus. The fluid and the powder represented urine, faeces, semen and blood, all of which, according to Erna's phantasies, her mother put inside herself in copulation through her mouth, anus and genitals.[10]

Such bizarre-sounding interpretations can unsettle readers today as much as they did the uneasy psychoanalysts who first heard them. Even the context of Freud's theory of infantile sexuality does not prepare for their impact. Can this impact be put down, perhaps, to Klein's exaggerated focus on libidinal issues? Greenberg and Mitchell believe so, and point out that while Freud had a 'proclivity for balanced, dualistic formulations' which present psychosexuality as 'juxtaposed with other motivational schemes', Klein's early interpretations have an exclusive sexual focus which can, at first sight, come across as a caricature of Freudian psychoanalysis. They point out that in the early years:

> Klein saw genital, Oedipal sexuality in every nook and cranny of the child's world. Letters and numbers have sexual meanings (strokes and circles in the construction of figures representing penis and vagina). Arithmetic (division as violent coitus, for example), history (fantasies of early sexual activities and battles) ... Music represents the sound of parental intercourse ...[11]

From a present perspective this kind of exaggeration does indeed come across as naive, and it should not be mistakenly imagined to feature in current child analytic practice.[12] When it comes to Klein's immediate colleagues, however, her exclusive sexual focus was not, in fact, consciously regarded by them as their main grounds for concern. Bearing in mind that the psychoanalytic community was operating under the impact of Freud's revolutionary thinking on sexuality, it was, as such, also receptive to its possible clinical permutations, however bizarre. There was an understanding that working with the unconscious mind necessarily involved working with the illogical, the strange, and above all the uncomfortable in human nature. Objections to Klein's early presentations were thus less a question of unthinking distaste for the more primitive aspects of human sexuality, than a question of theoretical issues of a very specific kind.

Still, her colleagues inevitably also reacted emotionally to what they heard, and no doubt experienced the kinds of concerns which still surface for today's reader. The major aspects of Klein's work which stirred up strong reactions in her colleagues amounted to the substance of her interpretations, and also her mode of delivering them. Klein spoke her mind to the children with a hitherto unknown directness and without any apparent kind of preparation or sexual education. In fact, these texts show Klein talking to her child patients as if they already know all the facts of sexuality. When Peter takes two toy carriages and bumps them against each other, Klein suggests that they represent his mother and father bumping their 'thingummies together' in order to make a baby. A toy man and a deer falling down repeatedly in his play are said to be 'his own penis and its inferiority in comparison to his father's erect member'.[13] Similar interpretations are echoed everywhere in the early papers.

Technique in psychoanalysis is obviously intimately related to the theory that gives rise to it, and with Melanie Klein this is no exception. Her forthright technique, based on what she called deep interpretations, consisted in addressing the child's unconscious mind directly, hence talking immediately about the hidden symbolic meaning of his play. This was done without first addressing the child's conscious frame of mind and own version of what his game meant. This technique still comes across as blunt because, as initially described by Klein, it appears to bypass the child's conscious participation in the process of exploration, and so trespass uninvited into the child's unconscious mind.

Once again, there are those who imagine that what they find in the early papers represents Klein's intended technique, and furthermore, that this technique is also adopted in contemporary Kleinian child analysis. Neither is the case, however. Klein's intention was not to barge into her child patient's mind, but to reach its more inaccessible crevices on the basis of carefully judged and fully contextualized observations. This is not evident in the publications of her work from the period. However, Klein was to find an opportunity to remedy the situation, spell out her intentions more clearly and defend her technique:

> I should never attempt such a 'wild' symbolic interpretation of children's play. On the contrary, I emphasized this very specially in my latest paper 'Early analysis'. Supposing that a child gives expression to the same psychic material in various repetitions – often actually through various media, i.e., toys, water, by cutting-out, drawing etc. – and supposing that, besides, I can observe that these particular activities are accompanied at the time by a sense of guilt, manifesting itself either as anxiety or in representations which imply over-compensation, which are the expression of reaction formations – supposing, then, that I arrive at an insight into certain connections: then I interpret these phenomena.[14]

The opportunity to thus defend herself arose for Klein when a direct critique of her work was published in detail, spelling out objections to her technique. This event did not altogether take her by surprise. Already in Klein's Berlin and early London years, when she was busy establishing her innovative work, she was no longer the sole and unrivalled occupant of the new field of child psychoanalysis. At some distance from her, in Vienna, Anna Freud was making progress with her own brand of child psychoanalysis, and in the process, was beginning to take issue with Klein's findings. Anna Freud's first comprehensive critique was articulated in her seminal 1927 publication *Introduction to the Technique of Child Analysis*, and, as noted by Young-Bruehl, this work was 'used to bring the differences between her own approach and Melanie Klein's into very stark light.'[15]

The attack on Klein, however, turned out to have one positive outcome. The fact that Anna Freud's reservations were published openly had the advantage of providing Klein with an opportunity to reply to her critic publicly, and so state her position for the record. This opportunity emerged in the same year, because Ernest Jones decided to sponsor a 'Symposium on Child Analysis' in London, devoted precisely to the divergence in thinking which was now emerging so explicitly. O'Shaughnessy suggests that Klein's presentation to the symposium sees her arguing 'forthrightly for her point of view', and indeed Klein spoke frankly.[16] To understand more fully the important nuances of this debate, it is useful first to have a brief assessment of Anna Freud's theoretical position relative to Klein's, especially as viewed in the context of their lifelong debate.

THE CONTROVERSY WITH ANNA FREUD

It is one of the strange twists in psychoanalytic history that Anna Freud and Melanie Klein were never able to collaborate professionally or indeed agree on very much. There was a great deal that might have united them, both professionally and personally. For a start, their fates coincided as the only two significant pioneers of child psychoanalysis working during the same period. At a personal level, Anna Freud and Melanie Klein also had to contend with issues that emerged from belonging to a minority group twice over, both ethnic and professional.

The difficulties that psychoanalysis initially encountered are well documented, along with some of the challenges faced by its women members. Perhaps less familiar is the ethnic dimension of the problem. The lives of Anna Freud and Melanie Klein followed a pattern that owed much to a shared female Jewish identity in a particular historical context. Paradoxically, they were not particularly conscious of the significance of their Jewish background. If anything, they lived as what Isaac Deutscher has called 'non-Jewish Jews', and belonged to a familiar genre of Jewish thinker who was concerned with universal issues and addressed the whole of society. Among such thinkers featured also radical women who had been taking up struggles for causes outside Jewish society since the late nineteenth century. Shepherd has shown how such women, who found it doubly difficult to gain recognition, tended to painful, confrontational, struggles and were sometimes prone to depression as a result.[17]

While Anna Freud and Melanie Klein did not regard themselves as rebels, just as they gave minimal thought to their Jewishness, they both none the less spent their lives pouring their considerable energies into a universal, and undoubtedly radical cause: revolutionizing the understanding of infancy and childhood through psychoanalytic knowledge. This cause also carried with it the pains of isolation and a lifelong struggle for acceptance, exacerbated for Anna Freud and Melanie Klein by each other, and by the fact that instead of joining forces they became each other's most unsparing critics. Among the determinants that contributed to this lifelong animosity between them were important personal factors which also shaped their whole approach to child psychoanalysis. While, as suggested, they had much in common, Anna Freud and Melanie Klein were also, in crucial respects, very different.

ANNA FREUD

Unlike Melanie Klein, Anna Freud had an upbringing that was privileged with a firsthand exposure to Freud's psychoanalysis. From adolescence onwards she was allowed to listen to discussions in Freud's Wednesday evening circle, and so had ready access to all the significant psychoanalytic thinkers who gathered around her father. As well as imbibing the essence of psychoanalysis in this immediate and also gradual way, she was increasingly allowed to help with tasks such as the translation of psychoanalytic works. Her professional progress was thus much more assured and also faster than Klein's. By the time Klein was publishing her findings in 1925, Anna Freud, who was thirteen years her junior, was both qualified and experienced with adult and child patients.

As well as growing up in the hub of the psychoanalytic movement, Anna Freud's loyalty to her father's thinking was intensified by further life circumstances. She chose never to marry, and instead devoted her life single-mindedly to the cause of psychoanalysis. She was later to find herself charged with the care of her frail father, when his suffering from oral cancer made him ever more dependent on her. At this time he not only relied on his daughter physically, but also began to look to her as his psychoanalytic 'heiress'. Freud's influence on his daughter must have received a decisive impetus by another significant factor. When, in her youth, she decided to undertake a personal psychoanalysis, it was to her father that she turned, and indeed he agreed to analyse her.

Not surprisingly, the main thrust of Anna Freud's efforts initially consisted in adapting her father's existing psychoanalytic method as faithfully as possible. It so happened that this suited Anna Freud for temperamental reasons as well. She was by tendency traditional, and so in any case inclined to follow in her father's footsteps. However, while it might be imagined that all these factors would add up to a deeply conservative personality, Anna Freud was, in fact, something of a contradiction. She turned out to be very strong minded and intellectually independent, a mixture that is aptly captured in Wallerstein's phrase 'radical innovator and staunch conservative'.[18] The continuity which Anna Freud sought with her father's thinking was thus far from a question of an uncritical devotion to him. She actually favoured an approach to her work that tended to be more scientific, in the sense that she saw it as her task to study existing models, proceed logically in applying these and systematically collect data to verify their value. Her personality and temperament were suited to this approach. She was by nature methodical and orderly, working with an exactitude that characterized everything she did, and that is aptly exemplified by the way in which she handled her literary estate: 'Anna Freud's own literary estate resembled an archaeological site, keyed precisely to the day-by-day, year-by-year living of her life. She filed away every piece of paper that came her way at 20 Maresfield Gardens from the end of the Second World War to 1982, and she kept carbon copies of every typewritten communication that left the house . . .'[19]

An orderly approach extended also to Anna Freud's clear written style as well as to the mode of training and research that she favoured. Within the Hampstead Clinic that she founded during her years in London, she developed a comprehensive indexing system that was taught to all the staff and used for the collection of an impressive archive. She also designed a profiling system that enabled a consistent, detailed approach to the diagnosis of children.

Given this background, it is perhaps not surprising that Anna Freud approached the profession conventionally, and so began with the logical first step of training as a teacher, before gaining experience with children. By 1922 she was already a member of the Vienna Psychoanalytic Society, but her professional interests remained broad. During the 1920s, she not only continued with clinical work, but also joined an informal study group of young medical students who were drawn to the Vienna Psychoanalytic Society. It is telling that these students were based in the *Ambulatorium*, which provided free medical treatment to the poor classes in Vienna, because this work resonated with Anna Freud's increasing interest in the provision of mental health to the public sector.

This interest intensified for Anna Freud when a psychoanalytic training institute became established in Vienna and she was asked to offer a child psychoanalysis seminar there. She was able to do so with great success, but it also provided her with an opportunity to offer joint teaching events with other child experts in the institute. It is thus that she joined with Aichhorn, Bernfeld and Hoffer, who between them had a wealth of experience in different child-care institutions, and together they taught a course in psychoanalytic pedagogy. Yet again Anna Freud found herself in a group which was oriented to public-sector work, but this time, the work was much more specifically targeted towards children, particularly those suffering from deprivation and delinquency. It was with this group of colleagues that Anna Freud began to share her reservations about Klein's new ideas. Her colleagues agreed that Klein was making a particularly blatant error: she was attributing asocial behaviour and delinquency in the child to personality factors such as neurosis, instead of environmental factors, such as the quality of care available to the child.

These beginnings left a lasting mark on Anna Freud's future work, which could never be confined entirely to a private consulting room. Indeed, even her London years were to be marked by her cultivation of community-based work, and she was to continue to extend her expertise to children who were deprived, traumatized, orphaned, handicapped and, for one reason or another, a concern of society as a whole. Anna Freud's conviction that children should be viewed in context when analysed, and her sensitivity to the significance of their external circumstances was rooted partly in this history, because she knew about the predicament of children who suffered blatantly from external afflictions and traumas, and therefore whose disturbed behaviour was evidently linked to their unfortunate life events. This meant that she always aimed at a balance and warned against '... viewing the child from one aspect only, whether this aspect concerns his object relations ... his social adaptation ... or his intellectual achievements.'[20]

In London, during the war years, Anna Freud was able to secure a grant from the American Foster Parents Plan for War Children, and open the Hampstead War Nursery, which was then attached to her training clinic. Children were sent to her by the Hampstead Billeting Authorities, by hospitals from poor parts of London and by psychiatric social workers from the East End Rest Centres. The Hampstead War Nursery offered places to children from bombed houses, 'tube sleepers' who had spent their nights on noisy platforms and developed sleep difficulties, children who had been sent back from evacuation after failing to settle down, children whose fathers had joined the armed services and whose mothers were at work, and other similar cases. Anna Freud not only organized expert care for those children but trained the staff engaged with them to observe and record all the important psychological details that emerged. This project typifies Anna Freud's vision of the ideal child mental health provision: it combined a humane public service with a rigorous scientific research programme.

Given this background, it is not surprising that Anna Freud found Melanie Klein's personality and lifestyle grating. When compared with her own orderly existence, Klein's life, with its frequent moves, its controversies and her divorce must have appeared turbulent and unconventional. Unlike Anna Freud, Klein had little patience for mundane details, and possessed a mind that though highly original, was none the less considered to be anarchic, or, in Ernest Jones's words, 'neither scientific nor orderly'. Indeed the approach that characterized Klein's work could be described more as artistic than scientific, proceeding through intuition and emotion, exploring the depths of primitive phantasy life and favouring evocative description as a main explanatory tool. In line with this Melanie Klein developed no systematic indexing or recording methods, and left behind only a handful of papers that expound her basic concepts. All this would have cut no ice with Anna Freud.

However, Anna Freud's background also had disadvantages as far as psychoanalytic pioneering was concerned. Her first observations of children were necessarily restricted by her formal and traditional approach, and she could not help thinking like a teacher and like Freud's daughter. By comparison, Melanie Klein's personal involvement in the first observations of children led to a much more free and also a closer look at their inner lives. Her observations were domestic, intimate and close to the source. Her experience was soon to show that psychoanalytic discoveries spring from unexpected quarters, and that the processes most likely to yield them are not so much scientific classification, as a particular kind of observation stance. It was important that this stance should not be hampered either by the psychoanalyst's external prejudices, nor by her internal defences against what emerged in the consulting room.

Without cumbersome affiliations, and in the privacy of her own consulting room, Klein was able to respond naturally and intuitively to the children whom she saw, and so develop the crucially important psychoanalytic play technique. Away from parents and in the private conditions of her consulting room, she was also more able to follow the child's subjective interpretation of his circumstances, and what his unconscious phantasy life made of his experiences. She was also not deterred by the way in which the child's strange reality became larger than life and overwhelming, and did not rush to impose an adult rationality on the meaning that emerged from his play. She felt that this subjective process was most powerful in shaping the essential characteristics of the child's psyche, and as such, should be the target of analytic efforts. As seen, this led her to address the child's unconscious mind directly, through deep interpretations. She argued that while it is often not possible to change the child's actual circumstances or environment, nor transform the child's parents, it is still possible to tackle the child's internal fragility through targeting his unconscious responses and releasing the related anxieties. She was convinced that doing so would alleviate the child's inner turmoil, and so empower him to cope with his imperfect environment from a position of greater inner strength: 'I have found that the children were enabled by analysis to adapt themselves better and therefore better to stand the test of an unfavourable milieu and to suffer less than before being analysed.'[21]

The emphasis on internal versus external dimensions of the child patient's predicament was one of the characteristic differences between the approaches of Melanie Klein and Anna Freud, but it is important to realize that these differences were symptomatic of their much more thoroughgoing disagreements on early mental life. As suggested, the disagreements were first aired in the 1927 London Symposium. However, this was only the first occasion for an open debate, and was succeeded, at a later date, by the much more ferocious professional confrontation of the Controversial Discussions. Not until 1938 were Melanie Klein and Anna Freud to find themselves living in the same place and working in the same, small psychoanalytic community. The war in Europe obliged the Freuds to flee from Vienna and move to London, where they now decided to make their home. It was here that the Freud-Klein differences came into the open yet again, and in a far more explosive way. It is worth moving forwards in time to 1941, for a brief overview of this major confrontation before focusing again on the earlier 1927 debate and its important links to Klein's clinical experience with child patients.

THE FREUD-KLEIN CONTROVERSIES

In 1938 Anna Freud and Melanie Klein came into close quarters at the same psychoanalytic society for the first time. For as long as there had still been a geographical distance between the two of them, it had been possible for them to sustain a reasonably conventional professional debate. But in London it became increasingly difficult to maintain such professional composure. Anna Freud increasingly took the devastating line that Klein's work could not really qualify as psychoanalysis, and within three years, they were to confront each other publicly in the Controversial Discussions.[22] The discussions, which took the form of a series of Kleinian presentations, were debated in the British Psychoanalytical Society between 1943 and 1945, and the debate lingered throughout this period without resolution.

Part of the difficulty in resolving the issues which emerged was that by the time Melanie Klein and Anna Freud confronted each other in the early 1940s, they were no longer doing so merely as child psychoanalysts, but as representatives of two opposing streams within the British psychoanalytic establishment. They were both experienced practitioners with well-formed views, and each commanded a small but dedicated following. Their insights, though clearly divergent, had immediate relevance to psychoanalysis in general, in as much as they were derived directly from data that held clues to the earliest and most formative experiences in life. Not surprisingly therefore, the discussions drew in not only their corresponding small circle of adherents, but the entire Society.

The content of the discussions remains a rich contribution to the history of ideas, but a consensus on key issues could not be reached, either by the two women, or by the Society itself. By this stage in her thinking, Klein's theory had evolved considerably. In its essence lay her belief that the human infant is born with a readiness for social interactions, and so is immediately capable of forming object relations, even though these are rudimentary and incomplete. The infant, Melanie Klein suggested, apprehends only 'parts and portions of the object world'.[23] But it does respond to maternal nurture, and becomes attached to a part of the mother that carries immediate significance for it – her feeding breast. This attachment is physical and libidinal, but also emotional and psychical. The breast represents not only food, but by virtue of offering also comfort and pleasure acquires the significance of 'good'. However, the maternal breast is also necessarily depriving, and when not available to the infant can provoke a frustrated aggression which endows it with the significance of 'bad'. The infant is thus equipped from birth to apprehend a qualitative essence in different kinds of life experiences, and so to make primary differentiations between good and bad, between what should be accepted and what should be rejected.

To Anna Freud such advanced differentiating capacities in the infant were hardly credible. They also threatened her father's model of development, which postulated instead an initial foetal-like primary narcissism. Sigmund Freud had envisaged the young infant as noticing very little of the outside world, its existence governed by the pleasure principle, and its primitive mind drifting into dream-like, hallucinatory states that hinder the full apprehension of worldly frustrations. Only gradually do such frustrations impinge on the infantile mind, thus enabling it to begin to accommodate the reality principle, and only then are object relations tenable.

Melanie Klein not only subverted this notion, but, on the basis of her beliefs, proceeded to hypothesize a rudimentary psychical activity that exists from birth and that she termed 'phantasy'. This concept was the first to be presented and debated in the Controversial Discussions, and was written up for this purpose by Klein's closest and most articulate adherent, Susan Isaacs.[24] In Klein's thinking, phantasy begins to operate at the very beginning of life. Its initial function is to both give form to infantile instinctual life, and also to elaborate and represent worldly events internally, gradually enabling the emergence of clearer cognitive capacities in the infant. In the adult, phantasy continues to be active in the deep, unconscious layers of the mind. It accompanies normal, everyday thinking, comprising a primitive, unconscious running commentary on the flow of conscious experience. In earliest infancy, well before the emergence of cognition and speech, phantasy is the main activity of the psyche, and in this sense, the earliest form of mental life.

During the time of the Controversial Discussions and in the succeeding years, Klein was to envisage an increasingly complex content to early phantasy, suggesting that it could also be used by the infant for defensive purposes. Accordingly, the newborn can feel overwhelmed by worldly impingements and react with anxiety. As a result, its phantasy life begins to elaborate archaic defence mechanisms which aim at fending off excessively disturbing or painful emotions. Klein felt that this archaic level of experience is the fixation point for some adult pathologies, and so helps to explain the mechanisms at work in psychiatric conditions including schizophrenia, manic depression and obsessional disorders. The revolutionary implications of this view are that all the important mental ingredients of adult psychotic illness are genetically present in early psychical life, and are, in fact, none other than the primary defences used by the human psyche. Healthy development is, by implication, a process which gradually mitigates such defences to the point at which they are no longer dominant, and so allow into the mind a sufficient reality sense for normal functioning.

This Kleinian model clearly indicated a radically different approach to analytic interpretations than the one favoured by Anna Freud, who continued to attribute complex processes and pathologies only to much later stages of development. As the early 1940s discussions could not be resolved, the situation was finally settled through a compromise whereby Klein's thinking was recognized as psychoanalytic, implying that she was allowed to keep her membership in the British Psychoanalytical Society. This also opened the way for her to develop her own line of work as a distinctive psychoanalytic school. Melanie Klein had survived professionally. The Controversies were an extremely serious threat to her position, and had the result been otherwise, she might well have lost the British Psychoanalytic Society's recognition of her status.

Moving back to consider the earlier 1927 Symposium confrontation between

Anna Freud and Melanie Klein, it is particularly interesting for revealing how their lifelong divergence was already then well in evidence. In hindsight, it is also possible to regard the symposium, and the arguments aired in it, as an early and more muffled precursor of the early 1940s controversies. As was to happen again later, it was Anna Freud who laid down the gauntlet with her 1927 publication *Introduction to the Technique of Child Analysis*.

THE 1927 SYMPOSIUM – KLEIN'S EARLY DISCOVERIES

For a start, Anna Freud was not at ease with the licence that Klein gave her little patients in the consulting room, nor with Klein's daring decision to make them conscious of their hostility towards their parents. Much to Klein's chagrin, Anna Freud voiced what adults had always tended to believe about children – that once allowed freedom, the child would lose her all too fragile impulse control and quickly deteriorate into delinquency. There was only one way to keep primitive, asocial childish impulses at bay. The adult in charge needed to restrain the child and thereby support her otherwise still fragile social and moral functioning. The psychic agency responsible for this functioning, or super-ego, had only recently been formulated by Freud in his new structural theory.

Freud's structural model represented a fresh approach to mental development. He now became aware that the child's overcoming of the Oedipus complex was more developmentally complex than he had appreciated. He realized that it is not enough for the child to surrender her desires uncomprehendingly, as this only leaves her feeling defeated and 'castrated'. A genuine resolution requires a fundamental psychical change which expands the child's mental horizons, enabling an altered and developmentally broadened perspective on her situation. Freud visualized this psychical change in structural terms. The mind's structure is altered and expanded when the child absorbs into herself aspects of parental authority. These are internalized to create an intrapsychic agency of a super-ego, which exerts an internal moral pressure on the child. The process gradually enables the child to accept the procreative sexual role of the parents and her own place within the family, thus making her socialized.

However, Freud felt that this was an achievement which could only happen with some degree of maturation, when the child was close to the age of five, and thus more in control of verbal and cognitive processes. In line with this, Anna Freud suggested that the younger child or toddler has not begun to develop a proper super-ego, and thus has no internal means of curbing her impulses. Even with older children, she suggested, the super-ego is newly formed and needs to develop in strength. In her view, the actual guidance of adults was therefore essential for children in all circumstances, whether outside or within the consulting room. In her own Symposium response, Klein clearly registered Anna Freud's conviction: '. . . when a child's instinctual tendencies have been brought into consciousness, the super-ego by itself should not be expected to assume complete responsibility for their direction. For she believes that children, left to themselves on this point, can only discover "one single short and convenient path – that of direct gratification".'[25]

Anna Freud's opinions were in direct continuity with her father's conviction that children's impulses have to be tamed, and that without threatening parents and nursemaids the child's behaviour and state of mind would disintegrate dangerously. Klein was chafing irritably with what she regarded as a mere feebleness on Anna Freud's part:

> Anna Freud had the feeling that she ought not to intervene between child and parents and that the home training would be endangered and conflicts aroused in the child if his opposition to his parents were brought to his consciousness ... She herself says that she feels uneasy in relation to the child's parents as her employers if she, as she calls it, sets herself against them.[26]

However, there was more to Anna Freud's critique. It was not quite so simplistic, nor was she concerned with a mere unleashing of naughtiness, even though it did trouble her. Anna Freud's objections clustered around a related issue which stirred in her particular misgivings. This was Klein's belief that the child patient is able to form a proper transference to her psychoanalyst, and exactly like the adult patient, transfer her typical patterns of relating to the arena of the analytic session. This added to the unacceptable view of the child's psyche as much more formed than it seemed to Anna Freud. Just as the young child was not sufficiently developed to have a super-ego and curb her own impulses, she was also not as yet sufficiently autonomous from her parents to have a clear internal sense of them as separate people. Anna Freud conceded that, 'The child indeed enters into the liveliest relations with the analyst' but emphasized that this should be taken at face value, and that the child definitely 'forms no transference neurosis'. She went on to explain that 'The child is not, like the adult, ready to produce a new edition of its love-relationships, because, as one might say, the old edition is not yet exhausted'.[27] This, Anna Freud reflected, is due to the fact that the child's

> ... original objects, the parents, are still real and present love-objects, not only in phantasy as with the adult neurotic; between them and the child exist all the relations of everyday life, and all its gratifications and disappointments still in reality depend on them. The analyst enters this situation as a new person ... but there is no necessity for the child to exchange the parents for him, since compared with them he has not the advantages which the adult finds when he can exchange his phantasy-objects for a real person.[28]

Melanie Klein was not swayed by this argument. In fact, the whole point of her Symposium presentation was precisely to challenge it. She believed that Anna Freud was wrong, and that there already was an 'old edition' of love-relationships in the child's mind, albeit not an obvious one. By the time of the Controversial Discussions, Klein was to become confirmed in this belief. Her more fully evolved theory at this later stage led her to think of this 'old edition' as composed of the archaic, rudimentary experiences of earliest infancy that had been absorbed into the infant's psyche to assume an internal form. Klein was to suggest that this archaic edition had already been internalized and integrated into the child's view of reality, colouring her relationships with all the adults in her life including the parents. It helped to explain why the small child's perception of ordinary parental behaviour was tinged with primitive elements that exaggerated its different facets; parental affection seemed more ideal to the young child than it was in reality, and by the same token, parental disapproval could be heard as more persecutory and threatening than it actually was. The process of phantasy enabled the young infant gradually to create primitive mental representations of the good and bad aspect of her first relationship with the mother. These representations, or internal objects, already integrated into the ego of the young child, were revived in the analytic relationship, endowing the child analyst with malevolent or ideal qualities, much as if the latter came to bear the mark of archaic features of the child patient's earliest environment.

While this understanding of 1940 was sophisticated and detailed, it is interesting to discover that even as early as 1927, with much of her understanding still to come, Klein was already adamant that the child patient forms a transference. Anna Freud immediately challenged her with further pragmatism. The adult, she argued, engaged with free associations voluntarily, while stopping other activities and lying down on the analytic couch. The child, however, could not easily separate meaningful play from her general activities and movements in the consulting room. How was one to ascertain which of her activities was a symbolic expression? Furthermore, in the child's play,

> ... [a] car collision may be reproducing some happening in the street; and the child who runs towards a lady visitor and opens her handbag is not necessarily, as Mrs Klein maintains, thereby symbolically expressing its curiosity as to whether its mother's womb conceals another little brother or sister, but may be connecting some experience of the previous day when someone brought it a little present in a similar receptacle.[29]

Anna Freud thus underscored the child's continuous engagement with her changing external environment. Often young children do not narrate external events coherently, and may indeed prefer to express the impact of these through play by repeating elements of what they had observed. Deep meaning, and sexual significance of the type that Klein appeared to discern should not be read into the child's ordinary need to repeat through play events that had been witnessed.

Logical though this thinking was, it failed to impress Melanie Klein, because it was not so much logic, as intuitive observation which guided her own thinking. She insisted that contrary to the prevailing Freudian belief, it was possible to discover a great deal about children without requiring them to lie on the couch or needing to elicit free associations from them. Play provided the solution, for it was the equivalent of adult free associating, making the child's deep unconscious readily available to the analyst. The phantasy elements revealed through play came from the same primitive source as adult dream material, hence also comprising a 'royal road to the unconscious'. Anna Freud was thus wrong to ignore the primitive unconscious elements that necessarily permeated the child's play. The play itself, by virtue of being unstructured and free-flowing, was a perfect vehicle for the unbridled meanderings of unconscious processes.

However, even with these explanations, Klein still needed to account convincingly for the child patient's ability to form a transference. Her early papers reveal how much this assumption was the product of direct experience, and emerged from her acute observation of what unfolded in the room with her patients. Klein's clinical observations yielded spectacular results because her child patients were uninhibited, and the fact that they were allowed to be so, was itself a link in the historical chain that culminated in her overall outlook in the early period.

In her applications of theory to her work, Klein was continuing to hold with some of Ferenczi's essential ideas. She had not lost her enthusiasm for his belief that, as far as child development was concerned, it was important to free the child from anxiety rather than increase her anxiety burden through coercive methods. This liberal principle was now resurrected by Klein, making an appearance in her new technique. She sought to give her child patients a sense of freedom in the consulting room so that they would lose their inhibitions and express more direct primitive impulses through their play. In accordance with this, she felt that the instinctual commotion which was unleashed in the child analytic session should not be curbed, but quite the contrary, understood and analysed. She referred to Erna, in whom analysis 'liberated enormous quantities of affect' leading to 'extraordinary abreactions', which included 'rages which were vented on objects in my room, such as cushions etc.; dirtying and destroying of playthings . . . and so forth'.[30]

In spite of this, Klein did not worry that the child's discharge of instinctual tension would weaken her moral fibre, because this discharge was not a simple question of degenerate behaviour: 'I discovered that it was not simply a case of "uninhibited" gratification . . . She was not by any means so "happy".' Rather, Klein suggested, 'what lay behind Erna's "lack of restraint" was anxiety'.[31] This way of viewing the child was indeed revolutionary. For the first time another factor besides naughtiness was pinpointed as disturbing children and making them unamenable to ordinary educative measures. If deep anxiety rather than amoral gratification was at source, then no amount of strict curbing was going to calm the child.

And indeed this was what Klein experienced directly with her little patients. Once given the freedom to express themselves with her, the children might, in theory, have expressed an array of different emotions, and yet in practice, the predominant emotions discharged in the room were those of anxiety and aggression. And it was when Klein observed how such emotions were vented, that she became convinced of the child's transference, for she could not help but notice that it was inevitably she who became the immediate target of the children's impulses. She was sometimes both hated and feared, but with her characteristic acuity, perceived that such negative emotions lacked a basis in the reality of her person or her manifest behaviour towards the children. For example, her little patient Ruth approached psychoanalysis with ideas about Klein which were predetermined even before they met. She arrived for her initial sessions in a terrified state, and refused to come into the room alone with Melanie Klein. Klein was obliged to analyse Ruth with her older sister present in the room, but no amount of niceness on her part, nor indeed any efforts to engage Ruth in play, prepared Klein for the terror that seized Ruth when her sister could not attend one day: 'I tried to comfort her and cheer her up and make her play with me, but in vain. When she was herself alone with me ... she went quite white and screamed, and showed all the signs of a severe attack of anxiety'.[32]

Klein astutely noticed that Ruth's reaction had little to do with what she had actually noticed or managed to learn about her analyst during their short acquaintance. Moreover, Ruth had made up her mind about her analyst even before their first meeting. And Klein would have countered any objection to the effect that children are normally cautious with strangers, by stressing the need to look for the primitive underpinnings of such childish caution.

According to Ferenczi, the child moved gradually from distortion to a full sense of reality, and this helped to explain why children can cling so tenaciously to certain irrational beliefs, and why, at times, all the reasoning in the world does not alter their distorted perceptions. While continuing with this line of Ferenczi's thinking, Klein was now able to add to it in the light of her new and direct experience of children. She felt that more was happening in her consulting room than the display of an incomplete reality-sense. Ruth was behaving as though Klein were a dangerous being, and Klein felt that Ruth had a definite subjective version of who her analyst was. Was this perhaps, after all, an 'old edition' of emotional relations which had come from within the child's unconscious mind, and if so, what was this an old edition of?

Klein had not, as yet, conceived of internal objects at this stage, and what is more, was still holding with Freud's key findings. She was thus led to her first revolutionary conclusion – the bad creature into which her anxious patient turned her was none other than a harsh super-ego, entirely internal to the child's mental structure. Contrary to Anna Freud's belief that the patient could only transfer fully understood parental figures on to the psychoanalyst, she suggested that the latter was only the case as far as adults were concerned. When it came to child patients, the transference consisted in 'transferring' on to the person of the psychoanalyst an aspect of their psyche – a harsh, infantile super-ego.

Here Klein began her first drastic departure from Freudian thinking. Ferenczi had argued convincingly that the young child only gradually acquires a reality sense, so the child would, in any case, distort its earliest perceptions of parental prohibitions. However, there was more that needed to be added to this thinking. Klein repeatedly witnessed how in the child's play, representations of parental punishments closely mirrored the savage cruelty characterizing the child's own aggressive phantasies. It seemed that the two were connected, and that the child's ferocious discharge of aggression determined the kind of parental response that she imagined. The parents were felt to reflect back to the child the very aggression which had been directed at them in the first place, and which was now assumed to have infiltrated their being. It was because of her own aggression that the child began to attribute similar impulses to the parents, and so greatly exaggerate and fear their ordinary disapproval or attempts at disciplining. It was thus the child's aggression which determined the kind of super-ego which first figured in her psyche. It was also this aggression that intensified the child's anxieties and inhibited her development.

In her debate with Anna Freud, Klein now delineated their diametrically opposed clinical conclusions: 'We find that what is needed is not to reinforce [the child's] super-ego but to tone it down.'[33]

Such thinking led Klein to a further emphasis on the child's internal world rather than the actual parents, and as seen, this was regarded as inappropriately one-sided by Anna Freud. However, the postulation of a super-ego at such early ages led her to an even more serious clash with the prevailing psychoanalytic orthodoxy. In Freud's model, the super-ego would only be formed later, when the child was nearly five and as a result of the resolution of the Oedipus complex. He believed that it is this latter which provides the child with the means of internalising parental values and authority, because it is only the Oedipus complex which can enable the child to master asocial, sexual and aggressive tendencies, such as incestuous desires for the mother and murderous hatred for the father. How was Klein to account for a super-ego at a time when the child was not supposed to have achieved any kind of Oedipal awareness?

Klein needed to concede that Freud was right. Without the Oedipus complex, it was hard to know why a restraining intrapsychic agency such as the super-ego would need to come into existence at all. With this in mind Klein continued to observe her patients. She began to wonder if the child's aggression, and corresponding phantasies of a sadistic parental retaliation, have their origin in the Oedipal situation after all, just as Freud had concluded. What this implied was not that Freud had been wrong about the relationship between the Oedipal situation and the formation of a super-ego, but that these processes began earlier than he had imagined.

Rather than assume that they would begin only when the child was near the age of five, perhaps it was possible to detect in children as young as two or three years old some sort of rudimentary Oedipal configuration. Klein was soon to become more convinced that this was indeed the case, and boldly ventured the hypothesis that the Oedipus complex begins much earlier than postulated by Freud and accepted as fact in psychoanalytic thinking: 'I conclude from this that the small child's anxiety and feelings of guilt have their origin in aggressive trends connected with the Oedipus conflict.'[34]

This assumption would also help to explain the corresponding existence of an early super-ego. But it inevitably courted intense controversy because it was completely at odds with the prevailing psychoanalytic view of development. However, it also led Klein into new territory. Bringing the super-ego forwards had substantial implications towards the viewing of early mental life, because it introduced the idea of archaic, primitive thought processes which shape the early

Oedipus complex and create a uniquely childish understanding of the world. In other words, Klein's idea of the child's transference now moved it firmly into the world of archaic experience which is subjective and distorted by internal, early Oedipal and pre-Oedipal phantasies.

NOTES

1. Petot, J. M. (1990) *Melanie Klein Vol. 1: First Discoveries and First System 1919–1932*. Madison, CT: International Universities Press.
2. Frank, C. and Weib, H. (1996) 'The origins of disquieting discoveries by Melanie Klein: the possible significance of the case of "Erna" ', *International Journal of Psycho-Analysis* 77, 6, p. 1102.
3. Frank, C. (1999) 'The discovery of the child as an object *sui generis* of cure and research by Melanie Klein as reflected in the notes of her first child analyses in Berlin 1921–26', in *Psychoanalysis and History*, 1, 2, p. 161.
4. Klein was invited to London with the initial specific aim of psychoanalysing Ernest Jones's children. (See P. Grosskurth (1985) *Melanie Klein*. London: Maresfield Library. p. 159)
5. Klein, M. (1975) 'A contribution to the psychogenesis of tics', in *Love, Guilt and Reparation*. London: The Hogarth Press. (First published 1927.)
6. Klein, M. (1975) 'An obsessional neurosis in a six-year-old girl', in *The Psychoanalysis of Children*. London: The Hogarth Press and the Institute of Psycho-Analysis. (First published 1932.)
7. Klein, M. (1975) 'Psychological principles of early analysis', in *Love, Guilt and Reparation*. London: The Hogarth Press and the Institute of Psycho-Analysis. (First published 1926.) p. 132.
8. ibid., p 131.
9. ibid., p. 28.
10. Klein, M. (1975) 'An obsessional neurosis in a six-year-old girl', in *The Psychoanalysis of Children*. London: The Hogarth Press and the Institute of Psycho-Analysis. (First published 1932.) p. 38.
11. Greenberg, J. R. and Mitchell, S. A. (1983) *Object Relations in Psychoanalytic Theory*. Cambridge, MA: Harvard University Press, p. 122.
12. For examples of contemporary child analytic technique see M. Rustin and M. Rhode (eds) (1999) *Psychotic States in Children*. Tavistock Series, London: Duckworth; D. Daws (1993) *Through the Night: Helping Parents with Sleepless Infants*. New York: Basic Books; A. Alvarez (1992) *Live Company*. London: Tavistock/Routledge.
13. Klein, M. (1975) 'The technique of early analysis', in *The Psychoanalysis of Children*. London: The Hogarth Press and the Institute of Psycho-Analysis. (First published in 1932.) pp. 19–20.
14. Klein, M. (1975) 'Symposium on child-analysis', in *Love, Guilt and Reparation*. London: The Hogarth Press and the Institute of Psycho-Analysis. (First published in 1927.) p. 147.
15. Young-Bruehl, E. (1988) *Anna Freud*. London: Macmillan. p. 165.

16. See 'Explanatory notes', prepared by E. O'Shaughnessy with H. Segal, B. Joseph and R. E. Money-Kyrle, in (1975) *Love, Guilt and Reparation*. London: The Hogarth Press and the Institute of Psycho-Analysis.

17. See Shepherd, N. (1993) *A Price Below Rubies: Jewish Women as Rebels and Radicals*. London: Weidenfeld & Nicolson.

18. Wallerstein, R. (1984) 'Anna Freud: radical innovator and staunch conservative', in *The Psychoanalytic Study of the Child*, 39, pp. 65–80.

19. Young-Bruehl, E. (1988) *Anna Freud*. London: Macmillan, p. 16.

20. Freud, A. (1962) 'Assessment of pathology in childhood, Part I' (1970), in *Writings 5*. London: The Hogarth Press and the Institute of Psycho-Analysis. pp. 26–37.

21. Klein, M. (1975) 'Symposium on child-analysis', in *Love, Guilt and Reparation*. London: The Hogarth Press and the Institute of Psycho-Analysis. (First published 1921.) p. 165.

22. King, P. and Steiner, R. (1991) *The Freud-Klein Controversies 1941–1945*. London: Tavistock/Routledge.

23. Klein, M. (1975) 'A contribution to the psychogenesis of manic-depressive states', in *Love, Guilt and Reparation*. London: The Hogarth Press and the Institute of Psycho-Analysis. (First published 1935.) p. 285.

24. Isaacs, S. (1991) 'The nature and the function of phantasy', in P. King and R. Steiner (eds) *The Freud-Klein Controversies 1941–1945*. London: Tavistock/Routledge. (First published 1941.) pp. 265–321.

25. Klein, M. (1975) 'Symposium on child-analysis', in *Love, Guilt and Reparation*. London: The Hogarth Press and the Institute of Psycho-Analysis. (First published 1927.) p. 159.

26. ibid., p. 163.

27. Freud, A. (1946) *The Psychoanalytical Treatment of Children*. London: Inigo.

28. ibid., p. 34.

29. ibid., p. 29.

30. Klein, M. (1975) 'Symposium on child-analysis', in *Love, Guilt and Reparation*. London: The Hogarth Press and the Institute of Psycho-Analysis. (First published 1927.) p. 160.

31. ibid., p. 160.

32. Klein, M. (1975) 'The technique of early analysis', in *The Psychoanalysis of Children*. London: The Hogarth Press and the Institute of Psycho-Analysis. (First published in 1932.) p. 27.

33. Klein, M. (1975) 'Symposium on child-analysis', in *Love, Guilt and Reparation*. London: The Hogarth Press and the Institute of Psycho-Analysis. (First published in 1927.) p. 164.

34. ibid., p. 5.

CHAPTER 5

'Figures wholly divorced from reality' – The Departure from Freud

I n the eight-year period between 1927 and 1935, Klein was able to expand substantially on her new theoretical ideas, accounting in much fuller detail for her controversial claims about the early onset of the Oedipus complex and super-ego. The writing from this period is often demanding. The psychoanalytic framework which has thus far been solidly Freudian, now becomes destabilized by shifts in the deeper strata of Klein's awareness. The implications of postulating an early Oedipus complex and super-ego are gradually discovered to be momentous. At a more immediate level, less important and more contentious issues claim the reader's attention. The strongest impression left by this period is both controversial and disturbing. Klein paints a picture of childhood sadism that is unprecedented in its ferocity, and that seems out of keeping with ordinary expectations. The picture is so stark that it has created, then and since, an unfortunate reputation for her theory. She has been charged with presenting a strange exaggeration, if not a downright distortion, of infantile mental life.

An initial examination of the texts from this period might surprise the reader, since it unexpectedly mitigates some of this reputation, if only a little. It is evident that the effect on Klein of her first extended period in London was far more lively. It awoke her interest in culture, history and evolution and also led her to think about creativity. While indeed suggesting that the human infant has particularly sadistic urges, she began to regard the infant's psyche as also essentially creative. She explored a mental mechanism of projection which leads the child to displace instinctual forces from the interior arena of his psyche outwards, and so invest the world with a qualitative variety of affect. In tandem with this, she postulated a process of introjection, whereby aspects of the external world are taken into the self and incorporated by the mind. Her vision from this period centralizes the human propensity not only to invest the world with subjective states, but also to take in, personify and dramatize what is encountered, thus creating a unique internal world.

Klein's exploration of this two-way, essentially creative dialogue between the world and the psyche was one of the important achievements of this period. However, at the same time, this achievement does not come across as vividly as it might, and does indeed suffer under the shadow of a melancholy outlook. In these years Klein repeatedly goes back to a grim theoretical scenario, almost as if she needs an opportunity to work through its sobering implications. This scenario, which has been compared with the notion of original sin, concerns the belief that the natural human state, as witnessed in infancy and before the advent of civilizing social influences, is a state of acute and exclusive sadism.

A powerful pessimistic streak undoubtedly runs through the texts of this period. However, to give it exclusive attention is also to miss the essence of Klein's overall development as a thinker, and the fact that her theory of sadism is embedded in a much broader framework. For a start, within Klein's overall oeuvre, the extreme beliefs of the 1927–35 period only marked a transitional point. Her controversial view on human sadism was to change significantly. What is more, it is the other thinking that develops during these years which poses an increasing challenge to it. What begins as a view of original sin is gradually transformed into its very opposite – a view of innate moral potentialities in the human individual.

Klein's emphasis on, and exploration of, sadism was none the less never abandoned. It kept reappearing in her writings in new guises late into her career, as if to raise again the same painful questions: why are human individuals capable of sadism, and how, in the process of socialization, does the mind find mechanisms to deal with its own cruelty? Important aspects of Kleinian theory are built around these questions and her unique mode of addressing them. It is therefore essential to have some understanding of the context into which Klein's beliefs during the 1927–35 years fit.

As might be anticipated, Klein continued to absorb the influences of her psychoanalytic mentors. However, she now ventured much further, and became even bolder with her conclusions. This affected the way in which she continued to carry forwards some of Ferenczi's thinking, specifically his ideas on the development of a reality sense. She explored revolutionary implications of this concept through her related notion of an infantile epistemophilic instinct, or instinct for seeking knowledge, which she now suggested as an addition to the array of libidinal and self-preservative instincts posited by Freud. The other influence which now increasingly gave impetus to her inventiveness was that of her second, and Berlin, psychoanalyst Karl Abraham, who had treated her until shortly before his death in the Christmas of 1925. The impact of his thinking on Klein resulted in a rush of extraordinary ideas. Yet while the influence of both her psychoanalysts came naturally, Klein found that she needed to continue to make a more conscious effort where a third, and more politically necessary influence was concerned, and this was Freud's.

Klein realized that in order to attach her discoveries securely to the theoretical body of psychoanalysis, it was not sufficient for her to offer clinical discoveries framed in her own terms, however original. She needed to find convincing ways of linking her emerging vision with the main body of Freudian thought. Initially she must have believed that this would be a relatively straightforward matter of applying relevant Freudian concepts to each of her findings in turn. She was, in any case, assuming that Freud's theory was providing the very lens through which she could observe, and make sense of, clinical data. However, this needed to be made more explicit, preferably by an overt tracing of her major clinical insights back to specific Freudian concepts.

The 1927–35 period is indeed characterized by Klein's repeated attempts to do just this. At the same time, it was becoming clear that the age group with which she was most concerned was not fully known to Freud. Before long, she found herself unable to resist the urge to fill in gaps in his thinking on infantile sexuality, and so extending Freudian theory. And because there were other important strands besides Freudian theory in her thinking as shown, Klein's evolving framework began to depart even further from classical Freudian conventions and take on a distinct character of its own. Some of the ways in which this happened will now be traced, showing the unexpected turns which led Klein to the unwitting creation of a new theory.

APPLYING FREUDIAN CONCEPTS

There were specific elements of Freudian theory which Klein was particularly keen to apply to her discoveries. As seen, her belief that child patients form a transference and her direct experience of such transference situations led to the supposition that there was a 'old edition' of emotional relations in the child's mind which could be transferred on to the psychoanalyst. Her conscious effort to interpret this finding along Freudian lines led her to assume that this edition was none other than an early super-ego, and as suggested, this, in turn, necessitated her postulation of an early Oedipus complex. The latter was felt by her to account for the source of the child's acute sadism and phantasy attacks on the mother.

However, in the process of accounting for an early Oedipus complex, Klein soon ran into theoretical difficulties, specifically because her new ideas seemed to tamper with the very framework that was supposed to give them sense – Freud's theory of infantile sexuality and its pre-genital stages. Freud did not regard the Oedipus complex as relevant to early infancy. His Oedipal subject is, as suggested, closer to the age of four or five, and has therefore already traversed and left behind the earlier, oral and anal, psychosexual stages of development, and is now in the most advanced stage – the genital one. The child is thus able to interpret what he observes of the parental relationship, and although still young and ignorant, can none the less form theories about sexual reproduction and pregnancy. By implication, both parents are perceived as they actually are, and it is within the context of such realism that the child activates Oedipal feelings of desire and hate for them respectively. For Freud, the Oedipal child's mental primitivism is mainly characterized by asocial incest wishes and infantile sexual theories, rather than by a mode of thinking which is wholly and essentially 'other' than adult.

Not so in Klein's view. The play of her small patients had already opened her eyes to the fact that the child's mode of thinking is not merely ignorant, or partially phantasy-dominated, but fundamentally different from the adult's. She now began to appreciate that it was much closer to the logic of the unconscious mind, with its characteristic dream-like quality of primary thought process. This awareness was to receive full realization later, in Klein's crucial concept of unconscious phantasy. However, while this concept was not fully formulated until 1943, its implicit early presence is crucial in the 1927 papers, and makes sense of her assertion that the Oedipus complex which Freud described was only the most visible, advanced form of a phenomenon that began much earlier than he realized.

Klein argued, with the help of clinical illustrations, that the Oedipus situation is not likely to emerge as a sudden discrete entity at an advanced developmental stage in childhood. She suggested instead that it is a phenomenon with archaic roots, and develops gradually and in an incremental manner rather than springing up suddenly at the age of four. In the play of her child patients and in the accounts of their parents, she found evidence that Oedipal patterns of behaviour could be expressed from as early as the second year of life. She gathered, for example, that from infancy onwards, her little patient Rita always showed a marked preference for one parent at a time, and that already by the age of fifteen months she 'used repeatedly to express a desire to be left alone in the room with her father and to sit on his knee and look at books with him.'[1]

Klein could also observe the kind of play that indicated Oedipal preoccupations in the sessions of all her child patients. For example, games about violent night-time events were commonplace, and typically played by children who suffered from night terrors and who repeatedly cried for their parents but without the ability to be easily reassured. As well as this, her little patients' games revolved time and again around the themes of adults, represented by dolls, who pair off in various permutations only to be repeatedly attacked by a third party. This symbolic play indicated that Oedipal states which were even earlier than the second year could not be ruled out.

However, as suggested, expressed purely in these terms, Klein's claims would not have been psychoanalytically tenable. Her colleagues would have argued that it was nonsensical to imagine early infantile thinking as defined by the logic of genital sexuality, and that it made no sense to regard the infant as capable of a recognizable incest wish. They would have agreed with Freud's view that psychosexual development begins with pre-Oedipal stages in which libidinal life is experienced, and also satisfied, via the agency of oral and anal pleasures. The object of these impulses is the mother, who is closely involved with the feeding and excretory processes of the infant's body, and the first psychosexual impulses are directly related to the physical preoccupations of early infancy. These pre-Oedipal stages would need to be traversed before the child's psyche could expand sufficiently for him to become aware of genital sensations, and so be able to grapple with the primal scene of parental sexual relations. If Klein was to undermine this order by bringing forwards the Oedipus complex, how would she make room in development for pre-Oedipal, oral and anal stages of psychosexuality?

However, Klein was decidedly not abandoning the idea of pre-genital, oral and anal stages. Quite the contrary. She was suggesting that locating the Oedipus complex at an earlier age had profound implications precisely because it was no longer aligned with the genital phase of development. Instead, Klein reasoned, the Oedipus complex coincided with earlier pre-genital mental life, and so took its character from the oral and anal processes that dominated early development: 'Intercourse comes to mean to the child a performance in which eating, cooking, exchange of faeces and sadistic acts of every kind ... play the principal part.'[2]

The fact that Oedipal experiences began much earlier complicated the picture of development in other ways. Where Freud suggested that the Oedipal child has genital desires for one parent and wishes to be rid of the other, Klein felt that the very early age at which the Oedipal process begins changes this. The younger child's desire is not so much for something that is genital and incestuous. His frustrated crying is not for withheld genital pleasures, as Freud assumed, but more for inaccessible oral and anal pleasures which are craved from both parents, but particularly from the feeding mother. The early Oedipal aggression is directed at the two parents when they are imagined to withhold the physical gratifications of feeding and handling from the child, and offer it to each other instead. Klein thus invokes the sense of a younger infant who craves elements of gratification and nurture more than outright genital incest. However, this craving takes on instinctual libidinal permutations, hence the early infantile scenario of the parental intercourse as a mutual exchange of precious bodily, oral and anal, substances.

It followed that since Oedipal jealousy is experienced in such pre-genital terms, so is the aggression that it stirs. Klein concluded that the parents are attacked in sadistic, oral and anal ways, that is, bitten, dirtied and devoured in phantasy. Her little patient Gerald, for example, though already four years old, showed in his games phantasies of penetrating the parental bedroom and castrating his father. He then played games in which the father's penis was 'bitten off, cooked and eaten', and later, the father's whole body was similarly cooked and eaten by the triumphant Gerald, who is joined in this feast by his mother.[3] It is revealing to compare these raw pre-genital phantasies with the much more sedate Oedipal material of Freud's 'Little Hans', who was of a comparable age to Gerald's. While Klein was able to witness Gerald's phantasy life in its elemental detail, the only material available to Freud amounted to Little Hans's reported wish to 'coax' with his mother, and his resulting displacement of a feared paternal retaliation on to horses.

The much more detailed material which was directly accessible to Klein reinforced her conviction that the first Oedipal aggression is particularly acute and sadistic. Pre-genital impulses were, by definition, primitive and unrestrained. They would become greatly provoked and intensified by the simultaneous onset of Oedipal feelings, and hence stirred to an extreme pitch, taking on polymorphous, oral and anal forms.

It is possible that, as developed thus far, Klein's ideas might have remained reasonably acceptable to her colleagues. Some might have thought it conceivable that Oedipal experiences can start as early as the second year of life, and that where this happens, it provokes in the infant an unusually ferocious pre-genital aggression. However, there was trouble in store for Klein, because this thinking was not the culmination of her research, but the mere beginnings of it. Her writings from this period unsettled her colleagues, yet she took her ideas on the Oedipus complex much further. She boldly suggested that since it develops gradually from primitive roots, it has a point of origin which goes even further back, all the way to an archaic Oedipal scenario which is first experienced in earliest infancy.

THE EARLY OEDIPUS SITUATION AND THE MOTHER'S BODY

Klein is now generally associated with a theory on the importance of the maternal breast for the infant. However, this thinking was not fully articulated until as late as 1936, in her paper, 'Weaning'. In the years leading up to this time, the essence of Klein's vision consisted of the idea that the infant's mental life grows around an archaic relationship with the mother's whole body. Furthermore, it is this relationship that comprises the first Oedipus situation. Klein's descriptions imply an early awareness of the actual maternal body. Essentially, however, she was concerned with a primordial phantasy experience of the mother's body as the site of sustenance and life. The first and most powerful infantile desires are directed at what is felt to be the global container of life resources, rather than a recognizable human body. Some of these desired life resources are accessible to the infant via direct experiences of the feeding breast. But the infant has a phantasy intuition of other, inaccessible maternal resources. Locked away in the secrecy of the maternal body are the mother's own gratifying possessions, signified by the internal contents of babies, faeces and an incorporated penis.

What turns this scenario into a specifically Oedipal one, is that far from experiencing the relationship with the maternal body as a comfortable twosome, the infant is aware of a third factor which interferes with his powerful urges. The life-giving space of the mother's body is inhabited by a formidable enemy, the generative penis which can fill it up with rival babies. It is therefore not surprising that the infant's initial reaction to the mother's body is fiercely acquisitive. He has an inherent intuition that rivals and usurpers can be created within the mother, and this activates his possessive and controlling impulses towards the source of life supplies. His instinctive possessiveness towards the maternal body is intensified by his epistemophilic instinct, which awakens his urges to discover and conquer the hidden territory of the mother's body.

The infant in this picture is a territorial being, whose first urges are to secure as much as possible for himself at the expense of feared rivals. The primary mental state invoked in this is of paranoia, as was indeed to be suggested by Klein much later. It is a perplexing yet strangely compelling picture, an anthropology of archaic symbolism which is so remote from self-conscious, verbal functioning as to seem incredible. But to understand Klein's rationale more fully, it is necessary to examine two other factors that influenced this particular vision. The first was Freud's allegiance to evolutionary theories, and the second was the theories of Karl Abraham.

EVOLUTIONARY THINKING

It is not always sufficiently appreciated how much Klein drew on the evolutionary aspects of Freud's thinking. She relied substantially on his belief in phylogenetic determinants that shape mental life. Like him, she thought of the infant's mental activity as owing much to inborn species characteristics that have accumulated over decades of evolution, and that could best be accounted for in terms of evolutionary theory. Klein never fully articulated an evolutionary explanation of her reasoning, but she did explicitly draw on Freud's phylogenetic hypothesis. He felt that the dictates of evolution have favoured a human propensity for rapid acculturation, and that therefore learnt behaviour patterns become inscribed in phylogenetically transmitted tendencies. As far as Klein was concerned, this thinking helped support the notion that because of survival needs, the infant's aggressive impulses are inscribed with an intuition both of maternal life resources, and of usurpers and rivals for these.

The normal baby in this second phase of Klein's thinking, is born with a readiness to fight others in order to control the access to vital life supplies. It is a baby who can aggressively defend his interests, and whose cry can be an angry battle cry, and not only the helpless whimper of dependency. The baby's initial way of securing life supplies is to direct his first attacks on the mother's whole body, since this is experienced as the site of nourishment and pleasure over which he must establish territorial control. Any interference in the infant's free access to the mother, such as normal delays in his care routine, triggers his apprehension of potential usurpers, and therefore stirs the most rudimentary Oedipal aggression.

As well as drawing on Freud's ideas on phylogeny, Klein continued to rely on her clinical experience. She had already discovered a degree of complex mental operations in small children which they could not have acquired via ordinary learning. Other evidence for her assumptions came from anthropological sources, which revealed the existence of pre-genital and primitive Oedipal patterns of behaviour in certain adult societies. She suggested that in the human child, 'We find repressed and unconscious, the stages which we still observe in primitive people: cannibalism and murderous tendencies.'[4]

As far as the infant was concerned, the horrendous quality of his primitive aggression could not be condemned on ethical grounds. It could not count as actual evil, because it arose at a time which pre-dates conceptual and verbal logic, and therefore necessarily pre-dates shame, guilt and civilized self-awareness: 'In phantasy the excreta are transformed into dangerous weapons:

wetting is regarded as cutting, stabbing, burning, drowning, while the faecal mass is equated with weapons and missiles. At a later stage ... the excreta are equated with poisonous substances',[5] and '... the child's sadistic attacks have for their object both father and mother, who are in phantasy bitten, torn, cut or stamped to bits.'[6]

Klein undoubtedly intended to look at such manifestations scientifically rather than in a judgemental mode. However, it was not possible to conceive of this scientifically exonerated phenomenon of infantile aggression, without realizing that its pre-genital destructiveness could outlive infancy, and so infiltrate the morality-bound world of adult life. The implication of this could be devastating.

The child's aggression leads him to attack with all the 'means at his disposal', that is, his body and its products. The child learns to bite, scratch, kick and soil, because his earliest angers emerge in the arena of bodily events of daily survival. However, pre-genital aggression is also mirrored in adult aggressive behaviour. Klein's attacking infant powerfully invokes an array of weaponry used in adult violence. This now appears to have a symbolical origin in the first bodily processes: oral attacks of biting underpin the adult violent behaviour of stabbing, while primitive anal attacks underpin the use of explosive bombs that blow up and mess the enemy's territory. While not actually articulating any of this in relation to adult violence, Klein did refer, as suggested, to evidence of symbolized pre-genital aggression in 'primitive' societies that had retained tribal habits such as cannibalism. She also believed that in more civilized societies primitive behaviour was seen in criminals, particularly psychotic ones who subject their victims' bodies to perverted sadism or cannibalism.

In the course of her life Klein was to learn that pre-genital, sadistic aggression is not confined to primitive people or perverse criminals, and that it could manifest, on a large and most brutal scale, in the midst of her own apparently civilized society. This awareness, though never openly articulated, makes a subtle yet unavoidable entry into Klein's account of an intensive child psychoanalysis that she conducted during the war and later published as her famous *Narrative of a Child Analysis*.[7]

The narrative concerns the ten-year-old 'Richard', whom Klein treated in 1941 when she took temporary refuge from the London Blitz in Pitlochry. Richard needed treatment because of his phobic school avoidance, which stemmed from his fear of other children. As well as this overall timidity, he clung tiresomely and dictatorially to his mother, and did not appear to feel particularly close to either his father or his older brother.

In Klein's makeshift consulting room, which was the local Girl Guide hut, Richard's deep anxieties became centred on the war, and he spent his sessions charting Hitler's terrifying progress in two ways. He noted actual war events on the map which covered the wall in the Girl Guide hut. Simultaneously with this, he expressed the situation imaginatively in his play. He executed manoeuvres with a toy fleet that he brought to the sessions, and he spent a great deal of time drawing an imaginary empire 'in which modifications appeared representing the changing in the course of events in the war'.[8]

Klein might have taken up this material in terms of an appropriate fear which was shared by all around him. After all, she was herself escaping from Hitler's bombs. Like Richard, she had to live daily with the terrifying question, never openly asked in the *Narrative*, of how much damage Hitler was actually going to cause.

However, this urgent question regarding external reality only served to intensify Klein's quest to discover more about internal wars and their outcomes. She was also aware that Richard's fear of Hitler, because of its very logic, was a perfect guise for the pathology that he had been referred for, which was a chronic and pervasive fear of others. Hitler was the convenient temporary receptacle for Richard's early anxiety situation, itself Oedipal in essence, and thus a horrifying social mirror for individual primitive states. Hitler's behaviour, as charted by Richard through his empire drawings, was therefore taken up entirely in relation to his infantile unconscious anxiety, which Klein traced to his Oedipal aggression.

Klein suggested that Richard clung to his mother and shied from the world because in his unconscious phantasies he wanted to dominate his mother as if she were a territory which was fought over by himself, his brother and his father. This early unmitigated aggressiveness was projected outwards and located in the schoolmates whom Richard avoided; it also took on a terrifying form in Hitler, who embodied the essence of pre-genital sadistic degeneracy of cutting, mutilating, burning, poisoning and bombing, as well as embodying the territorial aggression that comes with such attacks.

Klein's *Narrative of a Child Analysis* offers an extraordinary link between individual sadism and its projection onto a broader historical canvas of collective human behaviour. When Richard imitates Hitler's invasions in his empire drawings, and Klein takes this to represent his archaic attacks on his empire-mother, a link is suggested between the ambitions of warring nations and the first empire of the infant. The cruelty that features in both is a function of survival patterns which bear the mark of pre-genital sadism. While this is acceptable in the infant who cannot actually carry out phantasies, in an adult group, unmodified pre-genital aggression has catastrophic consequences.

Evolutionary ideas were helpful to Klein in all this thinking. They provided her with a framework that could make some sense of what she was perceiving in the play of her child patients. Evolutionary thinking also enabled a view of the mind as already containing hereditary predispositions that are manifest as primitive mental contents even before actual learning can take place. And yet when articulating her vision of infancy, Klein decided not to rely on evolutionary theory alone. Other factors influenced her deeply, and these enabled her to provide a psychoanalytic, as opposed to a purely evolutionary, account of her vision. In this she drew on the formative influence of Karl Abraham, her second psychoanalyst, who elaborated on the meaning of sadism in Freud's psychosexual model.

From Ferenczi Klein had learnt to think of development as a move towards a reality sense, and this helped her to conceive of the child's mode of thought as essentially other than the adult's. Her concern to explore of what such 'otherness' might consist, led her to look for symbolic meaning in play, to integrate Freud's ideas on dreams and to assign to infantile processes the essential otherness of the primary thought process. These ideas enabled her formulation of a primordial relationship with the mother's body shaped by pre-genital, primary thought process activity, and underpinned by evolutionary and phylogenetic characteristics. Yet these ideas alone cannot be understood separately from Abraham's contribution, which both blended with what was already there and enriched it.

KARL ABRAHAM

On the surface, Abraham may not have come across either as original, or indeed as idiosyncratic as Ferenczi. Described by Jones as 'the most normal' of the men around Freud,[9] he was, and preferred to be, a conservative figure, whose approach is best compared with traditional scholarship. He was methodical in his gathering of clinical evidence, and also in his drawing of conclusions. It is through a step-by-step analysis that the arguments in his papers accrue force and become convincing. In keeping with this, he chose not to present them as subversions of Freudian psychoanalysis. Unlike several of the thinkers around Freud who aspired to offer bold revisions of his theory, Abraham genuinely aspired to add to it.

However, within this apparently conservative framework, Abraham was able to be both creative and innovative. His papers testify to his substantial originality as an observer, and also to his ability to evoke the most intimate trust from others. The patient disclosures in his vignettes are among the most frank in early psychoanalytic writings. His patients, and no doubt Klein among them, appear to have sensed an ability to sustain a state of emotional openness even when faced with deeply disturbing or inaccessible material.

A decisive factor influenced Abraham's direction. After his medical training he had worked as part of the psychiatric team in Switzerland's progressive mental hospital, the Burghölzli, which also had on its staff Carl Jung and Eugen Bleuler. Abraham shared with this Swiss team a particular lifelong commitment. Being based in a large psychiatric institution inevitably focused awareness on severe psychiatric conditions such as schizophrenia and manic-depressive psychosis. When the Burghölzli team developed an interest in Freud's theories, it understandably wanted to discover what psychoanalysis could offer the most morbid pathologies. Bleuler used psychoanalytic thinking in his attempt to account for schizoid defences, and Jung dedicated a 1907 book to the psychology of dementia praecox (schizophrenia, as it was then known). Furthermore, according to Jacobi, Jung 'became one of the champions of the therapeutic approach to the treatment of schizophrenia'. Abraham's interest lay in a different area of pathology, which was equally serious, and this was that of depressive disorders. From 1911 onwards, when he was already in the Berlin Psychoanalytic Society, Abraham began to apply psychoanalytic thinking to an exploration of depressive and manic-depressive disorders.[10] This exploration was to influence Melanie Klein in a lasting and crucial way.

In a seminal 1924 publication, Abraham broadened Freud's libido theory in a way that sought to accommodate an explanation of melancholic illness.[11] Abraham had noticed for a while that his depressed patients conveyed a quality of fragility reminiscent of a helpless, unloved infant. Many of them also had early memories of disappointment in a trusted caregiver, and had since not overcome their tendency to feel hostile towards even the most loved and needed people in their lives. This combined with an unusually self-absorbed existence that indicated entrenched narcissistic grievances dating from the earliest years, resulting from what Abraham assumed to be 'a severe injury to infantile narcissism brought about by successive disappointments in love'.[12] Linking these clinical observations with Freud's theory, Abraham traced melancholia to the oral phase in earliest infancy, representing a deep regression. He hypothesized that in the melancholic individual, a fixation to early oral tendencies of incorporation persists at an unconscious level. This leads to unconscious oral attitudes which represent the continual aggressive cannibalizing of others, hence leaving the melancholic individual continually bereft, empty and depressed. On the basis of this thinking Abraham elaborated a complex theory of the underlying psychogenic factors of depressive states. It is both widely appreciated, and obvious from the texts, that Klein drew substantially on his linking of melancholia with early oral experience when formulating her concept of the depressive position in the 1935–40 years. But of equal importance to Klein was the exploration process which led Abraham to his conclusions. This process was strewn with insights that, added together, began to open her eyes to a psychoanalytic, as opposed to a merely evolutionary, account of archaic phantasy life.

For a start, Abraham's exploration of melancholia drew his attention to a particular conundrum. His hypothesis did not make it possible to account for the fact that oral fixations, which were common in many individuals, only sometimes led to melancholia, and that this always seemed to depend on the presence of destructive feelings towards a loved object. In more innocent situations, oral fixations could lead to not more than benign habits, such as a sweet tooth, or else reasonably acceptable degrees of greed.

This enigma obliged Abraham to re-examine Freud's view of psychosexual phases and to suggest necessary refinements to it. He reasoned that since oral urges manifest in both benign and destructive ways, it was appropriate to reclassify the pre-genital phases of development accordingly. Abraham accepted the particular developmental order posited in Freud's theory of psychosexual development. This held that a mature form of love, which alone enabled a morally responsible treatment of the object, can only begin when pre-genital development has completed its course and has successfully ushered in a genital phase of sexuality. With the genital phase, libidinal urges are directed to others not in primitive oral and anal ways, but as potential sexual love objects, hence triggering a host of loving and constructive behaviours, including affection, concern and esteem. By comparison, pre-genital phases in Freud's thinking come across as amoral, and as driven by a blind pursuit of primitive gratifications without regard for the object.

Abraham's research introduced changes to this picture in order to account for the existence both of benign and of destructive elements in pre-genital sexuality. He thus hypothesized a subdivision that would allow for an early and late period in each pre-genital phase, and this was to account for two periods, benign and destructive, in the oral and anal psychosexual stages respectively. Abraham suggested that in the oral phase, the benign subphase comes first, taking its character from the predominant activity of the earliest period, which is sucking. The infant's mental life is underpinned by urges to swallow the feeding object whole, and preserve it within himself. The infant is still pre-ambivalent and has no destructive urges towards the feeding object. This is an archaic form of an appreciative possessiveness, which underpins the desire to take in, and retain, goodness. However, a destructive phase sets in during the second period of oral libidinal life. With the appearance of teeth, oral sadism is triggered, and with it ambivalence. The infant now wants to bite, cannibalize and destroy the feeding object that he also desires.

The anal phase is similarly subdivided, except that the destructive subphase comes first. The earliest anal period, characterized by normal infantile incontinence, means that the infant is carelessly destructive towards his body contents, expelling his faecal object in an aggressive, annihilating manner. In the second anal subphase, a more benign approach sets in. The infant becomes aware of his body contents and possessive towards them. This archaic possessiveness, though it interferes with his cleanliness training, none the less represents an attempt to conserve an appreciated object within. In Abraham's thinking the tendencies to conserve and keep whole, whether expressed as oral swallowing or as anal possessive tendencies, are the foundation of benign human behaviour, the desire to accept from the world and grow. The tendencies to fragment and expel are associated with destructive mechanisms which aim at damaging and annihilating the object.

The most valuable aspect of this new thinking was not that it provided a taxonomic improvement on Freud's theory, but that it offered a different take on primitive mental life. Abraham redescribed the Freudian oral and anal stages as propelled by archaic relating mechanisms of preserving or expelling, and this was a significant addition to Freud's view that they were merely propelled by blind, pleasure-seeking drives.

ABRAHAM'S INFLUENCE ON KLEIN

Klein made abundant and diverse use of this refined model. At the most superficial level, she used Abraham's new categorization to lend further support to her view of the infant's sadism. In Abraham's suggestion, the two sadistic oral and anal subphases were adjacent in development. He had concluded that the human infant completes a cyclical developmental movement which begins and ends with benign preservative tendencies, the first being oral sucking and the last, anal preserving. The middle period saw two sadistic subphases follow in close succession: the oral cannibalistic subphase and the anal sadistic phase of expelling and destroying. It was in this middle period that Klein placed the infant's 'phase of maximal sadism' to which she repeatedly refers in the 1927–35 years. Abraham's refinement of Freud's theories on pre-genital sexuality thus added a specifically psychoanalytic, as opposed to a merely evolutionary, rationale for her vision of an attacking infant.

In this one instance of using Abraham's thinking, however, it arguably had a negative effect on Klein. It authorized a weakness in her reasoning during the 1927–35 period inasmuch as it lent support to a type of absolutist, original-sin outlook which characterized some of her thinking at the time. It thereby confirmed a view in which pre-genital mental life stood for amorality and unrestrained sadism, whereas maturation and genital sexuality stood for civilized morality. In important ways, this outlook was also an expression of an age-old human tendency to split-off and isolate badness, locating it in what is infantile and natural, while simultaneously privileging mature, and by implication, socially influenced and typically adult states of being.

However, Klein's Abraham-inspired thinking also led her to begin to balance this picture by adding the notion of early positive tendencies to her vision. In due course she was to revise her ideas in ways that led to increasing balance between positive and negative human tendencies. From 1935 onwards, she was to suggest that benign and destructive tendencies are not neatly separated in discrete developmental phases, and that it is simplistic to view the infant as proceeding from sadism to goodness. Klein was ultimately to conclude that destructive and loving impulses coexist from the beginning, living in continual conflict, and it is through this that a human mental life is shaped.

On the one hand, Abraham's influence appeared to delay such progress, by lending support to Klein's extreme beliefs on an infantile phase of maximal sadism. On the other hand, Abraham's influence was no less than instrumental to her progress, because she drew on it in ways that went well beyond the adoption of a single idea. In fact, Abraham's most far-reaching influence on Klein came not from his thinking on infantile sadism, but from his overall reframing of pre-genital mental life in a way that indicated its essentially relational nature.

This is not to suggest, however, that Abraham explicitly discussed infantile mental life in these terms. On the contrary, as suggested, he was focused on the task of addressing the relevance of pre-genital phases to particular pathologies. Abraham intended to do no more than forge clinically useful links between the former and the latter. The object relations element in his thinking was a byproduct of this broader endeavour, and furthermore, one of which he may not have been fully aware. It manifests most clearly in his texts not through his own deliberate reasoning process, but through the many poignant emotional states narrated by his patients. It is this – his particular mode of listening and his mode of transcribing patient narratives – that enables the to-and-fro movement of primitive object relations to first make itself felt. It is thus that in his texts, the language of instinctual gratification often gives way to a resonant language of emotional relationships, for example when he depicts 'the intense longing of the melancholic for the happy state when he was still at his mother's breast.'[13]

Abraham's theory crucially opened the way to discovering the object-directed nature of early oral and anal behaviours; this made it possible to understand the activities of incorporation and expulsion as modes of preserving or expelling objects, hence indicating urges to accept or reject. By the time that Abraham introduced his extended libidinal model, Freud had already conceived of the mental mechanisms of introjection and projection. He also linked the former to oral incorporation tendencies. However, Freud did not integrate his thinking on these mechanisms into a broader vision, nor did he link them to infantile mental development. And while Abraham was much more aware of these possibilities, his was also a half-glimpsed version of early mental life, and it was left to Klein to integrate all the available thinking in a full object relations theory.

PROJECTION AND INTROJECTION

Klein began to see that primitive psychic behaviours of incorporation and expulsion, derived from the first bodily processes of the human organism, play a key role in shaping a mind. She was now even more persuaded that infantile mental life is conducted as a continual relationship between the self and the world, in which objects of experience are accepted via introjection or rejected via projection. The value of such activity is that it equips the human mind for the lifelong necessities to discriminate and select, take in, or expel. More fundamentally though, the processes of introjection and projection link the mind with the world in a continual exchange which makes growth possible.

Thus far, Klein had opened the way to understanding an early Oedipal configuration which does not consist of an understood primal scene involving fully recognized parents. Instead, she showed the child as relating to parental bodies on phantasy levels that are saturated with archaic phantasy activity. Klein now began to consider this revelation in relation to the larger body of her theory. She realized that the mental mechanisms of projection and introjection were bound to affect even further the early Oedipal experience for which she was arguing with increasing conviction. She had already established that, because of its early origin, the Oedipal experience is coloured by the child's pre-genital life. It therefore distorts the child's view of the Oedipal couple, inasmuch as the child transmits pre-genital aggression to the parents and then views them as malevolently united against him. However, while Klein strongly believed in these ideas on the basis of her clinical evidence, they had remained psycho-analytically vague. She could not account for them in terms of intrapsychic processes, and could not explain which particular mental mechanism enabled the infant to transmit aggression to the parents in a way that so distorted his perception.

This was now rectified through the availability of ideas of projection and introjection. Klein suggested that the child projects and displaces impulses on to the parents, and that, in turn, he introjects parental figures, now felt to be saturated with pre-genital aggression and hence changed. Instead of a simple cognitive assimilation of parental representations, the child incorporates imagos which 'bear the stamp of the pregenital instinctual impulses'. It is these which gradually build up an early, ferocious super-ego. However, what the child takes in is not a complete distortion which amounts to a complete figment of his own imagination. Most importantly, the imagos 'are actually constructed on the basis of the real Oedipus objects'.[14]

The theoretical consequences to this new way of seeing the Oedipal child were decisive for Klein's direction. First, they led to a livelier and more rich-textured understanding of mental life. Introjected imagos, created through an elaboration and assimilation of worldly events, were now seen to be protagonists in the internal drama of unconscious phantasy, with crucial implications for the developing self. This immediately made sense of the perpetual activities of personification and symbol formation which Klein had always witnessed in the play of her child patients.

In Klein's understanding, early Oedipal experience is a particular mythology, created by the phantasy transposition of oral and anal events from the primitive life of the body to an infantile narrative about imagos and their relationships. For example, Erna's belief that her mother put inside herself 'blood, urine and semen' during sexual intercourse through her anus, mouth and genitalia, no longer refers to an advanced differentiation of an Oedipal couple. It is much more relevant to see it as a primitive Oedipal configuration which is fashioned by the language of the unconscious, or primary thought process. In this process, adults are felt to be the stuff of myths – strange supernatural creatures or powerful and fearful deities who use their bodies to exchange magical substances and bring forth new life.

For the first time, Klein began to portray mental life as creative in essence. Her descriptions conjure up all the key features of human creative activity, including the forging of new images to reflect life experience, the use of these in internal narratives, the creation of symbols as a central mental activity, and the mental creation of a subjective, personal mythology, an inner world inhabited by 'phantastic' beings and dominated by their adventures and relationships. Just as Klein's accounts were earlier suggestive of a link between the creation of weapons and pre-genital aggression, they now invoked links between the developing ego and a work of art.

Klein even provided such an analogy more overtly in a 1929 paper, in which she studied the story of the artist Ruth Kjär. In this paper, Klein describes how before discovering painting, Ruth Kjär suffered from depression and felt that she had 'an empty space within her'. Klein relates how a turning-point in Ruth Kjär's life occurred when her brother-in-law, himself a successful painter, took back one of the paintings he had loaned her, and she found herself staring at an empty space on her wall. Kjär at first despaired, experiencing this actual gap as a worldly reminder of her internal emptiness. However, she was suddenly inspired to fill the space left by the picture by painting a full female figure on the wall. Her depression simultaneously lifted, and she was discovered to have true artistic talent which led to further creative work. In Klein's understanding, Kjär's painting was symbolically representing her mother in her youth, while she was still in 'full possession of her strength and beauty'. Kjär was thereby trying to rectify the state of her internal maternal imago, felt to be destroyed through previous infantile phantasy attacks. Klein's understanding of Kjär's story invokes a sense that the human psyche creates meaning by filling the empty canvas of the mind with imagos fashioned through the artwork of phantasy elaborations. A further creative process which Klein now considered was reparation, which was represented in Ruth Kjär's ability to recreate a good maternal figure after its phantasy destruction within her. This process, which was to assume increasing importance in Klein's theory, addressed the psychic ability to repair and revive the object that had been attacked in phantasy, thus continually recreating internal goodness.

All these ideas introduced a new and more complex dimension to Klein's vision. By attributing such creative and reparative powers to the mind, she was beginning to introduce a greater balance into her hitherto one-sided, bleak picture of mental development. The reader, however, may not be easily aware of this change in the 1927–35 writings. While they show an undoubted shift in Klein's view of early life with the beginnings of an accommodation of positive elements, she does not abandon her sobering views of human sadism. The dark streak in her outlook continues to dwell on sadism and, as if this is not enough, she is also increasingly contemplating its consequences for the child, thus focusing more on acute anxiety. Klein had been convinced for a while that anxiety is derived from projected sadism and its reflection back to the infant, but her emphasis on anxiety was now becoming even greater.

She even went so far as to promote anxiety as the only instigator of symbolic thinking. In this unexpected line of reasoning, Klein suggested that the infant's first hostile projections not only affect his perception of the parents, but also of other worldly objects, some of them inanimate: 'We see then that the child's earliest reality is wholly phantastic; he is surrounded with objects of anxiety, and in this respect excrement, organs, objects, things animate and inanimate are to begin with equivalent to one another.'[15]

Klein explains symbol formation by suggesting that anxiety leads the child to abandon frightening objects and seek new reassuring ones in the world around him. But each new object needs to represent, or symbolize, what has been abandoned and thus lost through fear. In this way the infant hopes to re-find in the world what is lost through his aggressive attacks, much as Ruth Kjär needed to fill an empty space with a whole, beautiful maternal figure. The process described in this thinking is brilliantly conceived, until the improbable role that is allocated to anxiety is considered. Klein provides an inspired idea of the human quest to replace lost experience as the foundation of symbol formation. At the same time, she promotes the notion that anxiety is the only instigation for the process. She thus discounts the possibility that there might be other emotional spurs to the development of a symbolically functioning mind, such as, for instance, a pining and a love for what is lost. Is Klein's intensified emphasis on anxiety simply a further theoretical exaggeration, derived from her mistaken over-emphasis on sadism during this period?

ANXIETY AND THE SUPER-EGO

Klein developed her thinking on anxiety from her ideas on projection and introjection. The activity of these two processes implied that aggression always returned to the infant via introjection, and so necessarily caused anxiety. To begin with, Klein's interest in anxiety was induced by clinical observation. She noticed that her neurotic child patients could not tolerate even small amounts of anxiety. The fidgety, impulsive or demanding child was now newly understood to be not merely disobedient, but to be betraying his anxiety in these ways. Klein felt that where the tolerance threshold is low, the child is easily provoked by daily frustrations and hence prone to project excessive aggression. This in turn surrounds the child with a malevolent, anxiety-inducing world.

Klein concluded that the ability to tolerate some anxiety is a necessary condition for mental development, and that therefore, only the most ill children are devoid of some ability to bear anxiety. When this tragic circumstance affects a child, it brings his entire mental activity to a standstill because no anxiety-provoking experience is allowed to enter awareness. And since all human perceptions carry the risk of some anxiety, the mentally fragile child drastically restricts his ability to take in facts from the world, with catastrophic consequences for his entire mental functioning.[16]

However, the concept of anxiety contributed more than this important conclusion to Klein's developing framework. In particular, she could no longer believe that sadism can rage unhindered in the human heart. Introjection processes mean that mental activity is not a simple event of the passing moment, and its force, once expressed through projection, does not just vanish from the self into the world. The substance of each of the infant's sadistic attacks becomes located somewhere. By being projected and displaced on to the parents, it immediately confronts the infant with external embodiments of his own aggression. The introjection of these to form imagos is also the setting up of the first law-enforcement agency in the mind. By fearing attacked parents, the pre-condition is laid for the development of a social morality in the child. Anxiety thus provides a countervailing force to human sadism.

Klein now linked this insight with her earlier assertion that a super-ego is formed very early in the child's development. She suggested that the projection-laden Oedipal parents are not only transformed into internal imagos, but continue to function inside the child's psyche in the form of the mental agency of super-ego. The super-ego is thus earlier than Freud had anticipated, and emerges in archaic mental life as an immediate consequence of the introjection of harsh parental imagos. The earliest super-ego activity is therefore acutely sadistic, creating a measure of fear in direct proportion with the measure of projected infantile sadism.

In spite of the fact that Klein's thinking on infantile anxiety and the harsh, early super-ego continues to suggest a gloom-ridden view of development, a retrospective assessment reveals also that it offers the first glimpses of a more balanced theory of the mind; furthermore, it is one that ultimately abandons an original-sin colouring altogether. The imagos created through introjection introduce the idea that human beings are made afraid by their own aggression. This eventuality implies an inherent moral disposition in the human character, something which directly counters an original-sin outlook. It traces moral development not to social coercion, but to an internal situation, and to a psyche that begins to grapple with its own aggression no sooner than the latter is first expressed and projected.

If anything, this conclusion introduces a much more forgiving view of human nature. None the less, this is never very evident in the 1927–35 writings, which continue to suffer from a dark brooding on the worst in human nature. However, attention should not be detracted from a more benign element, and a much greater diversity of outlook that is slowly adding subtle layers to Klein's vision.

As suggested, she is beginning to set out how complex processes of projection and introjection help the child to invest the world with a symbolic meaning drawn from his immediate bodily and mental states. This is followed by processes of introjection and personification that create internal imagos. While Klein does speak of these as mostly harsh and punitive, she is becoming aware of other possibilities. She concedes that the infant internalizes imagos with 'phantastically good characteristics' and not only 'phantastically bad' ones.[17] In the play of her four-and-a-half-year-old patient, George, Klein notices the appearance of a 'fairy mama', who comes to him at night and brings 'nice things to eat which she shared with her little boy.'[18] And in another analysis, Klein notes that the 'fairy mama used to heal with a magic wand all the wounds which the boy's harsh parents had inflicted on him.' The bountiful, protective maternal body thus becomes a source of inspiration for introjecting helpful figures.

The end of the 1927–35 period sees Klein's interest in helpful imagos grow, and she now suggests that the infant introjects two kinds of extreme imagos: good and bad. The formation of such polarized imagos is felt by her to mark intermediary stages in the small child's development, leading from his experience of 'figures wholly divorced from reality' to 'identifications which approximate more closely to reality'. This process thus ushers in an increasing recognition of the actual, helpful parents, and mitigates the internally distorted, harsh parental imagos. Throughout the period, Klein's Ferenczi-inspired ideas on the child's desire for knowledge and move towards a reality sense thus become extended and elaborated. It is through projection and introjection that the child is able to invest the world with meaning drawn from personal life, but it is these processes that also initially distort his understanding. The thinking process is thus essentially creative in the sense that it personifies, dramatizes and forms symbols.

Significantly, this activity takes place in the context of a reality that does exist outside the life of the mind. Reality does not coincide with omnipotent phantasies, and so introduces frustration, anger and the need to tolerate some anxiety, presenting pivotal challenges for the growth of a mental apparatus. A healthy amount of anxiety spurs the mind on to a restless but productive quest for new rewarding objects. The infant is thus not only a territorial aggressor, but also an avid explorer and discoverer.

Above all, Klein began to see that the process of investing the experiencing self in the world does not simply amount to a mode of perceiving and organizing a mass of bewildering impingements from life. It is a mode of extracting a qualitative experience from an existence that would otherwise consist of a chain of meaningless events. It is therefore an emotional mode of constructing human meaning; of telling an early story of pleasure and pain, love and hate, good and bad.

NOTES

1. Klein, M. (1975) 'The psychological foundations of child analysis', in *Psychoanalysis of Children*. London: The Hogarth Press. (First published in 1932.) p. 3.
2. Klein, M. (1975) 'Criminal tendencies in normal children', in *Love, Guilt and Reparation*. London: The Hogarth Press. (First published in 1927.) p. 175.
3. ibid., p. 172.
4. ibid., p. 170.
5. ibid., p. 220.
6. Klein, M. (1975) 'The importance of symbol formation in the development of the ego', in *Love, Guilt and Reparation*. London: The Hogarth Press. (First published in 1930.) p. 219.
7. Klein, M. (1975) *Narrative of a Child Analysis*. London: The Hogarth Press. (First published posthumously in 1961.)
8. Grosskurth, P. (1985) *Melanie Klein*. London: Maresfield Library. p. 264.
9. ibid., p. 93.
10. Abraham, K. (1973) 'Notes on the psycho-analytical investigation and treatment of manic-depressive insanity and allied conditions', in *Selected Papers of Karl Abraham*. London: The Hogarth Press. (First published in 1911.)
11. Abraham, K. (1973) 'A short study of the development of the libido, viewed in the light of mental disorders', in *Selected Papers of Karl Abraham*. London: The Hogarth Press. (First published in 1924.)
12. ibid., p. 458.
13. ibid., p. 467.
14. Klein, M. (1975) 'Personification in the play of children', in *Love, Guilt and Reparation*. London: The Hogarth Press. (First published in 1929.) p. 204.
15. Klein, M. (1975) 'The importance of symbol formation in ego development', in *Love, Guilt and Reparation*. London: The Hogarth Press. (First published in 1930.) p. 221.
16. See Klein's description of her patient 'Dick' in the above, pp. 221–31.

17. Klein, M. (1975) 'Personification in the play of children', in *Love, Guilt and Reparation*. London: The Hogarth Press. (First published in 1929.) p. 203.
18. ibid., p. 203.

CHAPTER 6

'And who would doubt this?' – Early Object Love, Psychical Defences and Dissociation Processes

K lein's new ideas on early mental life were not well received by her colleagues, however diligently she continued to argue her case. It was also becoming increasingly apparent that she was not merely introducing a few small changes to Freudian theory, but radical revisions which had consequences for its entirety. In any case, each new idea had inevitable implications and necessitated further revisions. For example, it was not possible for Klein to suggest that the infant experiences acute anxiety and leave it at that. The idea that the fragile infant psyche could be swamped with powerful anxieties immediately begged further questions about what equipped the infant to deal with them. It is quite true that Klein regarded the child as needing a capacity to tolerate some anxiety, because in reasonable measure, it could act as a spur to turn to the world and seek new reassuring objects, hence setting development in motion. However, the idea of a modicum of tolerable anxiety did not address the issue of acute anxieties which Klein believed infants to experience as a result of their projected sadism.

Being obliged to give this further thought, Klein was logically led to consider the possibility of early mental defences, and this, in turn, introduced the even more disquieting possibility that some ego capacity may exist at birth. And indeed, Klein was becoming increasingly convinced about this, much to the chagrin of her colleagues. It has been noted that Klein tended to use the term 'ego' interchangeably with 'self', and yet, as Mitchell notes, 'from the very beginning it is the ego that interests Klein'.[1] Indeed from the early years until the time of the Controversial Discussions, it is the conventional sense of the term which most draws attention. The vision that Klein set out before her colleagues necessitated the assumption of an organizing mental agency, such as Freud's ego, in the baby. The ego implied in Klein's vision was not only capable of organizing chaotic worldly impingements into some coherent form, but could also identify danger, experience anxiety and perform defence manoeuvres to avoid mental distress. It was difficult for Klein's colleagues to translate what they had always regarded as developmentally acquired, sophisticated mental operations, such as experiencing anxiety and deploying defences, into the more archaic terms that Klein had in mind, and that her adherent Susan Isaacs would later come to describe as 'reflexive' mental behaviours. In order to do so, they would need to abandon the notion that the human mind can only create meaning after cognitive development has begun, and when much more reality is being accommodated by the psyche.

However, Klein was interested in the existence of ingrained mental characteristics which predispose the human infant to develop a mind in the first place. And while she did, indeed, conclude that anxiety results from the projection of sadism, she also felt that some anxiety is primary in the mind. The human organism would surely come into the world with a rudimentary ability to sense danger. Klein thus linked life's first experiences of anxiety not with acquired or learnt mental abilities, but with a reflexive internal registering of a particular phenomenon. This was the death instinct which Freud had postulated in 1920, and which she now began to regard as inscribed in the earliest experiences of the human organism and psyche. Survival meant that the baby was born knowing about death and sensing his internal destructive instincts, and this first knowledge took the form of a primordial terror of annihilation. Anxiety was thus basic to all living states, however immature.

This conceptualizing did little to improve the reception of Klein's ideas by her colleagues. They were already aware of Freud's concept of the death instinct, and, out of all his ideas, liked it least. But Klein did not enter into detailed philosophical debates on the issue. Instead, she turned pragmatically to the clinical situation, and built up her case from evidence which this provided. As seen, she had already begun to realize that the postulation of intense early anxiety necessitated some account of how the infant might deal with it. Otherwise, her theory would leave a picture of the infant as overwhelmed, unprotected and lacking the means to emerge from anxiety and so create a mental life at all.

Klein had already begun to consider psychic defences from the very beginnings of her psychoanalytic career. Her lifelong work on the subject was to make a most significant impact on psychoanalysis in the long run. During her entire career, her view of defences, which developed substantially, none the less retained a core element. This was her belief that the main principle which underpins defensive activity is based on primitive fight–flight responses. Freud had already pointed out that whereas human beings can actually flee from external danger, this is not an option where internal danger, such as surges of overwhelming instinctual activity, is concerned. Instead, the mind needs to find modes of avoiding or eliminating the internal source of danger, and this it does by trying, in various ways, to tamper with the psychic reception of it.

While Freud was led to explore the mechanism of repression, Klein's clinical observations led her in an alternative, but compatible, route. For example, she noted that her patient George, in whom 'anxiety was warded off by a noticeable exclusion of reality' enacted in his play interminable battles in which he was always the winner.[2] These served as an escape from his dissatisfactions with everyday situations. George could not handle the ordinary frustrations of daily life, was made excessively angry by them, and then, in turn, became convinced that it was all the fault of others who were deliberately getting at him. Klein realized that his daydreaming about heroic conquests was serving to distance from himself disturbing feelings created by his anger and paranoid anxieties. To this end, 'wish-fulfilment clearly predominated over recognition of reality'. However, far from helping George to cope, his escape into phantasies of omnipotent heroism only served to delay his adjustment to the world. Because his anger was excessive, it triggered, in turn, excessive anxiety and a prematurely rigid defensiveness. The particular defence mechanism that his mind employed tampered with his awareness of how the world actually was, and created in him an alternative phantasy of how it ought to be. It was thus that aspects of reality were fended off, and excessive phantasy activity replaced adequate intellectual alertness.

The same principle of reality disavowal could be observed much more clearly in an extreme example offered by the very disturbing situation of Dick, who was brought to Klein because of autistic-sounding defences that delayed his entire development. Dick was four years old, but functioned more like a fifteen-month-old child. He 'strung sounds together in a meaningless way' instead of speaking, was 'devoid of affect' and unable to play normally. He did not react at all to his mother or nurse, and also completely disregarded Klein's presence in the room, rushing past her as if she were an inanimate object. Klein worked hard to discover the root of the deep inhibitions that had brought his imaginative and affective life to such a standstill. Dick's limited activities in the consulting room and her own interactions with him, gradually enabled her to glean both his excessive sadism, and his complete intolerance of the anxiety provoked thereby.

Because of the extreme nature of his affects, Dick had to mobilize extreme defensive activity. His psyche needed to stifle even the most minimal degree of sadism, and with this stifling, his phantasy life was brought to a virtual standstill together with all the urges, ideation and even somatic experiences that would have otherwise carried potential threat. Dick could thus not bite his food or use scissors, but this blunting of potential aggression extended to the rest of his experiencing faculties. As a result, his stifled instinctual energies could not be directed outwards, he was unable to invest the world with aspects of his experiencing self and so form symbols. And when his symbol formation suffered, so, in turn, did his verbal development.

Klein found it difficult to account for the extremity of the situation, as there seemed to be nothing out of the ordinary in Dick's background. She also treated Dick at a time when autism was not understood. Klein none the less concluded that what she saw in front of her was out of the ordinary. Dick's defences were 'of a violent character' and 'different from repression'. She concluded that more than a stifling of urges and a disavowal of reality were taking place. Dick's mind continually and violently expelled his aggression and so destroyed his object, hence his bizarre unawareness of other people. This led her to think that Dick's defences were possibly schizophrenic.

While in Dick Klein provided an extreme and pathological example of defensive processes, they had something in common with more normal defences which she was considering. In her thinking all mental defences, whether mild or severe, had the same function: to rid the mind of portions of awareness that create excessive anxiety, disturbance or suffering. Klein was thus led to a crucial insight that now made sense of what she had observed repeatedly in the consulting room. She concluded that when the child seeks to distance and disown either hostile aspects of himself, or else the anxiety-inducing objects created by projections, he regularly resorts to defence mechanisms that are based on a dissociative psychic process.

Already at the time of her work with her son Erich, Klein noted how he tried to keep at bay negative feelings for his mother. He created a witch figure 'obtained by division of the mother imago'. Such a division was enabled through the witch-figure becoming 'split-off from his beloved mother, in order to maintain her as she is'.[3] The notion of such divisions in the object differed from the notion of repression, as they did not apply to isolated impulses, wishes or memories that were pushed away from consciousness. To Freud's theory of repression, Ferenczi had added the suggestion that some repressed impulses could 'drag into repression with them a great number of other ideas and tendencies associated with these complexes and dissociate them from the free interchange of thoughts …'.[4]

Klein built on this thinking when she realised that the child's mind was doing more than fending off and repressing individual impulses. The child was trying to protect himself from a whole aggregate of projected hostile elements, consisting of both oral and anal sadistic attacks, and collectively creating a bad imago. And because this amounted to a complex mental creation, it needed to be removed from consciousness in its entirety. However, like Freud's return of the repressed, the dissociated figure came back into consciousness in the guise of a witch. The child was now confronted with the more acceptable situation of two different figures, only one of which was encapsulating his projected aggression. This enabled the preservation of one figure, the mother, as loving and loved, and hence as safe.

These kinds of dissociation processes became even clearer to Klein when she realized that they are employed not only to create divisions in the object, but also corresponding ones in the self. In her analysis of the four-year-old Gerald, she observed how in his games he perpetrated cannibalistic Oedipal attacks on his father, and was left with the grim consequences of his own aggression. Klein noticed that Gerald had not only repressed his pre-genital aggressive impulses, but also, along with these, an aspect of himself that identified with the aggressive intent and was felt to be criminal. To this, his civilized self became opposed. Dissociation processes which were enlisted to remove Gerald's disturbing feelings, were now seen to lead to a coexistence of two conflicting selves in his personality. However, Klein emphasized the normality of this child as indicated by an aspect of himself to which the criminal, cannibalistic activity was abhorrent: 'It is difficult to illustrate how such a warm-hearted child, as this one was, in particular suffers through such phantasies, which the cultivated part of his personality strongly condemns. This boy could not show enough love and kindness to his father …'.[5]

Klein was to give increasing emphasis to the defensive principle of maintaining internal divisions that aim to isolate the source of disturbance, whether this be the bad, anxiety-inducing imago or the sadistic aspect of the self. However, she did not assume that such internal divisions could actually succeed in altogether removing the source of disturbance from awareness. Instead, they located it in a single entity which, though persecuting, could now be addressed at an ideational level. Klein also noted that such defences of dissociation have obvious links with natural developmental patterns. At the beginning of life the whole mode of experience is fragmented in nature, and psychic immaturity is none other than the young mind's inability to accommodate more than the experiential fragment of the moment:

> The object-world of the child in the first two or three months of its life could be described as consisting of hostile and persecuting, or else of gratifying parts and portions of the object world. Before long the child perceives more and more of the whole person of the mother, and this more realistic perception extends to the world beyond the mother.[6]

The dissociation defences which Klein was now exploring, thus appeared to be in the nature of simulation processes that repeated a fragmentation that had initially been the natural infantile mode of apprehending the world. But whereas the infant's earliest and undeveloped experiencing capacities responded passively to fragments of reality, defensive processes of dissociation were active strivings to separate certain portions of experience from the psyche. And yet in spite of their alarming-sounding activity, such defences were also normal in infancy. They could be observed when children struggled to keep the goodness of their loved objects safe and separate from the bad, hated aspects of these same objects, reflected also in experiences of helpful and hostile imagos. Klein now noted that 'the ego endeavours to keep the good apart from the bad' and that 'the result is a conception of extremely bad and extremely perfect objects ...'.[7]

Klein's view of early defences had important implications for her entire vision of development. Even before 1935, when these ideas were relatively undeveloped, they were already suggesting a new way of understanding child development. The early mind was prone to processes of fragmentation and dissociation, both because of its piecemeal mode of taking in the world, and because of dissociative defences that created extreme imagos. The task of maturation was thus newly understood as consisting of a gradual synthesis that helped the child to bring together disparate parts of experience and disparate self-aspects. Klein was now led to conclude that development is essentially a move from fragmentation to integration, and consists of the mind's ability to assimilate portions of experience into a whole picture of meaning and so begin to think. She also realized that this leads to an inherent paradox in the operation of mental defences. Defensive activity aids the process of integration by protecting the organism from overwhelming anxiety. However, it can also, by its very nature, hinder development, and where used in excess, annihilate large areas of awareness and so prevent the development of an adequate reality sense.

As she had already noted, the dynamic nature of early impulses not only spins phantasy versions, or imagos, based on the parents, but expresses an early intentionality that directs the mind to either accept, or flee from, what it encounters. Klein began to realize that it is within this movement of impulse and intentionality that an early, rudimentary ego functions and that a sense of identity begins to be structured. Yet the identity intimated in this vision is initially as changeable as the impulses that constitute it, and the result is a fragmented, multiple experience of a primitive sense of self.

It is this line of thinking that gradually led Klein to introduce her key concept of positions, which brings forward a particular kind of self at different times, such as a paranoid self, a depressed self or an obsessional self. She suggested that early states are organized around different positions and that these ebb and flow continually, bringing into focus a particular responding part of the self at different moments. In the light of this, Klein began to realize that the mind's move towards integration is essential for growth, for it creates a composite identity made up of self-aspects that are gathered over time into a more inclusive and stable identity. The principle of developmental integration was to inform all of Klein's later vision. But it soon confronted her with her most challenging and complex theoretical task yet, for she realized that the process of integration is far from simple. The more the infant perceives of reality, the more whole her understanding, the more she is obliged to face a distressing world which has loss and pain in it. The infant's broadening mental horizons create a new context for her experiences. Good experiences, though they dominate moments of pleasure, are no longer believed to come from a complete, purely good object. Moreover, they are increasingly understood to be only one aspect of an otherwise mixed reality. It is thus that Klein found herself on the threshold of her central concept of the depressive position. And it is here that her thinking turned to the development of human love.

EARLY OBJECT LOVE

With so many new and contentious ideas following on in close succession, it is not surprising to discover that quite shortly, when she was plunged into the turmoil of the 1940s Controversial Discussions, Klein came under extreme pressure to do much more than justify her theory: she was obliged to fight for its very survival. In the midst of this critical struggle, Klein chose a brief interlude in which to make her boldest and most concerted claims on the nature of love in early infancy. Her thinking on this was expressed succinctly, as part of a much broader 1944 presentation on infantile development. She none the less concluded that, 'we can assume that love towards the mother in some form exists from the beginning of life'.[8]

This conclusion represented a significant shift that had been taking place in Klein's thinking over the preceding decade, and that now advanced a substantial positive counter-force to the gloom of her early vision. To understand why

Klein's suggestion of love in early infancy was both revolutionary and dubious in terms of the prevailing psychoanalytic orthodoxy, it is necessary to place her thinking in the context of Freud's views. Without understanding how Klein's view on love had to change from the Freudian model, it is also not possible to make full sense of her conception of the depressive position.

In his thinking, Freud made room for two currents in human libidinal life, the sensual-erotic and the emotional: 'A normal sexual life is assured by an exact convergence of the affectionate current and the sensual current directed towards a sexual object and sexual aim.'[9] However, Freud did not regard the affectionate current as a primary, irreducible force. In his thinking it was a secondary phenomenon that mutates out of early erotogenic sexuality:

> The resultants of infantile object-choice are carried over into the later period ... but as a consequence of the repression ... their sexual aims have become mitigated and they now represent what may be described as the 'affectionate current' of sexual life. Only psychoanalytic investigation can show how behind this affection, admiration and respect there lie concealed the old sexual longings of the infantile component instincts.[10]

This view was rooted, as seen, in the definition of an infantile sexuality as moving gradually from pre-genital towards a genital and ultimately adult sexual organization. It is worth recalling the main features of this model briefly, because though familiar, they have a particular bearing on the present discussion. Freud believed that at the beginning of life sexuality is immediately present in germinal form, but that it is initially inchoate and unorganized, composed of component instincts, each of which 'goes its own way to achieving satisfaction'. Such fragmented, pleasure-seeking instincts make the young child polymorphously perverse. Freud invoked the sense of an infant as bringing into the world elemental aspects of her sexuality which infuse every aspect of her existence. Sensations, sights, smells, tastes and sounds all carry some sexual charge with a potential for excitation. Of particular intensity are sensations in the body orifices of mouth and anus where internal membranes are sensitive, hence becoming focal sexual centres around which pre-genital organizations take shape. In this view, it was the genital organization – the mature directed sexuality – that was regarded as integrating different currents, including emotional ones, towards a single object. Klein's second psychoanalyst, Abraham, was faithful to this view, suggesting that, 'Gradually [the individual] achieves a libidinal cathexis of his object-love as a whole ... if this has been achieved there arise in him expressions of his libidinal relation to his object that are inhibited in their aim – feelings of fondness, devotion and so on – and these coexist with his directly erotic desires for it.'[11]

This way of thinking on love and libido reached Klein in her early work, and she too believed that, 'In ontogenetic development sadism is overcome when the subject advances to the genital level. The more powerfully this phase sets in, the more capable does the child become of object love ...'[12] Since the child was thought to become capable of object love only upon reaching the genital phase, there was no notion of an earlier kind of love, and this was partly responsible for leaving the early Kleinian theoretical terrain under the unchallenged dominance of sadism. Klein gradually developed her thinking on anxiety as a counter-force to sadism, but a combination of sadism and anxiety also seemed to exacerbate rather than redress the gloomy view of the early years. It is partly this understanding of libido that gives Klein's early papers their negative slant. Klein was also aware that in the prevailing Freudian model even adult love was defined as a secondary, derivative phenomenon. In Freud's words, the 'affectionate current' was directed towards 'a sexual object and sexual aim', implying that genital sexuality is a prerequisite for object love. A considerable alteration in this vision was required before envisaging something different became possible, and in this the influences of both Abraham and Ferenczi were instrumental.

Klein, who became increasingly convinced that there was an early infantile love which existed in its own right rather than being a secondary, derivative phenomenon, initially wondered how to account for it. As seen, she had already placed the Oedipus complex early, and concluded that its early onset aligned it with pre-genital phases. Perhaps it was altogether more logical to think further along these lines, and conclude that human psychosexual phases do not follow one another in a completely neat succession. A more natural picture would also look more chaotic, showing that in early infancy all the psychosexual phases overlap to some extent, and only become more coherent stages when gradually organized with the predominance of one or other libidinal zone. This possibility would explain the appearance of genital elements and sensations early on, thus accounting for a very early onset of love. However, Klein was also aware that the notion of genital experiences so early in life was at odds with prevalent psychoanalytic beliefs: 'If we follow Abraham's hypothesis, there is an evolution of love, which starts at the phase of partial cannibalism ... that is to say, at a stage when according to both Freud and Abraham the genital libido does not yet play a part'.[13] This led Klein at once to a crucial question: 'Does love exist in the infant prior to the emergence of genital libido?''.

One way of conceiving of this possibility was to suppose that 'genital trends play a part in the sexual and emotional development of the infant' and that 'even from the beginning they influence, however dimly, the relation to objects'.[14] However, Klein now went further in her exploration. She suggested that 'whether it is due to the early activity of genital trends that elements of love are present' remained a theoretical issue, but that there were other ideas around her which accounted for the presence of early object love in a different way, and without relying on the need to postulate genital trends. Among the theories to which Klein refers are those of Michael and Alice Balint, who rejected the theory of a primary narcissism in favour of a view that the first stage is characterized by 'a passive aim – the desire to be loved'. In her presentation on love, Klein did not need to spell out the background to the Balint theory, because her colleagues were well aware that it was inspired directly by Ferenczi, who had also been the analyst of Michael Balint. Unlike Abraham and Freud, in 1933 Ferenczi became convinced that it was necessary to separate out an early love of 'tenderness' from a mature, partly sexual love of 'passion'. He thus introduced the idea that love had its own developmental phases and so opened the way to viewing it as a force in its own right that does not depend on genital libido and that can develop from the beginning of life:

> I should like to call this the stage of passive object love or of tenderness. Vestiges of object love are already apparent here but only in a playful way in fantasies. Thus . . . we find the hidden play of taking the place of the parent of the same sex in order to be married to the other parent, but it must be stressed that this is merely fantasy; in reality the children would not want to, in fact they cannot do without tenderness.[15]

In a 1933 Sandor Ferenczi Memorial volume,[16] Alice Balint began to explore early infantile love in a paper which was to take its final form in 1939. The date is significant, as is the fact that the occasion for exploring early object love was linked not only to commemorating Ferenczi's contribution to psychoanalysis, but in particular to his concept of passive object love and his conclusion that object relations exist from the beginning of life.[17] The thinking about early love as influenced by Ferenczi was thus already being articulated when Klein shortly afterwards in 1935 first described love as a phenomenon that exists in its own right from the beginning of life: 'Feelings of love and gratitude arise directly and spontaneously in the baby in response to the love and care of his mother'.[18]

This commonplace statement represents a crucial shift in Klein's thinking, for it marks an extension of her view of the early libido to include love, and her growing awareness that infantile libidinal states encompass emotion as well as physical pleasure. As shown earlier, prior to this Klein's views on love were in keeping with Freud's and Abraham's notions that it was a secondary, later phenomenon which belonged with genital sexuality. Yet the kind of love that Klein was to envisage went very much further than anything suggested in Ferenczi's works. Like her, he envisaged the breast as the first love object. But he thought of it as forced upon a passive baby who returns a passive love for it: 'The . . . activity of the newborn infant is limited principally to sucking at the mother's breast. Indeed this first love object is forced upon the child from the beginning by the mother, so that one may speak in the case of the child of a primary "passive object-love".'[19]

His vision had no room for an infant who seeks the breast actively, and who experiences it intensely and with libidinal gratification. Klein's thinking, on the other hand, had always attributed active instincts to the child. As seen, in her vision the child's epistemophilic instinct, combined with her aggression, implied a host of intense projective activities, both exploratory and defensive. Active introjection also led to symbol formation and the creation of an internal world. The idea of the breast being foisted on a passive infant did not sit well with this kind of model. Klein found that in this respect she needed to look for further inspiration. Indeed, the active intensity that was not explicit in Ferenczi's vision of infantile experience was none the less apparent in Abraham's, as was the notion of a relation to part objects. However, for Abraham early love remained a mostly erotogenic, sensual phenomenon. In a subtle integration of the views of both her analysts, Klein was to apply intensity to feelings as well, thus giving primitive positive emotions a power in psychical life hitherto reserved for either genital experience, or sadism. The conclusion was a picture of development in which love is central: 'First the whole interest and love focus on the nipple and on the breast; but very soon interest develops in the face and in the hands, which attend to [the infant's] needs and gratify them. Thus, step by step, the infant comes to perceive and love the mother as whole person'.[20]

Klein emphasizes again that 'love towards the mother in some form exists from the beginning of life', and completes her reasoning by referring back to evolutionary theory and to Freud's thinking on phylogenetic determinants in human nature:

> I have on several occasions expressed the view that the relation of the infant to his mother is based on phylogenetic inheritance and is ontogenetically the most fundamental of all human patterns. If there are such fundamentals acquired in the evolution of the race (and who would doubt this?) a relation of the infant to the mother who gives birth to him and attends to his first needs must be one of them.[21]

It is striking how the woman who had been writing so much about sadism and anxiety now concluded that early love takes its place among 'the most fundamental of all human patterns'. Furthermore, Klein's ideas on early love were to continue to develop significantly.

THE PRIMARY GOOD OBJECT

By the time Klein described the formation of the first good object in 1946, she had a new understanding of libido that made it into a substantial counterpart to the sadism in her theory. Accordingly, the first good object is created by 'the projection of loving feelings' that underlie 'the process of attaching libido to the object.' Not only was love felt to underlie libidinal activity, but libido itself was seen as 'the manifestation of forces which tend to preserve life' in keeping with Freud's coming to regard eros as representative of the life instinct.[22] The earliest libido thus moved away from being the infant's sensual oral gratification to being the essence of his quest for nourishment and life. In this sense early love can be regarded as inseparable from libido. This extension of the thinking on libido was to be elaborated further and in even more significant ways. By 1957 the libidinally invested breast was felt by Klein to be a principle of fulfilment that reflects the power of the life instinct, and is as such a boundless ideal source of mental sustenance: 'I would not assume that the breast is to [the infant] merely a physical object. The whole of his instinctual desires and his unconscious phantasies imbue the breast with qualities going far beyond the actual nourishment it affords.'[23]

In addition, the libidinally invested breast, when introjected, was believed to form the 'core of the ego'.[24] Not only did Klein add early love to her theory, she also gave it the central place in infantile mental life, and showed how the object upon which identity is modelled is none other than the good object, created by infantile object love. Since her new, and indeed her ultimate, understanding of libido came to be centred on love and the life instinct, it was logical for her to suggest that the original good object that embodies libidinal passion must be experienced in a primitive way as ideal. Nothing less would adequately express 'the whole of [the infant's] instinctual desires' or form an adequate core of his ego. All the life-craving intensity of the infant is part of his libido and contributes towards forming his original good object. And indeed, this compares well with Alice Balint's 1939 statement that 'there exists an archaic form of love of which the essential determinant is the lack of a reality sense towards the love-object ... The development of higher forms of love derives as a consequence of adaptation to reality.'[25]

As shown, when Klein talked of the earliest kind of love, she was referring to primitive states that amount to the 'whole of [the infant's] instinctual desires and unconscious phantasies'. The infant projects what amounts to his entire loving capacity, as well as his capacity for pleasure, on to the object, and this is then introjected together with the object's actual goodness to become his very core. This makes clear Klein's conclusion, towards the end of her life, that the good object is essential to sanity. In one of her last works Klein was to go so far as suggesting that 'without the good object at least to some extent becoming part of the ego, life cannot continue.'[26] Such thinking does bring her theory of early love close to that of Michael Balint, even though in other respects the theories are every different. Balint developed a concept of primary love which referred to what he described as a state of 'intense relatedness' in the infant.

THE GOOD AND THE IDEAL

Klein's concept of love should be easily evident in her works, but it is, on the whole, elusive and dispersed among writings which continue to emphasize the impact on development of sadism and anxiety. There is a further factor that obscures Klein's ideas on love in her texts. The last section of this chapter is devoted to noting a theoretical ambiguity in her thinking that further diminishes a clear impression of the kind of early love that she wished to convey and indeed explicitly described. The version of object love as outlined so far represents only one current that runs through Klein's writings. In another current, she turned her attention to something which directly contradicts it, because Klein also asserted that much of what the infant experiences as positive is in fact due to idealization, and that the latter is not the 'most fundamental of all human patterns' and a grateful response to a caring object, but another psychological defence. Idealization, she suggests, is none other than the result of a defensive exaggeration of the object's goodness: 'Idealization is bound up with the splitting of the object, for the good aspects of the breast are exaggerated as a safeguard against the fear of the persecuting breast.'[27]

There may appear to be no contradiction between these two versions if experience is regarded as a continuum that enables a defensive slide from a good (healthy) to an ideal (defensive) experience. This slide would imply a gradual distortion of reality. However, by implication, in such a situation the good experience would necessarily be moderate in relation to the ideal experience. And indeed some later thinkers took this to mean that a moderate, good experience amounts to a realistic, healthy love, whereas an intense experience indicates a pathological, defensive idealization. Since an ideal love is more primitive and thus earlier, one is led to conclude that according to Klein the infant does not love at first – she only idealizes. And yet to accept this version of positive experience in early infancy also has serious implications, as it resurrects the unchallenged power of sadism as the ruling force in infantile mental life.

In fact, Klein did not opt for this notion of idealization as the exclusive form of infantile love, but then nor did she make a clear space in her texts for the intensity of the feelings of love and gratitude that she postulated. There is an unresolved tension between the former and the latter which is bound to create a sense of ambiguity regarding Klein's ideas on the good object. The reason is that Klein also describes a good object that is, in fact, ideally experienced: 'We find in the analysis of our patients that the breast in its good aspect is the prototype of maternal goodness, inexhaustible patience and generosity, as well as of creativeness. It is these phantasies and instinctual needs that so enrich the primal object that it remains the foundation of hope, trust and belief in goodness.'[28]

It is necessary to conclude that the primary good object cannot be the core of the ego, embody the 'whole of [the infant's] instinctual desires and unconscious phantasies', and also form 'the foundation of hope, trust and belief in goodness' without being ideally experienced. But this kind of ideal cannot be due to a defensive exaggeration and the denial of persecution, for it represents the all-important core of the self. As Klein shows, it embodies the life principle and thus the source of psychical sustenance to the infant. It is difficult to imagine how the infant would be able to derive sustenance from this self-nourishing aspect of his psyche without drawing on its ideal essence.

By not terming it appropriately Klein gave the other half of experience – hate, sadism and envy – an apparently greater theoretical solidity. There is no doubt that Klein also noticed an idealization of a pathological kind, bound up with omnipotent phantasies, as was indeed noted and developed by her followers. However, while such idealization deserves exploration in its own right, it cannot be imputed to the earliest object love that underlies states of complete gratification. It is more logical to assume that only with a greater integration does defensive distortion come into play. In this situation the early primitive ideal is clung to, controlled and transfixed in its primitive, all-giving form in order to avoid reality. However, as shown by Klein the healthy ideal is also preserved by the psyche as its most important life resource, and is apparent as a source of hope in adult patients. It therefore cannot be the same as the pathological ideal that distorts reality.

In Klein's writings this is not resolved explicitly but implicitly. Her 'primary good object' and her 'loved object' acquire the significance of technical terms that involve a complex interaction of internal and external, libido and the world, whereas 'idealization' tends to retain its everyday linguistic sense of excessive valuation. Her term 'good object' is therefore in the nature of a technical term that implies in practice an ideal experience when referring to the earliest states.

This brings it close to some of Balint's descriptions of early infantile states. Both in their thinking went further than Ferenczi. However, Klein did not explicitly sanction the healthy ideal experience that her theory could not but indicate. Her infant was supposed to experience primary goodness and benefit from its unmodified essence but without feeling excessively for its object. Or rather, she did allow this excessive experience in her texts, but passed it off as moderate in her terminology.

The developments that have been described in this chapter were in full motion, but not complete, when Klein reached the most crucial theoretical period that was to give decisive form to her new model. This was the 1935–57 period that was to see the emergence of the key Kleinian concepts of the depressive and the paranoid-schizoid positions, as well as the concept of primary envy. By this stage Klein felt that love counteracts the force of sadism in mental life, that the good object, created by loving impulses, is essential for a secure internal environment, but also that sadism, anxiety and fragmentation processes abound in primitive mental life. She also felt that the task of growth entails a move from fragmentation to integration. However, also typical of her thinking was the fact that development was not deemed to be an uninterrupted progression. While the notion of an unhindered linear progression would form a comforting view of growth, Klein included in her vision insights into destructive obstacles that beset normal growth at every stage. In her model, therefore, each new stage in maturation is not simply welcomed by the ego. Increased awareness triggers new anxieties and conflicts in keeping with the infant's growing realism. An awareness of, and love for, a whole mother necessarily triggers the first serious crisis of infancy – the painful crisis of the depressive position.

NOTES

1. Mitchell, J. (1986) *The Selected Melanie Klein*. London: Penguin Books. p. 31.
2. Klein, M. (1975) 'Personification in the play of children', in *Love, Guilt and Reparation*. London: The Hogarth Press. (First published in 1929.) p. 201.
3. Klein, M. (1975) 'The development of a child', in *Love, Guilt and Reparation*. London: The Hogarth Press. (First published in 1921.) p. 52.
4. Ferenczi, S. (1952) 'Stages in the development of a sense of reality', in *First Contributions to Psycho-Analysis*. London: Maresfield Reprints. (First published in 1913.) p. 19.
5. Klein, M. (1975) 'Criminal tendencies in normal children', in *Love, Guilt and Reparation*. London: The Hogarth Press. (First published in 1927.) p. 172.

6. Klein, M. (1975) 'A contribution to the psychogenesis of manic-depressive states', in *Love, Guilt and Reparation*. London: The Hogarth Press. (First published in 1935.) p. 285.

7. ibid., p. 286.

8. Klein, M. (1991) 'The emotional life and ego-development of the infant with special reference to the depressive position', in P. King and R. Steiner (eds) *The Freud-Klein Controversies 1941–1945*. London: Tavistock/Routledge. (First presented in 1944.) p. 757.

9. Freud, S. (1905) 'Three essays on the theory of sexuality', *Standard Edition*, 7. London: The Hogarth Press. p. 207.

10. ibid., p. 200.

11. Abraham, K. (1973) 'Character-formation on the genital level of libido-development', in *Selected Papers of Karl Abraham*. London: The Hogarth Press. (First published in 1925.) p. 407.

12. Klein, M. (1975) 'Personification in the play of children', in *Love, Guilt and Reparation*. London: The Hogarth Press. (First published in 1929.) p. 214.

13. Klein, M. (1991) 'Early object love', in P. King and R. Steiner (eds) *The Freud-Klein Controversies 1941–1945*. London: Tavistock/Routledge. (First presented in 1944.) p. 756.

14. ibid., p. 756.

15. Ferenczi, S. (1955) 'Confusion of tongues between adults and the child', in *Final Contributions to Problems and Methods of Psycho-Analysis*. London: The Hogarth Press. (First published in 1933.) p. 165.

16. Parts of the Alice Balint paper were first published under the title: 'Reality sense and the development of the ability to love' in the Sandor Ferenczi Memorial volume *Lélekelemzési Tanulmányok*, in Budapest, 1933. A later version appeared under the title 'Love for the mother and mother love' in Balint, M. (1952) *Primary Love and Psycho-analytic Technique*. London: The Hogarth Press. pp. 109–27.

17. Balint, M. (1952) *Primary Love and Psycho-Analytic Technique*. London: The Hogarth Press. p. 127.

18. Klein, M. (1975) 'Love, guilt and reparation', in *Love, Guilt and Reparation*. London: The Hogarth Press. (First published in 1937.) p. 311.

19. Ferenczi, S. (1989) *Thalassa: A Theory of Genitality*. London: Karnak Books. (First published in 1938.) p. 21.

20. Klein, M. (1991) 'Early object love', in P. King and R. Steiner (eds) *The Freud-Klein Controversies 1941–1945*. London: Tavistock/Routledge. (First presented in 1944.) p. 757.

21. ibid., p. 757.

22. Klein, M. (1975) 'Love, guilt and reparation' in *Love, Guilt and Reparation*. London: The Hogarth Press. (First published in 1937.) p. 311.

23. Klein, M. (1975) 'Envy and gratitude', in *Envy and Gratitude*. London: The Hogarth Press. (First published in 1957.) p. 180.

24. ibid., p. 180.

25. Balint, A. (1952) 'Love for the mother and mother love', in *Primary Love and Psycho-Analytic Technique*. London: The Hogarth Press. (First published in 1949.) p. 125.

26. Klein, M. (1960) 'A note on depression in a schizophrenic' in *Envy and Gratitude*. London: The Hogarth Press. p. 265.
27. Klein, M. (1975) 'Notes on some schizoid mechanisms', in *Envy and Gratitude*. London: The Hogarth Press. (First published in 1946.) p. 7.
28. Klein, M. (1975) 'Envy and gratitude', in *Envy and Gratitude*. London: The Hogarth Press. (First published in 1957.) p. 180.

CHAPTER 7

'Loss of the loved object' – Ambivalence and Depressive States

K lein's assertion that love begins in infancy and in the context of an archaic, fragmented relationship with the object, had inescapable theoretical consequences. The infant, whose love creates an ego core on which psychical development depends, is also faced with this task of creating an ego core at the most precarious early stage. His mental grasp of experience and of the good object is partial and changeable, and this necessarily implies that the object which is loved can also be lost. It was this conclusion – that there exists an infantile experience of loss of the loved object – that demanded a consideration of depressive states, and ultimately led Klein to formulate her concept of the depressive position.

For a start, Klein noted the specific and evident loss of weaning. She was now able to emphasize something that mothers had always known intuitively – that weaning represents the first important loss in life, and therefore triggers in the infant states akin to mourning. A central event of infancy, which had received little attention hitherto, was now seen in a new light. But Klein emphasized that its significance is due not only to the immediate impact of the loss of breast feeding. This event is the culmination of numerous small-scale losses that had been experienced from the earliest time, externally through the mother's normal absences, and internally through sadistic attacks which had repeatedly annihilated her in phantasy.

Klein had believed for a while that the infant is born with a readiness for social interactions and is therefore immediately able to relate to his human milieu, even though this relationship is initially rudimentary and incomplete. She had suggested that the maternal body provides a focus for infantile phantasy life, and that the infant also responds to nurture by becoming attached specifically to the maternal breast. The latter is the first important love object; it is a part-object which represents not only food, but by virtue of offering comfort and pleasure, acquires the significance of 'good'.

Klein had also described how in earliest infancy there is an ability to apprehend good and bad portions of experience, but not, as yet, a conceptual capacity to link these to a whole that makes sense. Apprehensions of the good, nurturing aspects of the mother via the manifest presence of her feeding breast, form a separate entity in the infantile universe – an ideal part-object that exists solely for the purpose of fulfilling. By the same token, the withdrawn breast which is absent to the hungry infant is felt as a bad entity, tormenting the infant with hunger and privation and so eliciting sadistic phantasy attacks. Klein suggested that repeated experiences of maternal presence and absence, nurture and privation, build up in the infant's psyche an inner world populated with archaic, good and bad beings.

Klein now moved to consider the implications of the gradual synthesis of these part-objects. She realized that, for the first time, the mother is understood to be the sole site of both sustenance and privation, and while this is much closer to reality, it necessarily ushers in a sense of the painful imperfections and limitations of life. The infant loses the precious sense that there exists, somewhere, an ideal object of unlimited pleasure and satisfaction. This triggers an experience of a 'loss of the loved object'. The whole mother initially represents a despoiled perfection and provokes sorrow and indignant rage in turn. Recognizing a whole mother thus amounts to a psychical weaning from the partially recognized mother, the good breast of earliest infancy. And it is this recognition that triggers the depressive position.

The depth and extent of the infant's sense of loss was only just dawning on Klein's awareness. Her increasing appreciation of its significance was made possible through her growing understanding of a specific element of her framework, and this was her conception of internal objects. The more Klein realized the power and importance of internal objects, the more momentous was the depressive position seen to be. The concept of internal objects thus provides an essential gateway into the labyrinthine complexities of the two depressive position texts: 'A contribution to the psychogenesis of manic-depressive states', published in 1935, and 'Mourning and its relation to manic-depressive states', published in 1940.

DEPRESSIVE STATES IN ADULT PATIENTS

Segal has rightly emphasized that 'A contribution to the psychogenesis of manic-depressive states' was a watershed that marked the beginning of a distinctively Kleinian vision.[1] But surprisingly, the paper's most original Kleinian moments are relatively hidden in a structure which prominently displays ideas which were more commonplace and already circulating in the psychoanalytic community in relation to work with adult patients. Klein's understanding of depressive states, her linking of these to early oral experience, to weaning and to an infantile sense of loss, and also her inclusion of issues of ambivalence and introjection in this picture, are all, in important ways, less original features of her paper.

During the 1930s, a steady interest in depressive conditions resulted in a number of psychoanalytic publications, all of which contained the same cluster of conceptual elements. The most prominent of these was the tracing of depression to a loss suffered by the patient, and the conclusion that depression shares important elements with mourning. Mourning, however, was understood to be a normal process, whereas depression was clearly not. For a start, it was not a reasonable reaction to a real loss. The pathology of depression was felt instead to be rooted in a metaphorical loss, brought about by the patient's phantasy attacks on a strongly resented object. However, while this circumstance could have resulted in no more than anger or hatred, there was a crucial complicating factor that led specifically to depression.

The depressed patient's central relationship was intensely hostile, yet at the same time the resented object was emotionally indispensable to him. Psycho-analysts reasoned that the patient attempts to gain a mastery of the situation by introjecting the object, which, in Deutsch's words, amounted to its 'displacement from reality on to the psychic process'.[2] However, such a displacement exacerbates matters, because the patient redirects his resentment inwards towards his own ego, now identified with the resented object. As Fenichel remarked, 'the depressed patient says "I am bad because I am a liar" when he wants to say "I am angry with X because he has lied to me".'[3] The result of introjection was therefore felt to be the patient's identification with the hated object, his attacks on his self, a resultant lowering of his self-esteem and a depressive deterioration.

This framework of ideas was crucially influenced by Abraham's seminal work on depressive illness, and also by Freud's Abraham-inspired 1914 paper 'Mourning and melancholia'. The psychoanalytic community found these papers particularly inspiring because they vividly confirmed what was amply evident in the material on depressive patients. For a start, such patients invariably described a difficult relationship which was both very central in their lives yet caused them disappointment and grief. There was some uncertainty among psychoanalysts as to the causes of the patient's disappointment. Some noticed that their depressive patients were actually poorly treated by crucial others, and yet most psychoanalysts also noticed an over-sensitivity in such patients. They concluded that the depressive condition was rooted in a narcissistic pathology and that the individual who normally succumbed to it was likely to have a vulnerable self-image, take offence easily and be prone to grievance. In Abraham's thinking, infants who suffer repeated disappointments from their maternal object become narcissistically fragile, and prone to the kind of love-and-hate fluctuations that lead to depression. Either way, the depressive patient was understood to feel let down by his object, and his disappointment and resultant anger were considered to be the trigger points for the condition.

For example, in 1935 Marui described a twenty-five-year-old medical student in whom a melancholic illness was occasioned by the death of a strongly disliked grandmother.[4] The student's grandmother had participated with his mother in bringing him up, and both had been domineering, coercive and at times, sadistic. The patient was brought up to be compliant and timid, stifling his aggression throughout his childhood and adolescence. When he left home to go into higher education, the patient expressed his unconscious aggression towards both women through his sexual promiscuity and his inconsiderate treatment of his female partners. He also spent on prostitutes the money sent by his grandmother for study purposes. When the grandmother died, the student was guilt-stricken and yet unable to resolve his lingering hostility. Instead of being able to mourn the loss of his grandmother, the student was stuck with conflicting love, hate and guilt, and so succumbed to a depressive illness.

As early as 1927 Radó described how depression was typically preceded by the patient's 'rebellious state' towards his resented object,[5] and in 1930, Deutsch amplified this idea with her observations that the patient not only felt fury, but was inhibited and unable to express it. Deutsch gave the example of a female patient whose depression was accompanied by a delusional fantasy that she might find herself destitute and homeless, literally 'in the street'.

This patient had lost her parents at an early age and was left in charge of a younger sister. The patient sacrificed her life, working in menial occupations so that her sister could enjoy better prospects. In doing so, she strongly identified with her younger sister, obtaining vicarious pleasure from imagining the latter's successful future. However, when in due course the sister's life did improve and she found a good marriage partner, the sisterly relationship turned sour. The younger sister decided to leave behind her old life and her sacrificing older sister, and went alone to live with her husband. Deutsch noted how this event raised in her patient a storm of anger. Like Radó's 'rebellious state', it was also the forerunner of the patient's depressive crisis. The patient felt betrayed and abandoned, and yet was unable to resolve this by either wholly rejecting her sister, or else finding the means to seek a compromise and forgive her. The result was an introjection of the resented sister and a revenge fantasy attack on her in which she was imagined to be banished from her new home and made destitute in the street. But the introjection also meant an identification, and it was thus that the patient was tormented by a delusion that it was she who was actually in danger of destitution in the street.

In such typical clinical situations psychoanalysts began to note that the patient's anger was very severe, and in fact amounted to sadism and murderous tendencies. However, they also noticed that the depressive individual is trapped, able neither to confront and then accept and forgive his object, nor to reject and relinquish it. The patient continued to seek love and approval from the very object who was apparently repeatedly betraying. Inasmuch as the object was needed and sought, it was still loved, and yet strong resentment meant that it was equally hated. This tormented state, termed 'ambivalence' by Eugen Bleuler, was now seen to be crucial to the depressive predicament, as had indeed first been suggested by Abraham. It became clear that without ambivalence depression might never occur, since if either love or hate prevailed in the patient's mind, he would resolve the situation by being able to either reject or accept the object.

An awareness of the significance of ambivalence made sense of the patient's need to introject the object, because this offered an opportunity to master the situation by placing it within the orbit of the individual's phantasy control. But this also suggested a complexity which went beyond Freud's thinking in 'Mourning and melancholia'. If the purpose of introjection was to resolve ambivalence, then the patient's aim must be the transformation of the bad, disappointing aspects of the object into good ones. Radó thus suggested that even when the patient is disappointed he is aware of good aspects of his object, and in his effort to control the situation, he separates the good and the bad aspects and introjects them separately, the former into the super-ego, and the latter into the ego. The patient thus internalizes a battle between the two aspects of the object in the hope that the super-ego good object would win and destroy the bad object.

This struggle to keep apart good and bad aspects of the object was noted by other thinkers, including Deutsch and Fenichel. They also wanted to relate this understanding to Freud's theoretical model and hence to psychosexual fixation points in the patient's early development. Here they could rely once more on Abraham's work, since it was he who first linked depressive states to a fixation point in archaic oral experience. Accordingly, the individual first experiences murderous resentment towards a loved object in earliest infancy. Radó noted that when faced with the absent mother, the infant 'flies into an impotent rage', so that 'the deepest fixation point in the melancholic (depressive) disposition is to be found in the "situation of loss of love" ... more precisely, in the hunger situation of the infant'.[6] Fenichel showed how this made sense of the depressive patient's miscarried introjection. An aggressive introjection resurrected the oral sadism of infancy, incorporated a resented object cannibalistically, and so burdened the ego with a malevolent internal object, confirming Freud's crucial insight that 'the shadow of the object fell upon the ego'.[7]

This outlook confirmed also that the depressive patient had been predisposed to ambivalence since early childhood because of a fixation to early oral aggression. According to such thinking, the hungry infant who is unable to elicit a response from his object 'flies into an impotent rage'. When the object becomes available again the infant is simultaneously relieved yet vengeful. He tries to both appropriate and regain the object, and yet has urges to punish it. These two contradictory impulses are united in the single phantasy of a vengeful devouring. As seen, Abraham had already suggested that infants who are exposed to too much disappointment are more likely to become fixated to 'devouring', inconsiderate patterns of relating. He also traced this pattern to the first onset of depression in life because it left the individual with the sense of a destroyed object.

It is significant that all of these ideas, as expressed by the group of psychoanalysts who explored depressive states, reappear as key features of Klein's definition of the depressive position. She too focuses on early oral experience, on the hungry infant's impotent rage and sadism towards the maternal object, on the separation of good and bad object aspects, on ambivalence and on what Radó called the 'situation of loss of love'. Other features of Klein's depressive position were also anticipated in the works of the thinkers around her. For example, her conclusion that the infant experiences guilt and remorse as part of the depressive process and that this functions as the starting point of moral development, are both thoughts which were foreshadowed in Radó's statement: 'When the child passes from the period of suckling, he carries with him, indelibly stamped on his mind, a sequence of experience which later he works over so as to form the connection: guilt-atonement-forgiveness.'[8] Even the idea of an infantile position was germinally present in Deutsch's suggesting that 'the periodic changes of mood, to which most people are subject, probably correspond in a modified form to the periodicity of manic-depressive insanity.'[9]

What, then, did Klein add to the ideas of others, and in what way can her concept of the depressive position be considered as truly original? A reading of Klein's two key papers on it in the context of other thinking of the period undoubtedly reveals the substantial leap in understanding which she offered. Klein did make use of several existing insights on depressive states, but she linked their significance in a unique way, shedding light on an underlying reality of primitive mental functioning which she conceptualized with a hitherto unmatched depth. It was through the linking of psychoanalytic ideas on depressive states with her own original vision that Klein was able to shed unique light on the significance and place of depressive states in the human life cycle.

For a start, she suggested that depression is not an occasional aberration in adult mental life, but an inevitable part of the human condition. Furthermore, it is something that is first experienced by everyone in infancy and that finds an outward expression in the universal process of weaning. Typical elements of the adult depressive state such as ambivalence, separation of good and bad aspects of the object, introjection and other relevant mechanisms therefore make sense in the light of originally infantile processes. Klein justified the notion that depression can happen so early on the grounds that since depression is a prototypical human reaction to loss, it must have a point of origin in the earliest situations of loss, even if the loss experience itself is not initially framed in conceptual adult terms.

As suggested, Klein also emphasized the fact that loss is more than an occasional, random event in early life, because even in optimal conditions the infant has repeated and inevitable encounters with life's painful lacks, especially as conveyed via the normal limitations of maternal handling. Far from adapting easily to this knowledge, the human infant reacts with anger towards the object, and this sets the scene for an ambivalent conflict between love and hate, hence to typical features of depressive states.

The linking of adult depressive states to an infantile origin did not fit easily with the prevailing Freudian views on mental development. Freud was not persuaded that the newborn is able to have a significant recognition of the maternal object. Freud continued to believe instead that the infant's initial existence is sheltered in a state of primary narcissism, and that while the infant does imbibe maternal goodness, he does not differentiate it from the totality of his self-centred, bodily experiences. Freud conceded that worldly impingements are none the less gradually registered, and that this makes possible a growing recognition of the world. However, he continued to hold that it is only after mental maturation that the mother can be recognized, and that when this happens she is recognized entirely and fully. The child typically continues to love, desire and perceive her as good, at least until the onset of the Oedipus complex, when he begins to accommodate the significance of two parents. As Freud continually emphasized, within the Oedipal triangle one parent is loved and regarded as good, while the other is hated and treated as bad.

Contrary to his thinking, Klein now concluded that the notions of good and bad are not initially located in two fully recognized parents, but in partly recognized aspects of the mother. This also implied that the earliest recognitions of good and bad experiences are not conceptual, and so pre-date an ability to obtain a secure mental hold over what is experienced. The Freudian Oedipal child is nearly four years old, and can thus form a notion that goodness is securely located in the actual person of his mother or father. By comparison, the young infant with only rudimentary discriminating capacities can only experience a goodness that though intense, is also fleeting. Goodness materializes to him, and then vanishes, along with the feeding breast, leaving behind an impression which soon dissipates under the impact of new experiences. Retaining an inner sense of the object's goodness or indeed having an established notion of goodness as an inner resource are achievements for which all human individuals must struggle. This struggle is expressed in none other than the painful experience of the infantile depressive position. The most important psychic event that is invoked in the Kleinian texts of this period is the infant's successful introjection of the good breast to form a core for his still fragile and fragmented ego. This lays the basis for development, but not before a crisis of loss and grief is resolved.

Klein concurred with the idea that the hungry infant attacks the mother with rage and sadism, and suggested that such attacks induce him to keep apart in his mind the good and bad part-objects. But this temporary solution to anger cannot last, because development rapidly forces on the infant a growing awareness, hence a realization of the coexistence of good and bad in the same mother. Such an increased cognitive awareness is not, however, matched with an emotional ability to accept what is perceived. The infant is still not able to accommodate himself to the mother's absences and imperfections, and what Radó described as the 'rebellious state' of the depressive adult is, in fact, an old experience, and the earliest human rebelliousness against an imperfect existence conveyed via an imperfect mother.

Like adult depressive patients, the infant is disappointed in his object, yet continues to need and love it. He is, in fact, in the throes of ambivalence, struggling with equally forceful states of love and hate. At moments when sadism prevails, he attacks the object sadistically and annihilates it in phantasy, and when love prevails, he remembers his recent attacks and is devastated by a sense of a 'loss of the loved object', hence becoming depressive.

Furthermore, Klein suggested that these fluctuations of ambivalence are a necessary developmental event which, in optimal conditions, is overcome by the infant. The infant's intellectual development and increasingly secure grasp of reality enables him to observe that the mother who is repeatedly attacked in his phantasy none the less returns to him unharmed in reality. Continual reassurance gradually helps him to overcome his hostility; in his psyche the good internal object has overcome the bad one, and the notion of goodness is now established within him and henceforth available as a permanent source of emotional security.

Klein felt that two intrapsychic processes help the infant through the difficulties of the depressive position. The first is reparation, which enables him, after a bout of mistrust and sadistic attack, to restore the mother in his psyche to her wholesome, loved state. The second process is connected with mourning, and it enables the infant to work over in his mind a sense of loss entailed in the mother's actual imperfections. Both, as will be shown, amount to an overall view of overcoming the depressive position which was crucial to Klein.

With this complex picture Klein unravelled the earliest states of depression and mourning which are a part of every individual's experience. But her thinking also had important implications for adult mental illness, specifically the understanding of depressive and manic-depressive pathology. Klein showed that it was not only current disappointment or narcissistic fragility which triggered adult depression, and that Abraham's suggestion of a fixation point in early oral sadism, though crucial, was not specific enough. Her own framework offered the view of the adult depressive as someone who, as an infant, had failed to cope with the depressive position. He may have been too angry or too fragile to process his ambivalence towards the object, hence adopting rigid manic defences and a denial of his inner state, or psychic reality. Such an adult is not easily able to engage in psychical reparation, nor mourn the normal imperfections of others and of life, and so is also continually prone to disappointments and depressive bouts.

With her linking of adult pathology to infantile states Klein completed the first stage of her major theoretical innovation, which was to trace the essence of human sadness in its many forms to a prototypical early moment in life, and so underscore the ambivalent rebellion with which human individuals greet their first recognition of life's limitations and pains. Klein's other important achievement in defining the depressive position, and one which represents an even more distinctive hallmark of her thinking, was a further elaboration of her concept of internal objects. The concept, which had already appeared at a very early stage in her writing in the form of her thinking on imagos, none the less only acquired a sufficient theoretical depth within the context of the depressive position.

INTERNAL OBJECTS

When other psychoanalysts around Klein wrote about depressive states, they had in mind the patient's response to actual relationships, and when they wrote about introjection, they assumed that the patient's external objects were taken into the psyche in the sense of being lodged, through identification, in the existing mental agencies of ego or super-ego. In this understanding, the only way for an adult individual to absorb something external is via the presence and activity of already established psychic agencies. Klein, however, changed all this.

She suggested that the depressive condition is rooted in interactions with internalized objects that are based on actual ones, and furthermore, that such objects are experienced without the mediation of the mental agencies of super-ego and ego. In the patient's unconscious, the internal object assumes the form of a powerful anthropomorphic being that inhabits his internal domain, permeating both mind and body. This object is also felt in unconscious phantasy to have been devoured in the first instance, since introjection signified for Klein a type of taking in which was much more primitive and cannibalistic than an ideational representation of objects in the mind. Her thinking thus intimates a much more organic transaction between the subject and the world, in which parts of experience are more ingested by the mind than recorded in it. Defining the concept of internal object thus, meant that it was more likely to make sense to anthropologists than to psychiatrists; it had more in common with tribal beliefs about being possessed by spirits than with Western scientific views on the mental recall and representation of external events.

Hinshelwood has shown how the concept of internal objects was so central to Kleinian thinking that between 1934 and 1943 it was regarded as an almost defining characteristic of her theory, and so played a crucial role in the rapidly consolidating group of devotees around Klein.[10] However, the concept also caused considerable difficulties for non-Kleinian psychoanalysts, and was the focus of an intense debate within the British Psychoanalytic Society both before and during the Controversial Discussions. It is clear from this debate that internal objects provoked confusion and scepticism, and that Klein herself was far from indifferent to the problem: 'The psychoanalysis of young children ... led me to use a term which has not proved acceptable and clear enough to a number of my colleagues. It is the term "internal objects".'[11]

One of the main reasons for the confusion created by the concept was to surface during the Controversial Discussions. It was related to a theoretical idiosyncrasy that was becoming increasingly apparent, which was Klein's tendency to use a term both to describe the subject's internal experience and, simultaneously, to offer a technical psychoanalytic designation of a phenomenon. Some of Klein's colleagues felt that she was failing to follow Freud's logical procedure at her peril. Freud built models of the mind by trying to observe the experiencing patient from an objective stance, and then attempting to unearth universal rules that dictate the behaviours of our 'mental apparatus' and so underpin subjective states. His model thus advocated a completely different approach, and one which makes clear distinctions between the patient's subjective experiencing and the theoretical framing of his mental state by the psychoanalyst.

Freud saw it as his task to go beyond the description of human subjective experience and to find ways of theorizing its underlying principles. It was for this reason that he worked out different models of the mind which could help to conceptualize the forces that govern the mental apparatus. The terms used in such models, for instance, 'super-ego', were important as designators of phenomena, and were to be used as conceptual tools with which to try and understand the subjective states that patients presented in the clinical situation.

A term such as 'super-ego' was thus a theoretical construct used to refer to a specific mental function. The function in question could be described as a self-critical faculty which, in optimal conditions, helps to uphold morality and a social conscience. But in Freud's thinking, this theoretical view of the function had to be distinguished from the way in which the individual might experience it within himself. This latter could take the form of thoughts and beliefs that together amount to an inner voice of some kind, or even the sense of a critical inner presence.

While Freud's thinking distinguished between theoretical definitions and subjective descriptions, Klein's concept of internal objects appeared to offer no such distinction. It put emphasis on subjective phantasy, specifically on the subject's experiencing of the introjected object as an actual being within the self. To add to the difficulty, internal objects had never been defined specifically enough in, say, a paper fully devoted to the subject. When pressed about her precise meaning, Klein finally penned a brief definition, but significantly, one that was never published:

My reason for preferring this term to the classic definition, that of 'an object installed in the ego', is that the term 'inner object' is more specific since it exactly expresses what the child's unconscious and for that matter the adult's deep layers, feels about it. In these layers it is not felt to be part of the mind in the sense, as we have learned to understand it, of the super-ego being the parents' voice inside one's mind. This is the concept we find in the higher strata of the unconscious. In the deeper layers, however, it is felt to be a physical being, or rather, a multitude of beings, which with all their activities, friendly and hostile, lodge inside one's body, particularly inside the abdomen, a conception to which physiological processes of all kinds, in the past and in the present, have contributed.[12]

This response shows Klein reacting to a moment of pressure by over-stating her case, so that instead of finding a conceptual approach to the term, she tries to lend it substance by dwelling even more on its subjective phantasy content. The suggestion that internal objects are phantasized 'particularly inside the abdomen' moves the concept even further into the terrain of subjective irrationality, and does little to clarify the term's theoretical status or technical meaning.

However, Klein's attempted definition is also very revealing. There was a good reason for her difficulties in conveying why introjection resulted in more than a mere representation of objects inside the mind, and why it would still refer to a different process even in the event that the notion of representation was stretched to account for a full range of primitive psychic and somatic forms of registering external events.

As suggested, the Freudian psychoanalysts around Klein believed that objects could only be known internally via the mediation of psychical agencies. In keeping with Freud, they were separating the patient's subjective experience from a theoretical designation of its underlying structure and mental function. Looked at in these terms, an introjected object was felt to correspond to a form of identification which affects the functioning of the ego or super-ego. Radó, Deutsch and Fenichel thus viewed the mental changes responsible for depression in terms of alterations in the functioning of ego and super-ego, and from their point of view introjected objects would only be theoretically significant for instigating this change.

Klein's difficulty lay partly in the complexity she perceived when she came across the particular mental phenomenon which she designated as internal object. The phenomenon appeared to elude theorization because there was no easy way of framing it conceptually without resort to anthropomorphic props. If such an attempt were made, it would be possible to describe an internal object as a dynamic psychic entity which exerts a characteristic influence on the individual's way of experiencing life, and crucially affects relationships with others. The internal object is a part of the world lodged within, which both becomes identity and yet differs from what the individual feels to be himself. However, it is not visualized and static as a representation might be, but a dynamic process constantly touching individual mood and perception and psychosomatic sensations.

Thought of theoretically, an internal object can be described as a distinctive mental process which generates a characteristic emotional state. And yet it amounts to more, because, and this is where Klein felt challenged, its characteristic mode takes on a relational format. In other words, the mental process corresponding to an internal object continually treats the subject in a characteristic way. To take as an example a malevolent internal object, one firstly notes that it is subjectively experienced by the patient as a destructive inner being which spreads pain in the body and fear in the mind. Looked at theoretically, it can be said to correspond to a phantasy pattern which exerts a particular kind of anxiety. This pattern itself persecutes the subject with anxiety, and such persecution is intrinsic to its mode of manifesting.

The most distinctive essence of Klein's object relations approach is precisely her suggestion that mechanisms within the mind simulate human relationships. She showed that it was not enough to think of the human mental apparatus along Freudian lines, as having developed in response to the pressures of accruing stimulae. What had been missing in this picture was the suggestion that the mind reacts to pressure by framing its adaptive responses in relational terms, that is, by bringing different mental entities into a constant relational dialogue with one another. It is within the matrix of the mother-infant relationship that the human psyche comes into being, and thereafter its processes are shaped as relational patterns, in which various good and bad entities interact and thus define meaning.

The internal object is thus, confusingly, both a subjective experience of an internal presence, initially based on an introjected breast, and at the same time, the theoretical designation of a process which takes on a relational pattern, treating or maltreating the individual in various ways, and by the same token, being moulded by the individual's internal treatment of it. And because of the way in which such patterns are embedded in the very format of mental processes,

Klein's internal object is a very powerful entity that has a far-reaching effect on the mind. Not surprisingly, it was also felt by her to be experienced by the individual as actually living in and occupying his internal domain, and this power over the self needs to be appreciated as a prerequisite to understanding the depressive position. Because of the power of the internal object, its loss, as experienced in the depressive position, is an internal event of catastrophic, tragic proportions, as will now be discussed.

NOTES

1. Segal, H. (1978) *Introduction to the Work of Melanie Klein*. London: The Hogarth Press.
2. Deutsch, H. (1965) 'Melancholic and depressive states', in *Neurosis and Character Types*. London: The Hogarth Press. (First published in 1930.) p. 152.
3. Fenichel, O. (1945) 'Depression and mania', in *The Psycho-Analytic Theory of Neurosis*. New York: Norton.
4. Marui, K. (1935) 'The process of introjection in melancholia', *International Journal of Psychoanalysis*, 16, I, pp. 49–58.
5. Radó, S.(1927) 'The problem of melancholia', in *International Journal of Psychoanalysis*, 9, pp. 420–37.
6. Fenichel, O. (1945) 'Depression and mania', in *The Psycho-Analytic Theory of Neurosis*. New York: Norton. p. 425.
7. Freud, S. *Mourning and Melancholia, Standard Edition* 14. London: The Hogarth Press. p. 249.
8. Radó, S. (1927) 'The problem of melancholia', in *International Journal of Psychoanalysis*, 9, p. 425.
9. Deutsch, H. (1965) 'Melancholic and depressive states', in *Neurosis and Character Types*. London: The Hogarth Press. (First published in 1930.) p. 152.
10. Hinshelwood, R. D. (1997) 'The elusive concept of "internal objects" (1934–1943): its role in the formation of the Klein group', *International Journal of Psychoanalysis*, 78, 5, pp. 877–99.
11. ibid. D16, Melanie Klein Trust papers, Wellcome Library. London.
12. ibid. D16, Melanie Klein Trust papers, Wellcome Library. London.

CHAPTER 8

'Loss of the loved object' – Tragedy and Morality in the Depressive Position

K lein defined the depressive position in two stages over a five-year period beginning with the 1935 publication 'A contribution to the psychogenesis of manic-depressive states', and completing the process in the 1940 'Mourning and its relation to manic-depressive states'. The extended elaboration of the concept ideally should have helped to clarify it considerably. However, the reader is faced instead with a bewildering account of complex mental dynamics which can become something of an intellectual obstacle course. While Klein's startling ideas might still come across as intimately evocative and strangely accessible at an emotional level, they can still be disturbing and challenging to intellectual processes and to clear conceptual determination. Only later, in simplifying secondary sources does the concept gain some coherence, but not always without a cost. Secondary accounts may play down what is problematic, but also, inevitably, some of the crucial subtleties and depths of Klein's own formulation.

For a start, Klein's formless, intractable prose, while not an advantage, none the less reflects her struggle to articulate elements of unconscious life that elude language. By this stage in her understanding, she perceived mental functioning as a complex activity of simultaneous processes which is not easily captured in our secondary thought process with its conceptual and linguistic order. In the primordial chaos of the unconscious mind, anarchic mental phenomena overlap, refuse to fall into a coherent temporal sequence and defy the whole notion of developmental stages. A Kleinian position was later often described as a 'constellation' of interactive emotions, defences and psychic processes, all of which group around a particular object relationship.[1] In the case of the depressive position, such processes typically include the twin experiences of ambivalence and a loss of the loved object. But perhaps it is best to begin with the event that Klein regarded as the trigger for the depressive position, that is, the integration that she considered to be the main determinant of psychic growth in the early years.

Klein believed that the infant, with her fragmented mode of experiencing reality and relating to the mother, undergoes a crucial psychic integration towards the middle of the first year of life, thus being enabled to recognize the mother as a whole being. Klein's idiosyncratic way of theorizing, already evident in her thinking on internal objects, was even more pronounced in her ideas on integration. She was, yet again, addressing subjective experience while simultaneously seeking to offer an objective designation of a mental phenomenon. In fact, her two depressive-position papers show an increasing emphasis on the experiencing individual, so that powerful descriptions of subjective states are at the very heart of her endeavour, and partly used as explanatory tools. In line with this, the integration to which she refers is both a subjective experience, that is, an awareness of a mother who integrates in herself good and bad, but also simultaneously, an objective designation of a change in the infant's mental structure. In this second sense integration is an ego maturation, or a gathering of fragmented ego-parts into a more coordinated psychic entity. When the ego is thus capable of organized functioning, there is a corresponding growth in the infant's capacity to coordinate environmental impressions and make sense of the world. She is now able to experience it as a composite reality in which parts relate to a whole, and by the same token, apprehend a whole, good and bad mother.

It is sometimes not sufficiently appreciated that Klein did not equate the depressive position with integration. In fact, she did not even try to account for the maturational factors that lead to integration. Like Ferenczi, she believed that the infant's reality sense and maturation develop in predetermined ways. And while she suggested that development can be aided by the natural drive for knowledge (the epistemophilic instinct), or hampered by psychic defences, she did not believe that it depends on such active psychic manoeuvres. Psychic integration, much like such physical equivalents as learning to crawl, sit and walk, is an evolutionary given. As early as the middle of the first year of life, there develops naturally enough reality sense to begin to accommodate the emotional significance of a mother who does not respond flawlessly to needs, and by the same token, to notice a reality which has frustrations and gaps in it.

However, what concerned Klein above all was not so much the infant's integration and growing ability to notice a flawed reality. The most crucial element in her concept of the depressive position was the acute response that integration triggers in the infant. The recognition of an imperfect world and object necessarily inflict a shock, and so mobilize in the infant aggression and ambivalence as well as bereft, depressive states. Klein had already described some of these depressive phenomena, and she now proceeded to amplify on her description. She added that because of her conflicted, ambivalent state, the infant experiences not only anger and sorrow, but also primitive guilt, rooted in her attribution of the loved object's loss to her own destructive aggression. The perfect breast of earliest infancy, no longer available in its original, all-giving form, is believed by the infant to have been lost through her oral aggressive attacks. In its place, there is now a whole mother whose good, nurturing qualities are marred by frustrating limitations. The fully recognized mother, however loving in reality, is not initially experienced as an adequate substitute for the early feeding relationship. In the place of the lost archaic bliss, she introduces a reality of pain and ambivalent conflict.

Yet even with the addition of guilt, the definition of the depressive position was not complete. Klein felt that the aggression mobilized in the infant by the sense of a flawed mother is used partly to attack her in phantasy, but also to attack the depressive states themselves. Aggression thus contributes to the erection of psychic defences, specifically manic ones which seek to attack, negate and ultimately annihilate depressive states along with the awareness that they bring. Instead of feeling failed or abandoned by the lost, loved object, the infant becomes defensively manic and denying, reversing her bereft state into an omnipotent phantasy of control over the object. The actual autonomy of the object, which would otherwise present a threat, is kept at bay through psychic denial and an accompanying dictatorial omnipotence towards it. Such manic defences do mitigate the infant's grief and rage at extreme moments, and thus have the developmental function of providing a temporary refuge from pain. However, they cannot be adopted as a long-term developmental strategy. Used in excess, they can actually interfere with the natural progression of a reality sense and hamper mental growth.

Klein therefore concluded that the infantile psyche must negotiate a developmental path which ultimately enables a successful emergence out of the depressive and defensive chaos, and this negotiation is a protracted, yet natural process. It involves fluctuations between depressive and defensive/manic states, until a gradual diminution of grief and guilt becomes possible. Along with these processes the infant comes to terms with the object's flawed wholeness and so has a more grounded, secure experience of an object that is now loved in a new, more complex, mature and forgiving way. This is supported by reparative processes that salvage and preserve the internal object, establishing it securely in the mind as mostly good, and as a lasting presence that can be preserved.

Integration for Klein, though independent of the depressive condition, is none the less also the process that continues through the fluctuations of the depressive position and that ultimately helps to resolve it. While initially integration is a contact between good and bad which introduces the trauma of a flawed world, such contact, through its very repetitions and continuity, enables love gradually to absorb hate and diminish its force, making the loved, good object predominant in the internal world. This outcome is not possible where love and hate are equally poised in balance and where there is unresolved ambivalent tension. Klein therefore came to believe that the depressive position, which is marked by ambivalence, is overcome in infancy, with the exception that it can be reactivated in adult life in situations such as mourning.

However, after Klein's time there was a growing tendency to play down her belief that the depressive position must be overcome. This coincided with an altered emphasis whereby it has come to be regarded as a mostly progressive phenomenon. As such, it has been felt to mark the beginning of intersubjective awareness and so spell the infant's ability to recognize, and show consideration and concern for, a whole mother. In this understanding, the depressive position necessarily lays the foundation for internal moral structures, inasmuch as integration requires that the infant should be able to accept a mother who has lacks and badness in her. It thus ushers in the ability to accept others in the world as imperfect, and by implication, as fully human with needs and entitlements of their own. They are no longer seen as gratifying part-objects which exist solely for the benefit of the self and need to remain perfect for the purposes of selfish wish-fulfilment.

In such thinking, the infant's shift from an ego-centred to an object-centred state is emphasized, and held to be the crux of the depressive position. There is a further factor which might have reinforced such a view. Historically, the depressive position was formulated by Klein roughly in mid-career and before she had a full theory of development. A more completed account of infant development only became available in 1946, when she was able to theorize fully the earliest stages of life. With this she concluded that the depressive position is only the second important experience of childhood, and that it is preceded by a more archaic position which is equally complex. Klein already had in place ideas on the early fragmented functioning that precedes integration and the depressive position. But she was to re-evaluate this early situation in 1946, when she understood the infant's most archaic functioning anew as the expression of a paranoid-schizoid position, characterized by splitting mechanisms and primitive persecutory anxiety.

However, for over a decade Klein worked without this added knowledge and therefore with the assumption that the depressive position is the singular crucial event of infancy and early childhood. And because her view of development reached a stage of completion only in 1946, there is often a temptation to bypass the numerous details of the 1935 and 1940 depressive-position texts, and settle for secondary accounts which offer an overview of Klein's two positions together. Such descriptions typically reverse the historical sequence in which Klein's papers were actually written, and offer instead her completed developmental account which starts with the earliest, paranoid-schizoid position.

There are obvious advantages to this. It can certainly help to make sense of Klein's completed outlook which follows the infant's move from a fragmented paranoid-schizoid, to a depressive, mode of experiencing the world. However, such an account also carries a specific risk. When viewed together, the Kleinian positions invite us to impose a linear developmental order on them, and this has led some thinkers to view them as a move from an inferior, sadistic and 'psychotic' paranoid-schizoid position, to a progressive, developmentally desirable and 'sane' depressive position.

But, as will be discussed, Klein herself did not regard psychic growth as a move from a negative paranoid-schizoid position to a depressive position which is a purely positive phenomenon. Furthermore, this way of regarding the concept leaves out crucial dimensions of it. In its original formulation, the depressive phenomenon was set out as both developmentally progressive and positive and, simultaneously, as a dangerous crisis point which sets in motion ambivalence, a catastrophic sense of loss and also, psychotic anxieties and defences, all of which need to be overcome.

And yet, an emphasis on a progressive view of the depressive position continues to date, and has also ushered in other changes in contemporary Kleinian theory. While Klein focused on the depressive position as an event of infancy which she placed within the first six months of life, later psychoanalysts were led to re-evaluate it as a more permanent feature of adult mental life. Since the depressive position was reframed as a mostly evolved mode of intersubjective relating, it followed that its presence in psychic life does not need to be overcome. In 1963 Bion suggested that the two Kleinian positions continue into adult life and are a lifelong feature of psychic functioning. There are thus continual fluctuations between a depressive, intersubjective mode of functioning and a more primitive, ego-centric paranoid-schizoid one. He designated such fluctuations as PS <‹–›> D (paranoid-schizoid – depressive), and this has been broadly accepted as the principle which continually governs adult psychical life. A progressive-regressive slide between the two positions has thus been understood to be constantly operating even on the micro-level of everyday psychical experience. In 1981, Joseph analysed the importance of such fluctuations for Kleinian clinical technique:

> The notion of positions helps us as a framework, to orient ourselves in our listening to our patients. We need to get the feeling of the central position in which his mind is currently operating – whether for example, he is viewing his world ... more from a depressive stance with a sense of responsibility, pain, and guilt that has to be dealt with or from a more paranoid stance with much splitting-off and projection of impulses.[2]

This addition of responsibility to the typical range of depressive emotions has been broadly accepted, and it has the effect of tilting the concept from a definition in terms of anxiety and suffering to a definition which accentuates moral achievement. The term 'depressive' then becomes a perplexing choice, as was indeed noted originally by Winnicott, who wondered if a purely progressive developmental position did not deserve a more appropriate title, such as 'a stage of concern'.[3] And, indeed, with a positive emphasis, depressive phenomena assume the significance of vital features of object relations, representing the capacity to accept the loved object even when it is frustrating, refrain from excessive attacks on it and exercise concern towards its well-being and continuity. The focus on it as a moral achievement has been generally prevalent with Klein's followers, evident in the depiction of infantile and adult states alike.[4] It is exemplified in Segal's outlook: 'The shift from the paranoid-schizoid to the depressive position is a fundamental change from psychotic to sane functioning ... The sense of psychic reality develops – acknowledging and assuming responsibility for one's impulses and the state of one's internal objects.'[5] Such sentiments have been echoed in Meltzer's approach: '... the values of the paranoid-schizoid position are gradually replaced by those of the depressive position, with relinquishment of egocentricity in favour of concern for the welfare of the loved objects.'[6] This kind of thinking has also informed clinical observation and practice, as is evident in Steiner's outlook, where the progressive moment in the psychoanalytic encounter is deemed to be an essentially depressive one: '. . . if the patient makes meaningful progress, a gradual shift towards depressive-position functioning is observed, while if he deteriorates we see a reversion to paranoid-schizoid functioning such as occurs in negative therapeutic reactions'.[7]

Klein's original notion of overcoming the depressive position does not sit well with such thinking. It has even led later Kleinians to wonder if Klein actually believed that depressive emotions must be overcome. Segal, for instance, wonders if what is overcome is not depressive states themselves, but traces of earlier, paranoid-schizoid anxieties that are still active in the depressive position:

> Clinically and developmentally it is certainly true that persecutory anxieties persist in the depressive position. It is, however, useful to . . . consider the persecutory fears still operative in the depressive position as belonging to the paranoid-schizoid position; the working-through of the depressive position could then be considered precisely as the overcoming of the paranoid-schizoid elements *by* the depressive ones. (Emphasis added.)[8]

Meltzer has made another, similar suggestion. Namely, that overcoming the depressive position amounts to an acceptance of depressive anxieties: 'I take it that by "overcoming" the depressive position [Klein] meant learning to tolerate the depressive anxieties about the destruction of the good object.'[9]

Such an understanding of overcoming fits in well with later, post-Bion insights that are now integrated into Kleinian theory. However, Klein worked without this hindsight, and her texts therefore reveal her conviction that it is crucial to overcome, rather than merely tolerate, the depressive position: 'I have shown here and in my previous paper the deeper reasons for the individual's incapacity to overcome successfully the infantile depressive position. Failure to do so may result in depressive illness . . .'[10] The texts also reveal that it was specifically depressive anxieties such as grief, depression and feelings of loss (rather than paranoid-schizoid anxieties), which Klein assigned to the class of emotions that needed to be overcome: 'the diminishing of fears through happy experiences helps the baby step-by-step to overcome his *depression and feelings of loss*'[11] [and] 'In normal development these *feelings of grief and fears* are overcome.'[12] (Emphasis added.)

Klein's intentions are reinforced by the context in which she made such assertions. Anyone who might imagine that her emphasis on overcoming depressive anxieties was only an early feature of her thinking and purely a function of her pre-1946 theoretical framework, discovers from the texts that this is not the case. It is significant that even with her completed post-1946 framework, Klein regularly made little differentiation between the status of depressive anxieties and anxieties belonging to an earlier paranoid-schizoid level. Both could lead to illness: 'To repeat my conclusion expressed in earlier writings: persecutory and depressive anxieties, if excessive, may lead to severe mental illness and mental deficiency in childhood. These two forms of anxiety also provide the fixation points for paranoic, schizophrenic and manic-depressive illnesses in adult life.'[13] Klein's clinical conclusions, both early and late in her career, also reinforced this point. For example, when discussing her patient Rita's difficulties, she emphasized that these were due to both depressive and persecutory anxieties: 'Rita's relation to her mother was dominated by two great sources of anxiety: persecutory fear and depressive anxiety ... she was therefore overwhelmed by the fear of losing her.'[14] Klein related this to her observations of how typical depressive anxieties deeply undermined Rita's security: 'Her feelings of guilt and unhappiness expressed themselves in constant questions to her mother: "Am I good ?" "Do you love me?" and so on.'[15]

Thus, interestingly, a pathological fear of abandonment was seen by Klein as depressive in origin. As suggested, such thinking was not an early passing phase in her theory, but evident in her writings until the end of her life. Klein continued to group depressive and persecutory anxieties together in writings as late as her last published paper, where, for example, she describes a patient who 'reached a fair level of integration but this was disturbed by persecutory and depressive anxiety ...'[16]

The fact that the notion of overcoming the depressive position does not figure in a more contemporary, post-Bion view, might lead some to argue that Klein's thinking on 'overcoming' is a clinical anachronism that has little to offer today. Yet the texts reveal that more is involved in Klein's argument. Hinshelwood notes that Klein felt that primitive guilt, a central feature of the depressive position, must be overcome if the infant is to avoid a slavish dependence on the object and later become a guilt-ridden, weak individual. In addition, Klein suggested that other depressive emotions, listed by her specifically as sorrow, grief, depression and fear of loss, are initially psychotic in content.[17] As such they amount together to a germ of a depressive illness, or a 'melancholia in statu nascendi.'[18]

This aspect of Klein's thinking is familiar, but the idea that anxieties should be altogether overcome in the process of growth would not make sense with a post-Bion awareness. Psychic pain, with some depression, guilt and fear of loss are seen as essential to normal adult object relations, especially when experienced in the normal fluctuations as summed up by Bion's PS $\leftrightarrow$ D. Ogden, for example, suggests that without such fluctuations psychical life would stagnate.[19] And yet in her thinking, Klein had already laid the foundation for this later understanding. Her description of how infantile states change with development implied a great deal about the nature of the mature psychical states that evolve from them. The notion of overcoming is central to this. However, Klein's notion of overcoming is also not a simple one. It touches on a problematic area in her definition of the depressive position, that points, in turn, to the contradictory nature of the phenomenon which she tried to articulate. Specifically, overcoming in the texts applies to a level of depressive experience that is submerged in the process of growth but that continues none the less to represent a powerful psychical reality. As such, it affects the more evolved mode of psychical functioning that replaces it.

TRAGEDY AND MORALITY

There is a contradictory tension in the texts between some of the mental states grouped by Klein under her concept of the depressive position. This theoretical problem both complicates the concept, and yet enriches it in a way that warrants a re-examination of its history. More specifically, in Klein's description of the position, two main conflicting strands emerge. In order to focus more easily on these it is useful to think of them as tragic and moral, respectively. The tragic strand centres on an experience of irrevocable loss or damage. This is felt to have been brought about through the subject's own aggression. The moral theme centres on the infantile capacity to experience guilt for attacks on the imperfect and frustrating object, and so accept responsibility for personal aggression. This enables also a capacity to engage in reparation after aggressive attacks, and so salvage the internal object and restore it to its loved, cared-for state. Such moral processes correspond to an attitude of concern for the object, an ability to forgive and accept its normal limitations and so emerge from a purely ego-centred outlook.

The terms 'tragic' and 'moral' are useful in relation to the Kleinian texts for designating basic, universal configurations of psychical experience that emerge in her vision. They are not intended to suggest that Klein actually chose to use cultural and historical references in the same way that Freud, for example, deliberately made use of the original Oedipus story. In the Kleinian texts, tragedy – the irrevocable loss at the heart of the depressive phenomenon – is a psychic state representing a loss of the loved object. The catastrophic, tragic quality of this loss reverberates throughout life with the significance of the loss, at birth, of the original intrauterine perfection. However, the experience of the loss of the loved object derives its essence not so much from regressive intrauterine longings, as from the initial impact of life itself, presented to the infant through its first good object. As seen, the good, nurturing object of earliest infancy, the breast, is loved in the most primitive, over-powering sense. It is invested with the whole of the infant's 'instinctual desires and his unconscious phantasies', which as such amount to 'the manifestation of forces which tend to preserve life.'[20] The essence of the infant's quest for psychical nourishment and life is projected at moments of contact with the nurturing object. The latter is invested with a fundamental life-giving significance and introjected to form the core of the ego. It develops to provide 'the foundation for hope, trust and belief in goodness', as well as becoming the 'prototype of maternal goodness, inexhaustible patience and generosity.'[21]

The good internal object is structured on the basis of introjected maternal goodness, and represents the phantasy objectification of such goodness, hence an endowment of a central aspect of the psyche, its core, with an identity that can be experienced in primitive phantasy. Losing such an object amounts to the profound loss of the life-orientated, self-nourishing aspect of the psyche, the core of the self. Thus the loss of the loved object is an internal event related to the internal object, as well as being bound up with the perceived loss of the external object or its qualities due to separations, frustrations and weaning.

Because the loved internal object was now understood by Klein to be so essential to the infant's functioning, it followed from this that its loss implied an internal catastrophe. In Segal's words, 'the infant's internal world is felt to be in bits'.[22] The result was what Riviere described as 'a nightmare of desolation' that threatens breakdown.[23] Indeed, Klein concluded late in her life that 'without the good object at least to some extent becoming part of the ego, life cannot continue', thus underscoring the formidable impact of the good internal object on the psyche.[24]

While the world of tragic, irrevocable loss suggests a world that has been overwhelmed by destruction and guilt, the world where a moral framework is secure is one in which an order has been set up precisely to prevent tragic consequences. As suggested, in the Kleinian texts its essence is the capacity to bear some guilt, experience the state of the internal object, continually make good any damage inflicted on it, and thus preserve it. Within such a system damage is not allowed to reach absolute proportions, for a continual internal awareness implies a continual reparative activity.

Theoretically, there may appear to be little difficulty in relating the infantile tragedy of the loss of the loved object to the object-related morality that emerges from it. But in experiential terms, the kind of depressive position depicted by Klein is constructed of two mental states that negate each other. The moral aspect reverses the result of its tragic aspect, in the sense that the object is no longer experienced as irrevocably damaged or lost but, quite the opposite, restored and safeguarded. The early depressive phantasy of harbouring a dying or dead object which Klein describes, is replaced by a new and opposite experience of a live object that is successfully preserved. Some might argue that this negation is insignificant, since tragic anxieties are merely temporary, and soon replaced by more mature awareness. However, such a temporary significance can only be experienced retrospectively by the individual. From the infantile perspective each part of the depressive experience is characterized by its very completeness as a world view, its comprising 'a total situation'.[25] And indeed Klein was increasingly referring to the most archaic experience of the internal object as of a total situation rather than a recognized entity. This implies that when the tragedy of loss of the loved object is first experienced, it cannot be modified by what lies ahead and out of its present orbit – the future development of a stable object-related morality. In a primitive psychical state there is no such experience as a potential loss, or a mere fear of losing the object, before there is a subjective internal state that gives full meaning to actual loss. Remaining within the bounds of mere fear for the object is in any case a theoretical fiction, as Klein was aware: 'A hungry infant cannot ascertain the limit to which his aggression is justified and beyond which it becomes murderous and destructive ... Moreover, in the early mind desires and phantasies are felt to be omnipotent.'[26]

Klein did indeed stress that in reality the caring mother continually shields the infant from the devastation of tragic anxieties. Although the mother is periodically lost to the infant – externally through separations and internally through infantile aggression – she is also continually regained. But however limited or temporary its duration, tragedy can only be known initially as a total situation that dominates experience and is a subjective but powerful psychical reality. This means that underlying the narrative of morality with its powers of reparation, hope and continuity, and with its measure of control over events, is a hidden stratum of a completely different order – the tragedy that ends in destruction and loss and that leads to despair and madness. The psychical realities of tragedy and morality are simultaneous narratives that work on two levels within the Kleinian texts. Her vision intimates that in the socialized individual a continual underlying level of tragedy ensures that the secondary, higher level of morality retains its sense, for morality must assume the possibility of irrevocable loss all the time.

AMBIVALENCE

Klein's definition of the depressive position was partly structured descriptively, as shown, through her depiction of a series of subjective internal scenarios, representing a loss of the loved object. However, she also approached it conceptually, and for this the term 'ambivalence' is most relevant. It is Klein's approach to the process of primitive ambivalence that further illuminates the nature of both levels of the depressive position in her thinking. As suggested, Klein's understanding of ambivalence was in keeping with that of psychoanalysts who were studying adult depressive states. As such, it was regarded as an insoluble hostility towards a disappointing, but none the less intensely needed and loved object. This irreconcilable conflict was shown by her to have an early origin, and in her formulation of the depressive position she provided an account of how it might first be experienced by the infant.

In the thinking of later Kleinians, the increasing emphasis on the depressive position as a progressive phenomenon required also some re-evaluation of infantile ambivalence. Since there was no longer a sense that the depressive position needs to be overcome, it was correspondingly necessary to depict ambivalence as desirable for development. In the 1960s, for example, Rosenfeld discussed ambivalence not as an intractable archaic conflict, but as an infantile state in which love can coexist with aggression: 'The infant soon begins to realize that his love and hate are directed towards one and the same object. This enables him to experience guilt and depression and the anxieties that centre around the fear of losing the good object.'[27]

Although Rosenfeld's thinking in the 1960s was clearly Kleinian, what he depicts here is more evolved than the kind of primitive ambivalence which features in Klein's vision. For Rosenfeld, the infant realizes that his love and hate for the object coexist, and this enables him to experience a range of depressive states. By comparison, in Klein's descriptions the infant is not initially able to realize ambivalence, nor accommodate depressive states in a single mental framework. Rather, the infant initially lives out ambivalence by undergoing powerful swings between hatred and love, sadistic attacks and acutely anxious states of primitive concern: 'We must not lose sight of the fact that sadistic impulses ... are a most potent factor in the infant's conflicts arising at this stage.'[28] To such sadism is added overwhelming greed: 'Greed ... is felt to be uncontrollable and destructive and to endanger the loved external and internal objects.'[29]

Uncontrollable and destructive greed corresponds to irrevocable damage or loss. For Klein infantile ambivalence is thus characterized by volatile states in which overpowering sadism and greed periodically swamp the infantile psyche, endangering love and so triggering acute, psychotic anxiety. Klein was increasingly convinced that within the infant's most primitive framework each part of the ambivalent relationship is a total situation that overwhelms him in turn. This pattern to some extent fits into the earlier fragmented, paranoid-schizoid framework from which the infantile psyche is still in the process of emerging, so that 'the ... splitting processes characteristic of the paranoid-schizoid position continue, though changed in strength and form, into the depressive position.'[30]

The infant does now recognize a whole object which is also identified as the loved and needed mother. But this initially makes the infant even more impatient with maternal lacks and imperfections. While infantile aggression has begun to diminish, the very gradual nature of this change means that at the early stages of the depressive position sadism continues to feature with a primitive ferociousness: 'In my opinion, the paranoiac mechanism of destroying the objects ... by every means derived from oral, urethral and anal sadism, persists, but still in a lesser degree and with a certain modification due to the change in the subject's relations to his objects.'[31] Ambivalence thus evolves gradually from early fragmentation and splitting and is in organic continuity with such archaic states. Klein suggested that it therefore continues to be 'carried out in the splitting of the imagos',[32] as was indeed held by thinkers such as Radó, and this is linked also to Klein's emphatic assertion that, 'I must again make clear that in my view the depressive state is based on the paranoid state and genetically derived from it.'[33]

The implication of such thinking is that the process of psychic integration which leads to the recognition of a whole object is extended and gradual. Its beginnings are most logically thought of as a qualitative change in each of the fragmented, split-off parts of early experience. Within the paranoid-schizoid state each fragmented, momentary experience of the object saturates the infantile psyche obliterating all trace of adjacent or previous impressions. It is a total situation, leading Klein to conclude that, 'young infants alternate swiftly between states of complete gratification and of great distress.'[34] With psychical development each new experience is no longer so global and so severed from other experiences. In Klein's words it has become 'porous' to preceding and adjacent impressions, enabling love and hatred to 'come much closer together'.[35]

With development, the impact of aggressive moments gradually begins to linger for longer periods after the aggression itself has subsided. The significance of such moments necessarily seeps into the now more porous, new moments of object love affecting their nature. By implication ambivalence is initially not so much a reasoning act of realizing as an emotional experience. The crux of tragedy is thus derived from the processes of primitive ambivalence. It is at moments of moving from aggression to love that the infant is likely to grapple with the psychical effects of recent sadism; in as much as the latter has still been of an overwhelming quality, its consequences continue to correspond to experiences of irrevocable damage and loss.

FEAR AND OVERCOMING

Klein believed that such states of volatile fluctuations between uncontrollable aggression and the resulting 'nightmare of desolation' are gradually outgrown, but that this depends on the infant's secure instating of the good object within his inner world. 'Overcoming' thus has two facets in Klein's vision. It represents the mastering of hate by love, a process that corresponds to the secure establishing of the good object within the ego as a strong core which underpins security. The subjective internal scenario which corresponds to this is the overcoming of tragic states, so that when primitive ambivalence subsides, so do the acute fears of catastrophe which it instigates: '. . . [the infant's] confidence in his own as well as in other people's goodness becomes strengthened, his hope that his "good" objects and his own ego can be saved and preserved increases, at the same time as his ambivalence and acute fears of internal destruction diminish.'[36] And, from the angle of subjective experience, overcoming also applies to more than the initial emergence from tragic anxieties. As a first step in growth, there is a shift from a helpless experiencing of the object's absolute damage or loss, to a capacity to anticipate such a possibility. A new experience enters the infant's world – fear for the object's safety. Fear indicates the growing ability to retain the significance of destructive aggression and so anticipate it, rather than succumbing to its effects helplessly at the moment when it arises and swamps the mind. This corresponds to a greater awareness of internal threats to the object, and an acknowledgement that in the face of these the psyche might lack the means to protect the object: 'Here we see one of the situations which I described above, as being fundamental for "the loss of the loved object"; the situation, namely when the ego becomes fully identified with its good internalized objects and at the same time becomes aware of its own incapacity to protect and preserve them.'[37]

Fear thus corresponds to a progressive developmental step, the beginnings of moral concern, but it is also initially a primitive, overwhelming phenomenon. When aggression is still unmodified, its fearful anticipation necessarily takes on an acute, psychotic quality. The good, needed object is continually felt to be at the mercy of imminent dangers, and such anxiety, though on the object's behalf, is therefore persecutory in quality: 'The dread of persecution, which was at first felt on the ego's account, now relates to the good object as well.'[38]

Klein vividly describes an early depressive state of mind in which there is no respite from incessant dread on the good object's behalf. Disappointment and anger with the ambivalently experienced object means that there are continual sadistic attacks on it, with the result that the entire mind is felt to be poisonous. Neither phantasies of expelling nor of incorporating the object provide a solution, as the object is threatened within and without, and there does not appear to be an enduring way of situating it safely: '. . . there is, furthermore, a deep anxiety as to the dangers that await the object inside the ego. It cannot be safely maintained there, as the inside is felt to be a dangerous and poisonous place.'[39]

In Klein's vision of development, such primitive fears of imminent catastrophe are also overcome. As with tragic states, the infant must emerge from states of mind governed by near-tragic fears if development is to be satisfactory and psychotic anxieties modified. In this picture, the most important developmental struggle hinges on the ability to gain a psychic possession of the principle of goodness. Positive experiences are not simply visited on a receptive individual who is automatically able to extract maximal value, pleasure and satisfaction from them. In fact, there is no lasting ability to do so without introjecting a prototype of goodness, and then identifying with it in a way that informs the entire functioning of the ego. It is appropriate that the infant should fear the possible failure of this process, since frequent ambivalent rages can destroy its basis.

TRAGIC ELEMENTS IN A MORAL FRAMEWORK

The notion of overcoming infantile tragic states and anxieties is none the less conceptually complicated, as, in the Kleinian papers, the tragic level of the depressive position is not always easily differentiated from its more evolved moral mode. As suggested, 'overcoming' means that an internal scenario of tragedy ceases to dominate experience, but not that its significance recedes altogether. While tragic anxieties become gradually overlaid in the process of growth, their presence in the primitive strata of the psyche continues to give them the power of an emblematic tale of warning. This tale is essential to a moral framework that protects the good internal object, even though in its essence it represents a negation of the security and progress achieved through morality.

This would indicate that there are implications for the Bion-inspired view of lifelong fluctuations between the depressive and paranoid-schizoid positions. It suggests that a dialectical tension needs to be maintained in the mature psyche, which neither annihilates nor completely succumbs to the significance of primitive tragic anxieties. Such a tension is itself an inseparable aspect of the moral level of the depressive position. There is a difference between this tension and the kind of tragic scenario that figures in the Kleinian texts, or between moral and tragic depressive states. A focus on the 'morality' mode of the depressive position involves the depiction of tragic emotions that are not of a catastrophic primary nature, but of a secondary and tolerable variety that is tempered and contained by the simultaneous presence of object love, and that can be safely mobilized by the analyst. Rosenfeld, for example, discussed how '. . . the analyst has to try to mobilize the patient's capacity to experience love, depression and guilt ... depression will then emerge in the transference situation and the whole problem of acting out will diminish ...'[40]

In Rosenfeld's description, the patient can experience depression safely because it is both tolerable, and also takes its place alongside love for the object. However, this kind of description does not represent the full and hence regressive significance of the most primitive and catastrophic depressive states which Klein depicted. As suggested, she also discussed a fearful apprehension of irrevocable damage or loss, that is, a threat of potential tragedy. The more this threat is described as counter-balanced by love and reparative capacities within a mental framework, the more secure is the state that is depicted, and the more this security upholds morality. On the other hand, the more it is tragedy that is envisaged, the less would other elements be seen to coexist with, and hence modify, its irrevocable quality, turning internal experience into the 'nightmare of desolation' that is depressive illness.

If the regressive, tragic significance of the depressive position has been of less interest in later Kleinian thinking, part of the reason may well be linked with the fact that Klein herself made no explicit differentiation between two levels that none the less emerge in her textual descriptions. While at times she equated the depressive position more with morality, describing a fear of losing the loved object and the simultaneous urge to repair it, at other times she conveyed the sense of full tragedy, as is exemplified in the following depictions of depressive states: 'It seems to me that only when the ego has introjected the object as a whole ... is it able fully to realize the disaster created through its sadism ... The ego then finds itself confronted with the psychic reality that its loved objects are in a state of dissolution.'[41] And also: 'the anxiety and guilt which the patient experiences relate to his hatred which in his mind injured and destroyed the people he loved and caused his world to decompose.'[42] And further: 'both in adults and in children suffering from depression, I have discovered the dread of harbouring dying or dead objects.'[43]

OVERCOMING THE DEPRESSIVE POSITION – EXTERNAL REALITY AND REPARATION

However, it is not only in direct references of this kind that the respective significance of tragedy and morality are indicated. The full subtleties of Klein's vision of two levels of the depressive position emerge in her detailed accounts of the process of overcoming. In this account, external reality and its recognition assume a prime importance, something that would surprise those who hold that Kleinian theory places no value on external events. Klein conceived of overcoming not as a single event, but as a process that extends over the entire period of early childhood: 'It takes the child years to *overcome* his persecutory and depressive anxieties. They are again and again activated and *overcome* in the course of the infantile neurosis.'[44] (Emphasis added.)

The dual use of the term 'overcome' in this passage indicates that repeated, small-scale experiences of overcoming gradually build up to a comprehensive, large-scale overcoming. As shown, Klein felt that the latter is achieved when 'love for the real and the internalized objects and trust in them are well established',[45] that is, when primitive ambivalence recedes, so that 'when the infant is able to feel that his mother will return, because his experience of regaining the loved object has proved this to him ... he is ... beginning to overcome his depressive position.'[46]

As this indicates, the term 'overcoming' does not imply an annihilation of early psychical states, but addresses a facet of experience that involves the outgrowing of primitive modes of psychical functioning. But the latter manifest as not only paranoid-schizoid, but also tragic-depressive perceptions of the world. As far as Klein was concerned, the normal child develops a capacity to counter both persecutory and tragic perceptions of the object. The more small-scale, periodic type of overcoming, enabled through the actual mother's comforting, involves the infant's growing capacity to continually reinterpret primitive subjectivity in the light of reassuring external proof to the contrary: 'In normal circumstances the infant's growing capacity to perceive the external world and to understand it increases his confidence in it, and his experience of external reality becomes his most important means of overcoming his phantastic fears and his depressive feelings.'[47]

Ultimately this capacity 'to perceive the external world and understand it', much as in Ferenczi's thinking on the development of a reality sense, is essential for normality: 'The extent to which external reality is able to disprove anxieties and sorrow relating to the internal reality ... could be taken as one of the criteria for normality.'[48] Furthermore, Klein was convinced that the external mother has a central role in this process: 'There is, as we know, no better means of allaying a child's fears than the presence and love of his mother ... the accumulation of such beneficial experiences is one of the main factors in his overcoming his infantile neurosis.'[49] In addition, Klein envisaged such processes as operating continually in the minutiae of ordinary daily interactions between the infant and its mother: 'Already in the fifth or sixth month many infants respond with pleasure to "peep-bo" ... The mother of infant B made a bed-time habit of this game, thus leaving the child to go to sleep in a happy mood. It seems that the repetition of such experiences is an important factor in helping the infant to overcome his feelings of grief and loss.'[50]

Klein understood such external reassurance to accompany internal processes of restitution to the loved object. The latter were central to the instating of the loved object inside the ego. However, even those internal processes were felt by her to depend on a continual reality-testing process specifically linked to external reality: 'The diminishing of fears through happy experiences ... enables [the infant] to test his inner reality by means of outer reality.'[51]

Such thinking bears the mark of Freud's belief that the loss of mourning can only be overcome through continual reality testing. But whereas Freud suggested that this process had the function of finally bringing home the permanent absence of the mourned person, Klein conceived of it in reverse. In other words, with the infant finding reassurance in a safe world that contradicts the terrors of phantasy.

This marked importance that Klein attributed to environmental influence has not been broadly appreciated, but she regarded such influence as the very factor which helps the infant to overcome early anxieties. Repeated reassuring contacts with an actual, loving and undamaged mother gradually correct internal distortions in the infant's psyche. Her internal object is modified through further alignments with the actual mother, her reality sense increases and her primitive anxieties diminish. The importance of reality in Klein's thinking is also a function of the value for the psyche of a model that contradicts primitive subjectivity. Thus for the purpose of overcoming the depressive position, what matters about external reality is not merely its actuality, but the fact that through it the infant discovers a version of events that is governed by alternative principles. The principles are those of duration, and signify a world that is beyond the dictates of primitive omnipotence. Since the principles of duration are introjected, an inner life that begins as a series of ephemeral creations of momentary omnipotent whims, gradually gives way to a world that outlives the omnipotent moment. It is only when this independent continuity of the external world is accepted, that the infant can establish within her psyche a good object that can outlive her temporary rages.

In this view reality itself offers healing by asserting the duration, in time and space, of good objects and life's goodness. This also implies that such goodness can be subject to temporal processes that dissipate or disperse it, and the infant, having experienced the tragic results of her sadism or greed, is also now motivated to preserve her resources and sources of sustenance, both material and psychical. Klein's concept of reparation grows from this, showing the infant as making restoring, compensating gestures towards the attacked object when there is hope that this object can be recovered. In Klein's vision, a temporal awareness enables the human individual to address the destructive consequences of his own sadism through a lifelong activity of restoration, and this complements the essential need for human beings to be aware of the importance of preserving the resources, both psychical and worldly, on which life depends.

OVERCOMING THE DEPRESSIVE POSITION AND THE OEDIPUS COMPLEX

Klein's belief in the need to overcome the depressive position received further emphasis five years later, in a 1945 paper devoted to linking her theory of the depressive position with the fundamental Freudian premise of the Oedipus complex. In her publication 'The Oedipus complex in the light of early anxieties', she showed subtle, but crucial, links between an ability to overcome depressive anxiety and a healthy libidinal development which leads to a normal Oedipus complex. It is most illuminating to examine this paper, both for its ample confirmation of the importance for Klein of overcoming the depressive position, but equally because the paper shows how Klein intended to fit her concept into the main body of Freudian psychoanalysis.

Klein decided to choose clinical examples to illustrate this new link, and for this purpose drew on two cases that she had already described in earlier years: the ten-year-old Richard from her *Narrative of a Child Analysis*, and her troubled patient Rita, nearly three years old at the time of analysis, and originally described in *The Psychoanalysis of Children*. Both these case examples now provided evidence of children who failed to overcome depressive states and, as a result, were ill-equipped to face the challenges of a healthy Oedipal rivalry.

In revisiting these two cases, Klein now realized the extent to which the symptoms that she had noted years earlier had their origin in unprocessed depressive states. Richard, who was school phobic, hypochondriacal and emotionally fragile, was now understood with a renewed depth in the light of being also 'frequently subject to depressed moods.'[52] For various external and internal reasons, Richard had not been able to establish securely a good, loved object in his inner world, hence not sufficiently overcoming the depressive position. Richard thus fluctuated between periods of positive feelings for his maternal object and periods of great anxiety, when ordinary life stresses due to 'illness or other causes' meant that 'his feeling of confidence was shaken' and as a result 'depression and hypochondriacal anxieties increased'. At such times, Richard feared that he could not protect his loved internal object from his grievance, his phantasy attacks and therefore 'the danger of destruction and death'. Such death 'inevitably meant the end of his own life', and this, asserts Klein, is the 'fundamental anxiety of the depressive individual' which 'derives from the infantile depressive position'.

The same attention to unprocessed depressive states is given to the retrospective evaluation of Rita's symptoms. Rita had been originally brought to Klein because she was plagued by obsessional compulsions, deep anxieties and an inability to tolerate ordinary frustrations. Her symptoms were now significantly redescribed also in the light of her 'frequent states of unhappiness', the fact that she often cried, complained that she was sad and needed constant reassurance that she was loved. Indeed, Klein suggests that 'Rita's depressive feelings were a marked feature in her neurosis. Her states of sadness and crying without cause, her constant questions whether her mother loved her – all these were indications of her depressive anxieties.'[53] Put even more directly, Klein suggests that Rita was unable to deal with her acute anxieties and 'could not overcome her depressive position.'[54]

In both children, Klein suggested, these depressive difficulties mired the personality in anxieties and aggression, as well as a sense that a good object was only precariously available to restore safety. This prevented an ability to cope with the conflicts of rivalry that the Oedipus complex normally ushers in. However, before proceeding to examine what Klein meant, it is necessary to note one ambiguity. The reader, already aware that Klein had brought Freud's Oedipus complex forwards and had situated it in an archaic infantile scenario, may wonder why Klein is now discussing it as an event that emerges after the struggles of the depressive position, and furthermore, why she suggests that the depressive position prepares the ground for it. And while, indeed, this anomaly does create some confusion, it is one that is soon cleared by Klein.

What becomes apparent in the course of Klein's 1945 paper on the Oedipus complex, is that she has not given up any of her ideas on the early onset of an archaic Oedipus situation. She still believes that 'the Oedipus complex starts during the first year of life'. While conceding that 'the picture of its earliest stages is necessarily more obscure, as the infant's ego is immature and under the full sway of unconscious phantasy', she none the less sees no contradiction between her own views, and Freud's belief that the infant's instinctual life is 'at its most polymorphous phase', and that 'early stages are characterized by swift fluctuations between different objects and aims, with corresponding fluctuations in the nature of the defences'.[55] This Freudian scenario is fully compatible with her suggestion of an early Oedipal situation that consists of an archaic relationship with the maternal body and its contents. What is more, the archaic Oedipus situation is not at odds with what Klein is exploring now. Her 1945 paper is addressing not the earliest Oedipal configurations, but a different level of Oedipal development, that is, the fully Freudian Oedipal situation of the older child, which takes place around the fourth or fifth year of life.

The thinking in the 1945 paper amply confirms that Klein has not abandoned essential features of Freud's theory of libidinal development. While she has indeed concluded that Oedipal feelings begin early and initially assume an archaic form, as well as coinciding with pre-genital phases, her overall model still requires Freud's assumption of a psychosexual development that leads the child from pre-genital existence to a genital phase. It is clear from this that Klein's theory of the infant's relationship to the breast, of the early processes of projection and introjection, of archaic phantasy life and of the depressive position are not meant to have replaced Freud's idea of libidinal development, nor do away with the Freudian theory of sexuality, as some have mistakenly assumed. Rather, they are meant to be features of object relations that operate alongside libidinal life and sexuality. Klein thus continues to hold that the infant needs to progress from pre-genital, oral and anal phases to a genital phase, and that during this stage of genital primacy the child's hitherto archaic Oedipal situation assumes its fullest and most evolved expression. It thus becomes the familiar Freudian Oedipus complex which involves an incest wish and two recognized whole parents.

Furthermore, Klein continues to consider this classical Freudian Oedipus complex as a crucial destination of early development. The child's ability to enter a rivalrous relationship with one of the parents is a healthy moment, and one that is to ultimately enable self-assertion and, more crucially, the formation of gender identity. However, Klein now realizes that, both for the boy and for the girl, the ability to experience an Oedipus complex in the first place crucially depends on the child's resolution of earlier anxieties, particularly the ability to have emerged from catastrophic and tragic depressive states. Klein explains that with Richard, pre-genital 'oral, urethral and anal sadistic anxieties were excessive', and 'fixation to these levels was very strong'. As a result, 'his genital organization was weak' so that the transition from pre-genital to genital modes of functioning was incomplete and unsatisfactory. Fixation to early pre-genital sadism contributed towards Richard's excessive projection of aggression into his maternal object, and the resulting reintrojection of a bad object. Continual attacks on this frustrating object required a flight to an idealized phantasy breast, and this prevented an ability to integrate good and bad in a way that accepted a whole internal object and the actual mother's normal limitations. Thus, left with only a precarious good inner object, Richard found it impossible to engage with the challenges of Oedipal rivalry. It was for this reason that he remained timid, fearful, over-dependent on his mother in an infantile way and unable to face other children at school. Klein suggests that in earliest infancy, and when first faced with archaic Oedipal moments, Richard transferred his sense of a bad breast and object also on to his first atavistic sense of the paternal penis, which was therefore greatly feared. This archaic layer of feelings which had not been resolved in Richard now infused his recognition of a whole father. In his unconscious, his father, equated with a terrifying penis, threatened to become too dangerous and formidable an enemy and was disproportionately feared.

Klein noticed that each time Richard made progress in his therapy, he became reassured that he could engage in a reparation of his internal object, and this demonstrated to him that he could 'cope more successfully with his aggression'. With such reassurance, he regained 'an ability to experience his genital desires more strongly'. Therefore, Klein noted that 'his anxiety was lessened' and 'he could turn his aggression outwards and take up in phantasy the fight with his brother and father for the possession of his mother'.[56] However, at times when Richard was overcome with primitive anxieties, he retreated from this confrontation. His terror of the bad breast led him to an infantile regression, so that instead of a growing ability to accept a mixed, good and bad reality, he found solace in the anti-developmental shelter of an infantile dependency on the idealized breast. The more Richard felt dominated by his bad internal objects, the more he retreated from development and from the world, to the point at which he literally avoided leaving the house or going to school.

Rita's pathology reflected the same dynamic from a female perspective. Her unusual oral-sadistic impulses reinforced her early frustrations, and this affected the relationship with her mother. Rita's internal good object was also precarious rather than securely established, and when Oedipal desires 'came to the fore' they were so over-determined by a previous layer of hatred and frustration that she simply 'was unable to cope with these manifold conflicts', or indeed 'maintain her genital desires'.[57] As with Richard, Rita's poor relationship with her maternal object led her to transfer feelings of grievance and hatred to the paternal penis, and so feel aggressive and castrating towards her father.

With both children Klein envisaged developmental difficulties in terms of an initial inability to establish within the ego core a good object. The child then transfers the hostility and frustration felt in relation to the breast on to the father's penis, which now becomes saturated with early oral-sadistic character-istics. As a result, the child does not feel that she inhabits a safe world. Her perceptions are distorted by archaic phantasies and she is not at ease to confront her rival parent. The dangerous, sadistic penis created through these difficulties exacerbates the child's insecurity. It is felt not only to endanger the child, but also to endanger the mother through a sadistic, devouring intercourse.

Klein's 1945 paper traces a line from this unresolved and more primitive notion of an intercourse, to an experience that typifies a more optimal Oedipal situation. In the latter, the child has enough love for the mother, and is able to integrate her aspects sufficiently to transfer positive feelings from her breast to the father's penis. This is now felt to be potent but also reparative, with the powers to protect and heal the mother. A positive early development makes way for a healthy Oedipus complex, which then becomes a competition to display good attributes to the mother and to demonstrate an ability for creativity and reparation that is superior to that of rivals. For the boy it implies a masculine struggle to offer the most potency, reparation and protection. Accordingly, poor male development results in a resentful, infantile man who wants to take from the woman rather than give to her, and who clings to the existence of a demanding, oral infant rather than becoming a generous, impregnating father. In a similar way, positive female development results in an ability to transfer positive feelings on to the penis and so desire children from it. Failed female development is manifest in the transferring of hatred and frustration from the breast to the penis, and the resultant rejection of the penis. In this the female retreats from the responsibility for creating new life and offering nurture, and, like the undeveloped male, wants to retain an infantile position in which she continues through life to demand resources from others, and to take rather than give.

The vision whereby the Oedipus complex depends on the ability to establish a good object within and so overcome the depressive position, highlighted for Klein crucial gender differences in the development of the boy and the girl. Unlike Freud's unilateral model that focuses on the penis and on a phallic phase, her model focuses on the mother's breast and body as heralding the relationship with the penis. This implies a move in both male and female development from pre-genital stages to a genital stage where the position taken by the child relates to the procreative characteristics of both parents. Klein thus used her concept of the depressive position to shed new light on Freud's theory of libidinal development. She suggested that since love and hate interact in the child from the beginning of life, libidinal development depends on the child's ability to resolve their conflicted existence in a way that would allow two good objects, the breast and the penis, as well as two good parents, to take predominance in the inner world. With this, normal Oedipal rivalry becomes possible, and is expressed by a desire to rival the capabilities and strengths of adults. On the other hand, failed development results from a lack of resolution. It expresses itself in a desire to retain an infantile, omnipotent dominance over a providing mother. In this immature state, the individual continues to demand substantial emotional resources from the parents and from parental figures, while at the same time withholding personal and emotional resources from others in society. Both love and work become a problem, thus addressing Freud's two criteria for mental dysfunction.

There is a further significance to these insights, since the ability to experience a good breast and penis, and, respectively, two good parents, also establishes an all-important primal scene in the child's unconscious. The parents, united in a good intercourse, signify a basic emotional security in the child, albeit that it also sets in motion Oedipal rivalry. In fact, the ability to display Oedipal rivalry depends on such security, and on the sense of a parental couple that is sufficiently united to merit jealousy, but also to withstand aggressive expressions. The child's ability to engage in reparation after Oedipal attacks becomes another important factor for preserving and maintaining an internal sense of a good primal scene. Reparation thus continues to be of crucial importance for the growing child. By comparison, the inner world of the insecure child is dominated by a sadistic parental intercourse which exacerbates insecurity and makes rivalry impossible.

There is an inevitable logic in this picture, since a malevolent parental intercourse is not likely to elicit jealousy and rivalry, and is indeed likely to exacerbate chronic, catastrophic fears for the integrity of the family and so for personal safety. Klein's idea thus sheds light on the chief desire of children of divorced parents; it has been widely and consistently noted that, far from an incestuous rejoicing in the absence of one parent, such children typically desire that the parents should be, above all, reunited.

There is no doubt that in formulating the depressive position, its overcoming remains essential to Klein's vision. Only such overcoming would imply an integration of good and bad aspects of the object whereby the good absorbs and modifies the bad, thus being established securely within the core of the ego. Klein never suggested that adult life consists in fluctuations between paranoid-schizoid and depressive states, as some still believe, nor that the depressive position is a purely progressive developmental phenomenon which should be achieved or aimed for in psychoanalysis. An inability to overcome tragic depressive anxieties would leave the child in the throes of primitive ambivalence, and thus with a constant reexperiencing of a catastrophic loss of the good object, and the resultant excessive anxiety. In 1945, Klein added that this failure affects the ability to progress to the genital phase, enter a normal rivalry for the loved object and so identify with the adult energies of growth, reparation and a gendered responsibility for the creation and protection of new life.

This suggests that it is necessary to differentiate Klein's original ideas from some of the Kleinian developments that post-date them. Such differentiation has already happened in relation to technique. It is widely accepted for example, that although Klein herself was not persuaded that the analytic counter-transference was the result of projected patient emotions, this is now none the less a key feature of Kleinian technique. While there is no case for privileging either Klein's original views or the views of the Kleinian thinkers who followed, the two do need to be distinguished. Without doing so, it would be impossible to make full sense of Klein's own vision. As shown, part of this confusion might be exacerbated by the fact that it is difficult to isolate a tragic mode of the depressive position implied in Klein's concept from a more advanced moral one, since an initial tragic scenario of irrevocable loss together with its emblematic significance, continue to be essential for the sustenance of a moral system as depicted in the texts. But while in one sense the emergence of tragic anxieties is the first step in moral development, and thus a prerequisite for healthy object relations, another such prerequisite is the overcoming of tragic states. In the Kleinian model mental illness results from an early, and later an overall, failure successfully to do so. Without taking account of such failure, it is not possible to understand Klein's assertion that the depressive position is the fixation point of manic-depressive illness and of melancholia. This leaves Kleinian theory without a full explanation of the latter, whereas Klein explicitly offered such an explanation: '... persecutory and depressive anxieties, if excessive, may lead to severe mental illness ... These two forms of anxiety also provide the fixation points for paranoiac, schizophrenic and manic-depressive illness in adult life.'[58]

NOTES

1. Spillius, E. B. (1988) *Melanie Klein Today, Volume 1: Mainly Theory*. London: Routledge. p. 4.
2. Joseph, B. (1989) *Psychic Equilibrium and Psychic Change*. London: Tavistock/Routledge. p. 117.
3. Winnicott, D. W. (1958) 'The depressive position in normal development', in *Through Paediatrics to Psycho-Analysis*. London: The Hogarth Press. (First published in 1954.) p. 264.
4. See Greenberg, J. R. and Mitchell, S. A. (1983) *Object Relations in Psychoanalytic Theory*. Cambridge, MA: Harvard University Press.
5. Segal, H. (1978) *Klein*. London: Karnac Books. (First published in 1979.) p. 132.
6. Meltzer, D. (1988) *The Apprehension of Beauty*. Strath Tay: Clunie Press. p. 1.
7. Steiner, J. (1992) 'The interplay between the paranoid-schizoid and depressive position', in R. Anderson (ed.) *Clinical Lectures on Klein and Bion*. London: Tavistock/Routledge. (First published in 1990.) p. 48.
8. Segal, H. (1978) *Klein*. London: Karnac Books. (First published in 1979.) p. 123.
9. Meltzer, D. (1978) *The Kleinian Development*. Part 2. Strath Tay: Clunie Press. p. 10.
10. Klein, M. (1975) 'Mourning and its relation to manic-depressive states', in *Love, Guilt and Reparation*. London: The Hogarth Press. (First published in 1940.) p. 368.
11. ibid., p. 347.
12. ibid., p. 345.
13. Klein, M. (1952) 'On observing the behaviour of young infants', in *Developments in Psycho-Analysis*. London: The Hogarth Press. p. 269.
14. Klein, M. (1975) 'The Oedipus complex in the light of early anxieties', in *Love, Guilt and Reparation*. London: The Hogarth Press. (First published in 1945.) p. 400.
15. ibid., p. 398.
16. Klein, M. (1975) 'On the sense of loneliness', in *Envy and Gratitude*. London: The Hogarth Press. (First published in 1963.) p. 308.
17. Klein, M. (1975) 'Mourning and its relation to manic-depressive states', in *Love, Guilt and Reparation*. London: The Hogarth Press. (First published in 1940.) p. 347.
18. ibid., p. 345.

19. Ogden, T. (1992) 'The dialectically constituted-decentred subject of psychoanalysis. II: The contribution of Klein and Winnicott', in *International Journal of Psychoanalysis* 73, 4, pp. 517–27.
20. Klein, M. (1975) 'Love, guilt and reparation', in *Love, Guilt and Reparation*. London: The Hogarth Press. (First published in 1937.) p. 311.
21. Klein, M. (1975) 'Envy and gratitude', in *Envy and Gratitude*. London: The Hogarth Press. (First published in 1957.) p. 180.
22. Segal, H. (1978) *Introduction to the Work of Melanie Klein*. London: The Hogarth Press. p. 70.
23. Riviere, J. (1991) 'A contribution to the analysis of the negative therapeutic reaction', in M. A. Hughes (ed.) *The Inner World and Joan Riviere, Collected Papers 1920–1958*. London: Karnac Books. (First published in 1936.) p. 145.
24. Klein, M. (1975) 'A note on depression in a schizophrenic', in *Envy and Gratitude*. London: The Hogarth Press. (First published in 1960.) p. 265.
25. Klein, M. (1991) 'Tenth discussion of scientific differences', in P. King and R. Steiner (eds) *The Freud-Klein Controversies 1941–1945*. London: Tavistock/Routledge. (First published in 1944.) p. 839.
26. ibid., p. 836.
27. ibid., p. 201.
28. Klein, M. (1952) 'On observing the behaviour of young infants', in *Developments in Psycho-Analysis*. London: The Hogarth Press. p. 92.
29. ibid., p. 73.
30. Klein, M. (1975) 'A contribution to the psychogenesis of manic-depressive states', in *Love, Guilt and Reparation*. London: The Hogarth Press. (First published in 1935.) p. 264.
31. ibid., p. 265.
32. Klein, M. (1975) 'Mourning and its relation to manic-depressive states', in *Love, Guilt and Reparation*. London: The Hogarth Press. (First published in 1940.) p. 350.
33. Klein, M. (1975) 'A contribution to the psychogenesis of manic-depressive states', in *Love, Guilt and Reparation*. London: The Hogarth Press. (First published in 1935.) p. 275.
34. Klein, M. (1952) 'On observing the behaviour of young infants', in *Developments in Psycho-Analysis*. London: The Hogarth Press. p. 71.
35. ibid., p. 66.
36. Klein, M. (1975) 'A contribution to the psychogenesis of manic-depressive states', in *Love, Guilt and Reparation*. London: The Hogarth Press. (First published in 1940.) p. 347.
37. ibid., p. 265.
38. ibid., p. 264.
39. ibid., p. 265.
40. Rosenfeld, H. (1965) 'An investigation into the need of neurotic and psychotic patients to act out during analysis', in *Psychotic States*. London: Maresfield Reprints. (First published in 1964.) p. 205.
41. Klein, M. (1975) 'A contribution to the psychogenesis of manic-depressive states', in *Love, Guilt and Reparation*. London: The Hogarth Press. (First published in 1935.) p. 269.

42. Klein, M. (1990) 'Tenth discussion of scientific differences', in P. King and R. Steiner (eds) *The Freud-Klein Controversies 1941–1945*. London: Tavistock/Routledge. (First published in 1944.) p. 837.

43. Klein, M. (1975) 'A contribution to the psychogenesis of manic-depressive states', in *Love, Guilt and Reparation*. London: The Hogarth Press. (First published in 1935.) p. 266.

44. Klein, M. (1952) 'On observing the behaviour of young infants', in *Developments in Psycho-Analysis*. London: The Hogarth Press. p. 260.

45. Klein, M. (1975) 'A contribution to the psychogenesis of manic-depressive states', in *Love, Guilt and Reparation*. London: The Hogarth Press. (First published in 1935.) p. 288.

46. Klein, M. (1991) 'The emotional life and ego-development of the infant', in P. King and R. Steiner (eds) *The Freud-Klein Controversies 1941–1945*. London: Tavistock/Routledge. (First published in 1944.) p. 779.

47. ibid., p. 780.

48. Klein, M. (1975) 'Mourning and its relation to manic-depressive states', in *Love, Guilt and Reparation*. London: The Hogarth Press. (First published in 1940.) p. 346.

49. Klein, M. (1991) 'The emotional life and ego-development of the infant' in P. King and R. Steiner (eds) *The Freud-Klein Controversies 1941–1945*. London: Tavistock/Routledge. (First published in 1944.) p. 772.

50. Klein, M. (1952) 'On observing the behaviour of young infants', in *Developments in Psycho-Analysis*. London: The Hogarth Press. p. 258.

51. Klein, M. (1975) 'Mourning and its relation to manic-depressive states', in *Love, Guilt and Reparation*. London: The Hogarth Press. (First published in 1940.) p. 347.

52. Klein, M. (1975) 'The Oedipus complex in the light of early anxieties', in *Love, Guilt and Reparation*. London: The Hogarth Press. (First published in 1945.) p. 371.

53. ibid., p. 403.

54. ibid., p. 404.

55. ibid., p. 407.

56. ibid., p. 382.

57. ibid., p. 400.

58. Klein, M. (1952) 'On observing the behaviour of young infants', in *Developments in Psycho-Analysis*. London: The Hogarth Press. p. 269.

CHAPTER 9

'This unreal reality' – Klein's Concept of Phantasy

We see then that the child's earliest reality is wholly phantastic ... As the ego develops, a true relation to reality is gradually established out of this unreal reality.[1]

The question of what Klein might have meant by an 'unreal reality' was addressed only as late as 1943, when her concept of unconscious phantasy was fully presented to the British Psychoanalytic Society for the first time. Yet this concept had been present, if unexplained, in her theory almost from the beginning of her career. It was enlisted into Klein's vocabulary through sheer necessity, when she was first confronted with the imaginative contents of her child patients' play. It continued to prove useful, and was, in turn, further illuminated when Klein formulated ideas on projection and introjection, personification, symbol formation and internal imagos. It was to become increasingly necessary to Klein's thinking with the formulation of her concept of the depressive position. By this time, Klein's rapidly proliferating insights began to form a dense web of connecting theoretical themes. At the heart of this, and essential to its logic, lay her notion of unconscious phantasy.

While it was presented after Klein completed her two papers on the depressive position, the concept had, as suggested, a forceful latent presence in the texts well before this time. And since it did not come into being in Klein's thinking at a single, easily demarcated moment, the best way to understand it is through examining the only paper ever written about it. Considering that ideas about unconscious phantasy were so central to Klein's developing theory, it is all the more surprising to discover that she was not the presenter of this single paper, entitled 'The nature and the function of phantasy'. The paper was written and presented instead by Klein's articulate, scientifically-minded adherent, Susan Isaacs. It is also noteworthy that the paper was written under some pressure. It formed the first presentation in the Controversial Discussions, and was the starting-point of this decisive moment in Klein's career. It is possibly the taxing nature of the situation that obliged Klein to hand over the writing to Isaacs;

Klein needed to condense her complex thinking into a concise format; she also needed to demonstrate that her theory was, by now, used by a new, Kleinian, school of thought. It made sense to distribute the workload among her adherents, and several of them took responsibility for presenting her ideas during the Controversial Discussions. And since Isaacs was a particularly strong and articulate supporter, it was natural for the British Society to look to her for some explanations. During the Extraordinary Meetings leading up to the presentations, Isaacs was requested by the Society's programme committee to begin the proceedings with a written presentation on projection and introjection. She chose, instead, to write about phantasy, realizing that without first doing so, it would be almost impossible to explain Kleinian theory.

The paper thus carried the full responsibility of an opening manoeuvre, and a great deal hinged on its reception. As suggested, the Controversial Discussions focused on several Kleinian presentations which were intended to enable a review of her theoretical innovations via open debate. It was also widely recognized that the unspoken agenda was more disturbing than this. The debate, which was to establish whether Kleinian ideas were psychoanalytically valid, would be bound to have implications for Klein's continuing membership of the British Psychoanalytical Society. As it happens, the phantasy paper was an excellent opening gambit. Already with this first presentation and debate, the Society discovered that the task of determining the psychoanalytic validity of Klein's ideas was unachievable. It was impossible either collectively to dismiss, or wholly accept Klein's thinking on unconscious phantasy, and the debates on it lingered without resolution for four months, before being abandoned for the second presentation and debate. This collective indecision was the function of converging political, professional and personal factors,[2] but Klein none the less managed to articulate one of the underlying sentiments that worked in her favour: 'Considering that psychoanalysis is still a young science and in its developmental stages, we should not be surprised that inferences from Freud's work must differ according to which particular aspect of his discoveries is taken up and pursued further.'[3]

The appeal for intellectual tolerance, and so for some creative licence, must have found support with most of the British group. It indicated that a concept of unconscious phantasy was worth exploring even if only to formulate further questions. At a deeper level, members of the Society must have also found the subject irresistible. The debates show the discussants repeatedly noting the sheer futility of trying to discover the actuality of infantile experience. And yet they appear not to be able to let go of the subject, and each, in contradicting Klein, sets out an alternative, equally enticing vision of early mental life. It appears that the mind's point of origin is a subject that is as irresistible as it is out of bounds.

Isaacs' paper, as noted, was entirely devoted to Klein's conception, and she was mostly acting the role of messenger. But her analytical acuity and lucid prose equipped her admirably for this difficult task. Her paper reflects the continuing theoretical refinements of Klein's vision of internal life, and in the light of these, elucidates the intricacies of unconscious phantasy. Isaacs highlights yet again the significance of Freud's ideas on dreams and on unconscious life. Klein had already claimed an equal status for childish play and dreams as both offering 'a royal road to the unconscious'. Isaacs now showed that the wishing, libidinal mind, governed by primary thought process was the inspiration for Klein's concept of phantasy. And because Klein's concept needed to be differentiated from the more conventional sense of conscious fantasy such as daydreaming, Isaacs suggested that it should be demarcated by the spelling of 'ph' instead of 'f'.

When Freud considered two different kinds of mental process, he conceived of the secondary one as bound by the reality principle, and so by conceptual and verbal logic which makes possible an accurate appraisal of the world. By comparison, the primary thought process which is the characteristic of dreams, is the more primitive and less rational human mental activity. It is based on what is desired, on omnipotence and on elaborations of wishing experiences at the expense of noticing reality as it is. Primary thought process was thus felt by Freud to be dream-like, and to negate all the rules of conscious logic. He felt that under the dominance of the pleasure principle, it plays havoc with facts. They are condensed into strange composite creations, or else fragmented and displaced, thus producing the typical irrationality of the dreaming mind. This is further exacerbated because incompatible ideas coexist without contradiction, negation of any kind does not figure, and nor does the defining structure of a temporal order. If there is a dominant direction in this otherwise chaotic mixture, it is the simulation of continual fulfilment and the obliteration of painful needs and desires.

This led Freud to observe a link between the dream's chaotic process and infantile mental life. '*Dreaming*', he suggested, '*is a piece of infantile mental life that has been superseded.*' (Original emphasis.)[4] He went on to posit a typical form of infantile hallucinatory thinking. He suggested that the newborn almost immediately forms associative links between pleasurable experience and the satisfying object. The latter is stored as a visual and sensory memory, and is instinctively sought by the sensory organs when the infant next experiences a state of painful need. And since the archaic mind is not bound by the strictures of reality, the infant can actually experience his anticipation so intensely and vividly as to conjure up the desired satisfaction in the form of an hallucination. Freud likened this to adult states of extreme hunger, in which an individual can be driven virtually to smelling or tasting food. In the infant, this ability to conjure up satisfaction is normal. It serves to fend off frustration for a short while, hopefully giving adults some time to respond to the infant. However, if environmental response is unduly delayed, the infant's capacity to hallucinate is, in Freud's words, 'exhausted', and reality breaks into his awareness. Hallucination enables the pleasure principle to dominate in the infant's mind during the vulnerable months of early infancy, but it also dictates his bizarre, primary-process logic.

Isaacs showed how Klein built on this idea by linking unconscious phantasy with the infant's hallucinatory wish-fulfilment. In line with Freud's thinking on the latter, she suggested that unconscious phantasy involves imaginal, sensory and somatic states. In the face of painful need, the infantile body together with the wishing, instinctual psyche, produces a particular phantasy. Although it belongs in the normal awake functioning of the infant, phantasy is therefore, in a sense, a species of dream life. But Isaacs went further in her description. She suggested that phantasy is 'the primary content of all mental processes' and so the raw material of the psyche which is 'latent in impulse affect and sensation'.[5]

What is more, the existence of phantasy is not gratuitous, because it has a crucial function. Phantasy is also '... the content of the archaic mental processes by means of which the primary libidinal wishes and aggressive impulses ... are experienced and ordered in the psyche.' In other words, libidinal wishes are registered by the psyche not as mere perturbations, but assume a mental form. No mental process or experience of any kind is possible without an accompanying activity that gives it content: '... every impulse, every feeling, every mode of defence is expressed and experienced in such a specific phantasy.'[6]

Before the infant is even able to recognize his own blind urges, his mind creates an internal scenario out of their activity. This scenario is also not created arbitrarily because it '... expresses the specific content of the urge ... which is dominating to the child's mind at the moment.' Isaacs' account intimates that phantasy creates the earliest system of meaning in the psyche. It is the element that gives blind human urges a direction, and so is an instinctual mode of thinking based on the response to worldly impingements. Out of this primordial mental activity, a more mature cognitive capacity later develops.

The implications of suggesting such a concept are profound. Klein offers a link between the blind, biological striving of the young human organism, and the narrative, ideational faculties that emerge out of it. Isaacs was aware of this when she moved from describing phantasy to an attempted definition of the concept. She offered a definition of phantasy as '... the mental corollary, the psychic representative of instinct', and added that, '... there is no impulse, no instinctual urge, which is not experienced as (unconscious) phantasy.'[7]

Freud had already referred to 'the mental expression of instinctual needs'. Furthermore, instincts were particularly important in his thinking. He regarded them as the fundamental motivational forces in mental life. He thought of their origin as neither purely physiological nor purely mental, but as being on the border between the two. The survival necessities of the human organism affect both body and mind, and the first energies activated to cope with the world must border alike on the psychic and the somatic, lying between the two. Klein's concept was now shown by Isaacs to give a fuller account of this Freudian vision. The specifically psychic element in the psychosomatic amalgam of the instinct was none other than phantasy.

Having set out this particular extension of Freud's instinct theory, Isaacs proceeded to elaborate a further aspect of the concept, and one that was more typically Kleinian in origin in the sense that it concerned object relations. In keeping with her description of unconscious phantasy as underlying human urges and giving them form, she went into some detail: 'When [the child] feels desires towards his mother, he experiences these as "I want to suck the nipple, to stroke her face, to eat her up, to keep her inside me". Negative expressions are experienced as "to bite the breast, to tear her to bits ... to throw her out of me.".'[8]

Such a description was not meant to imply a sophisticated conceptual content to the child's early phantasy life, and Isaacs also quoted another of Klein's adherents, Joan Riviere, on this topic:

When we speak of 'phantasies' in babies or small children, we do not imply an elaborate *mise-en-scène* or coherent dramatizations in them, nor of course to begin with psychic or verbal representations. We surmise that the child feels as if it were carrying out a desired action, and that this affective feeling is accompanied by a corresponding physical excitation in certain organs, e.g., mouth or musculature.[9]

Isaacs continued to emphasize that on the basis of such very rudimentary phantasy activity, a later and more complex internal visual imagery develops. However, what she was reaching after was the Kleinian belief that the particular scenario of which a phantasy is composed is always and specifically based on object relations, in which an object is either treated in a particular way, or else itself meting out a particular kind of treatment to the subject. Although Isaacs did not spell out the implications of this, it provides a quintessentially Kleinian originality. It portrays the basis of our mental operations as relational in nature, and suggests that we cannot make sense of our experiences, nor indeed our identity, without referring continually to an internal scenario in which meaning is actualized in an exchange between a subject and an object.

Klein's concept of unconscious phantasy had strong links with her ideas on the child's archaic Oedipal phantasies. By the time of the Controversial Discussions, her thinking had evolved substantially, with increasing refinements on the first relationship with the mother. She was now thinking in terms which even went beyond a global sense of the maternal body. She suggested that from the beginning of life the infant is able to discern quality in his exchanges with the mother, and he does so with both emotional and sensory equipment. She felt that quality can only be interpreted internally through some form of representation, however rudimentary. In her thinking, phantasy is a process which accurately gives shape to an internal reality. By now Klein was aware that phantasy is much more than the external object represented inwardly, and therefore affects levels of experience that are far more rudimentary than the recognition of a whole mother. Unconscious phantasy was better understood as 'ingested' parts of the world, or 'ingested' aspects of the mother, taken in by the psyche repeatedly through exchanges with the actual mother, and absorbed into the individual's growing identity.

Klein's early emphasis on a whole maternal body had already given way to a vision of part-objects, or aspects of mothering sensed by the infant and introjected as portions of experience. A better representative or prototype for this was the mother's feeding breast, and this tied the infant's first libidinal experience with the breast-feeding relationship. She now thought of the first infantile sadistic attacks as directed specifically at the mother's breast, and this led to her central formulation of the depressive position. It was also possible to understand the loss of weaning and the resultant sadness as states that are experienced in the six-month-old child's phantasies. Klein's thinking on the depressive position was not brought into Isaacs' phantasy paper very much. But some of the critiques of her colleagues did refer to the depressive position none the less, and furthermore, based objections to the concept of phantasy on the grounds that with her view of the depressive position, Klein had gone too far.

ANNA FREUD'S CRITIQUE

At first it was clear from the debate that followed Isaacs' presentation that, on the whole, the concept of unconscious phantasy had some significant appeal for an analytical audience. However, there were also some sharp critiques of it, most prominent of which was Anna Freud's. She attacked it on a number of scores, but one particular aspect of Isaacs' paper must have riled her more than the rest. It seemed that Klein, as represented by Isaacs, was smuggling improbably mature, secondary processes into the domain of infantile primary thinking. How could Klein claim that phantasy was the 'primary content' of all mental processes, Anna Freud wondered, when it actually failed to conform to her father's ideas on primary thought process? For a start, Klein's ideas on the depressive position undoubtedly included secondary thinking, such as a sense of time, conflict, contradiction and negation:

> There is, in Mrs Isaacs' description of the unconscious, no free and independent flow of instinctual urges. The integration of an 'early pleasure ego' occurs so soon that it is practically in existence from the beginning of life. Impulses enter into *conflict* with each other: the baby cannot feel rage against its mother without feeling its love for her threatened ... Its *ambivalent* feelings cannot exist side by side but have to be projected outwards in part ... Negation exists, as shown for instance on page [302]. There even seems to be a sense of time, as indicated on page [280] in 'the phantasy of the mother's permanent absence' as opposed to our idea that no difference exists for the child between temporary and permanent.[10]

What would have seemed worst to Anna Freud was Klein's postulation of an improbably early emergence of the ego. This was required by Klein's framework because she postulated the use of early defence mechanisms to fend off depressive states. Defences necessitated an organizing centre in the personality which would be capable of experiencing threat and mobilizing defensive activity:

> It is not easy to see how an early pleasure ego can assume the functions of a central personality within the unconscious, but only the existence of such an active centre could account for the presence of so-called early defence. Unconscious life, according to this paper, thus combines qualities of the primary with important characteristics of the secondary process.[11]

The charge against Klein's conception of phantasy was that it presented not primary thought process, but an unlikely confusion between primary and secondary thought process. When Isaacs was given an opportunity to reply, she rebutted this latter point energetically. She began by conceding that Anna Freud was right. However, Isaacs also proceeded to correct an important misapprehension. She explained that Klein's unconscious phantasy had never been intended to equate phantasy with pure primary thought process. What is more, Freud himself doubted that primary process could exist in pure form and without a constant interaction with organizing, secondary mental processes. Isaacs was able to quote from Freud:

> So far as we know a psychic apparatus possessing only the primary process does not exist, and is to that extent a theoretical fiction; but this at least is a fact, that the primary processes are present in the apparatus from the beginning, while the secondary processes only take shape gradually during the course of life, inhibiting and overlaying the primary, while gaining complete control over them perhaps only in the prime of life.[12]

In the light of this, Isaacs suggested that secondary processes begin early, and that their 'rudimentary beginnings' necessarily figure in infantile phantasy. As far as the postulation of an early ego that uses defence mechanism, she stated somewhat evasively that '. . . the child is born with the capacity for reflex defences against painful or disagreeable stimulae. He shows such reflex defences from the beginning, and could not survive without them.'[13] This argument affirmed Klein's conviction that a rudimentary ego exists from birth, and that it does indeed organize an archaic, reflexive fending-off of pain. Klein's concept of phantasy means that even this reflexive activity must be represented internally in the psyche, hence assuming the form of phantasies in which aggression is felt to have annihilated sources of pain. And even before phantasizing such destruction, the infant would have personified his experience of pain and presented it internally as a persecuting being.

Klein's concept comes out of these discussions as indicating an open system, in which the primary process is not hermetically sealed behind a barrier of unconscious life. A flow of information from the world to the psyche is constant, and continues to affect internal instinctual energies. The postulation of an early ego also suggested an added function for phantasy: it was to aid the ego to organize defensive activity by imagining and hallucinating such activity. As Isaacs put it, phantasies can act as the operative link between instinct and defence mechanism. If the child receives a fright, his phantasy will create ideation that is in the nature of 'suggestions' for defensive manoeuvring, such as an aggressive elimination of the source of fear.

The concept of unconscious phantasy rounded off many of Klein's most difficult early ideas. It made more sense of her conception of internal objects, her ideas of projection and introjection, and also her thinking on the internal experience of the loss of the loved object. While the concept of phantasy was neither fully accepted nor fully rejected by Klein's colleagues, it was soon to be further emphasized by Klein. When she proceeded to reconsider the beginning of life and the mental state that precedes the depressive position, she named it the paranoid-schizoid position. Essential to her conception of this position was the idea that phantasy can begin in earliest infancy, can operate in the most primitive psychosomatic, reflexive ways, can give mental expression to instincts, but above all, that it can also be an operative link between instinctual urges and the earliest defences of the psyche, now re-evaluated by her as specifically schizoid in nature.

NOTES

1. Klein, M. (1975) 'Notes on symbol formation', in *Love, Guilt and Reparation*. London: The Hogarth Press. (First published in 1930.) p. 221.
2. Steiner, R. (1990) 'Background to the scientific controversies', in P. King and R. Steiner (eds) *The Freud-Klein Controversies 1941–1945*. London: Tavistock/Routledge.
3. Klein, M. (1991) 'The second Extraordinary Business Meeting', in P. King and R. Steiner (eds) *The Freud-Klein Controversies 1941–1945*. London: Tavistock/Routledge. (First published in 1942.) p. 91.
4. Freud, S. (1901) 'On dreams', *Standard Edition* 5. London: The Hogarth Press. p. 567.
5. Isaacs, S. (1991) 'The nature and the function of phantasy', in P. King and R. Steiner (eds) *The Freud-Klein Controversies 1941–1945*. London: Tavistock/Routledge. (First published in 1943.) p. 272.
6. ibid., p. 278.
7. ibid., p. 277.
8. ibid., p. 277.
9. Riviere, J. (1936), quoted in ibid., p. 283.
10. Freud, A. (1991) 'First discussion of the scientific controversies', in P. King and R. Steiner (eds) *The Freud-Klein Controversies 1941–1945*. London: Tavistock/Routledge. (First published in 1943.) p. 330.
11. ibid., p. 330.
12. Freud, S. (1991) Quoted in 'The nature and the function of phantasy', in P. King and R. Steiner (eds) *The Freud-Klein Controversies 1941–1945*. London: Tavistock/Routledge. (First published in 1900.) p. 374.
13. Isaacs, S. 'The nature and the function of phantasy'. ibid., p. 375.

CHAPTER 10

'A kind of detached hostility' – The Paranoid-Schizoid Position

When the Controversial Discussions were over in 1946 with a positive outcome for Klein, she may have certainly experienced relief. However, far from wishing to use this moment for a pause, her newly established professional security had a particularly stimulating effect. Klein now felt freed to take her ideas to their furthest conclusion and to delve into the deepest obscurities of the mind, formulating her most challenging ideas yet. Within eleven years from this time, and three years before her death in 1960, her vision would stand complete in all its essentials. In 1946, however, there was the formidable task of developing to the full her thinking on what preceded the depressive position in infantile mental life. In a seminal 1946 paper, 'Notes on some schizoid mechanisms', which will be examined in the next two chapters, Klein suggested that before the onset of the depressive position and in the earliest months of infancy, a paranoid-schizoid position dominates the first evolutionary phase of mental life.

Klein's paper on schizoid mechanisms is both one of her most complicated works and, simultaneously, one that has proved to be hugely applicable to clinical work, with substantial contributions to the development of technique in twentieth-century psychoanalysis. In the paper, Klein sets out in much fuller detail her thinking on the first moments of infancy. She portrays mental life as emerging gradually out of a primordial chaos in which life-enhancing and destructive tendencies initially mingle, and suggests that these cohere to form a paranoid-schizoid position. Klein had already suggested that the infant engages in a rudimentary relationship with the feeding breast. She had concluded that the first relationship is therefore to a part-object, even though this is experienced in phantasy as a whole experience or what Klein termed a 'total situation'. However, essential to her vision had also been her belief that any stability that the infant achieves is always temporary, and threatened from external and internal sources which include environmental frustrations and disturbances, as well as intense instinctual activity that begins at birth.

Klein had also already considered infantile defences. She believed that the infant has a rudimentary awareness of disturbances and sufficient ego activity to react to them with anxiety. And since her psyche is not sufficiently mature to process large quantities of anxiety, she resorts repeatedly to primitive defence mechanisms. Such mechanisms, as well as being 'reflexive', are only serviceable for a limited period of life, since, in keeping with their archaic nature, they are easily triggered and charged with indiscriminate aggression, hence being paranoid in essence. Because they are untempered, they aim to annihilate not only pain and anxiety but the very awareness that leads to them. They thus aim to sever portions of painful experience from the self, and with it remove the malevolently experienced aspect of the object from its loved manifestation. They are therefore not only paranoid, but schizoid.

With her thoughts on the paranoid-schizoid position, Klein now aimed to show the earliest strata of experience, and to link these with her existing concept of the later depressive position. She had already charted a course of development that takes the infant from states of fragmentation, of taking in only 'parts and portions' of the object and the world, to states of integration that enable the mental accommodation of a whole rather than parts. She had suggested that the extreme phantastically good and phantastically bad internal imagos of earliest infancy gradually draw closer and achieve a synthesis, this coinciding with a reduction in infantile ambivalence and the secure establishment of the loved object in the psyche. Already with the depressive position, Klein showed how this developmental path is fraught with dangers, inasmuch as ambivalence can lead to tragic states of loss of the loved object, which , if not overcome, can become the fixation point for later manic-depressive psychosis. As seen, this presented difficulties with her colleagues, and there seemed to be little room in her theory to add yet more complexity to early mental life. But this was just what Klein proceeded to do with her new concept of the paranoid-schizoid position.

While the complexity in her thinking on the depressive position emerges from the many simultaneous processes set in motion by the struggles of weaning and of psychical separation from the maternal object, the paranoid-schizoid position owes its complexity to a different factor. Klein tries to account for several kinds of fragmentation processes which operate simultaneously in earliest infancy and which have different origins. But her terminology suggests that she is investigating only one such process with a single origin that is defensive – that is, a schizoid defence. To add to these difficulties, even this apparently single focus is multiple, because Klein is investigating not one, but several kinds of schizoid mechanisms. The reader is thus presented with a confusing array of similar phenomena, and this aptly mirrors Klein's portrayal of archaic mental life as a bewildering chaos, crowded with fragmentation processes which lack a coherent order. In order to differentiate the various fragmentation processes that Klein had in mind, it is necessary first to examine the basis of her new addition to her conceptual repertoire – the notion of a primitive schizoid mechanism.

For a start, a conspicuous feature of this thinking was the continuing adoption of psychiatric terminology for the purpose of psychoanalytic definitions. Already with the depressive position, Klein forged a link between early mental experience and later psychiatric illness. She showed how it is the primitive experience of the world that exposes the infant to intolerable anxiety and how this, in turn, sets in motion defences that, when excessively reinforced, have all the hallmarks of mental illness. Human pathology is thus accounted for through the very problems of living and of survival. Klein's thinking about depressive pathology and infancy was inspired by Abraham. She was able to draw on his thinking with confidence because of his direct experience with psychiatric patients within a hospital setting, something that was not available to her. When it came to her use of the concept of schizoid, she was yet again aware of the need to rely on the conclusions of someone with relevant psychiatric experience, and this she found in two of her contemporaries, Fairbairn and Winnicott. Klein's exploration of schizoid conditions in adult patients forms a subject in itself, and is a substantial subtopic in her 1946 paper. However, her discussion of what comprises a pathological schizoid state in the adult is essential for making sense of how she applied this understanding to her vision of infancy, and will therefore be discussed in this chapter.

THE INFLUENCE OF FAIRBAIRN

Between 1940 and 1945, the Scottish psychoanalyst Ronald Fairbairn concluded, on the basis of his psychiatric experience, that '*the basic position in the psyche is invariably a schizoid position.*'[1] (Original emphasis.) Klein, who had not previously thought in terms of schizoid phenomena, immediately realized the implications of this suggestion for her own theory:

> He called the earliest phase the schizoid position; he stated that it forms part of normal development and is the basis for adult schizoid and schizophrenic illness. I agree with this contention and consider his description of developmental schizoid phenomena as significant and revealing, and of great value to our understanding of schizoid behaviour and of schizophrenia.[2]

There was much in Klein's own pre-1946 work that anticipated Fairbairn's concept of a schizoid position. Her thinking on how the normal psyche develops suggested a piecemeal assimilation of experience, to which were added dissociation processes that segmented both the object and the self, aiming to split-off and isolate disturbing experience. Klein had thus already challenged the notion that the normal ego is a unified entity, and posited that dissociation processes were profuse in ordinary child development. Klein's fullest pre-1946 exploration of psychical dichotomies was evident in her two papers on the depressive position, in which she added the idea that the early ego fluctuates between positions that correspond in essence to depressive and manic conditions, but are each only partial aspects of the whole infantile self. In this thinking development was no longer seen as a simple linear progression, but as a complex effort to accommodate fragments of a self that is by turns distressed, manic, depressed, settled or contented.

When Klein became acquainted with Fairbairn's work, she logically perceived the factor that would add a definitive depth to her earlier conclusions. She now thought not merely in terms of various positions or fragmentation processes, but in terms of an underlying mechanism, the schizoid defence, which determined the primary position taken up by the subject at the most archaic level.

However, she had already accounted for the most rudimentary psychic scenario before 1946. She felt that prior to taking up a depressive position, the infant can take up a number of different earlier positions, including a paranoid one, believed by her at the time to be the most archaic and earliest of all positions. Since earliest infancy is characterized by the most extreme reactions to gaps or omissions in maternal care, these trigger an instinctive sense of danger created through the death instinct, hence amounting to a persecutory state, or paranoid position.

When faced with Fairbairn's inspiring ideas, Klein realized that the earliest phases were not fully captured by the notion of a paranoid position. She was, none the less, unwilling to dispense with it. She did not change her mind about the acute quality of infantile anxiety, nor about the sense of terror and rage that it engenders. However, she recognized that anxiety alone could not account for the fragmentation and incompleteness that seemed to be the hallmark of primitive mental life. Klein thus kept her concept of paranoid, adding Fairbairn's suggestion of schizoid to it.

However, it was not possible simply to append a portion of Fairbairn's theoretical framework without consequent shifts that affected the entire existing theoretical structure. Klein's struggle to integrate the concept of schizoid to her framework thus resulted in the formulation of a paranoid-schizoid position that is particularly complicated. For a start, at the time when Fairbairn was publishing his findings, Klein's colleague Donald Winnicott also became interested in schizoid phenomena. In 1940 he explored schizoid states as related to what he termed a 'primary unintegration'. Klein was also influenced by his thinking, since he too had psychiatric experience on which he drew in his psychoanalytic writings.

Klein's 1946 paper not only sets out to embrace their two rather contradictory suggestions, but to do so along with an integration of a host of other splitting processes that she had explored earlier in her career. But why was Klein drawn to psychiatric terminology yet again, and did this imply that she viewed the infant as psychotic? If this had been the case, it would imply that a kind of original-sin belief was reappearing in her theory, this time in the guise of a theory of original psychosis as the supposed state of nature. Indeed, it is all too easy to fall into the error of assuming that Klein equated psychosis with infancy, as happened with some of her psychoanalytic colleagues during the Controversial Discussions.

It is significant, however, that Klein went to some lengths to underscore the fact that she did not equate the two. During the Controversies, she supplied as evidence for this her explicit recorded diagnosis of eighteen child patients whose treatment formed the core of her earlier publication *The Psychoanalysis of Children*. It was clear that out of eighteen children, only two had been diagnosed by her as schizoid or incipient schizophrenic. The rest were diagnosed as suffering from a range of conditions such as 'severe neurosis' or 'obsessional symptoms.'[3] Klein took the opportunity of the Controversial Discussions to reiterate her belief that since some children are indeed mentally ill, a crass equation of infancy with psychosis would preclude the ability to identify them, as well as preventing the ability to distinguish normal from pathological development.

Her use of psychiatric concepts to describe normal developmental phenomena was thus not so much a question of equating the two, as forging links between early anxiety situations and the development of a personality prone to illness. This concern also needs to be understood in the context of the psychoanalytic community's growing interest in adult psychiatric illness.

THE INTEREST IN SCHIZOID PHENOMENA

As suggested, some psychoanalytic interest in schizoid phenomena became evident towards the 1940s. This interest represented a growing sense that mechanisms which underpin psychotic illness, such as schizoid mechanisms, held clues to processes that were central to mental life, and that a discovery of these would have a twofold significance – revealing the nature of development and revealing the meaning and cause of mental illness.

This ambitious aim was at odds with Freud's inclinations. Freud's efforts throughout his life had been centred on the classical neurosis and on what it indicated about normal development. Fine points out that in the course of its development, psychoanalysis made contact with a host of scientific and humanistic disciplines including psychiatry, psychology, sociology, biology, anthropology and others.[4] Freud gave importance to all of them. He was interested in the entire spectrum of disciplines that study human nature, attempting to synthesize them into a vision of mental life that was global and multidimensional. However, he was not persuaded that schizophrenia was amenable to psychoanalysis. Freud's tendency to centralize the classical neurosis meant that both his texts and his work were not geared towards chronic psychiatric conditions such as schizophrenia, and psychiatrists of all persuasions continued to suspect organic origins for the severity which they witnessed.

However, the growth of psychoanalysis coincided with an era of substantial progress in psychiatric thinking that began in the late nineteenth century, and was crucial to the understanding of schizoid states. The first important step towards understanding such states was taken in 1883, when Emil Kraepelin was able to demonstrate the kindred nature of a range of conditions that he grouped under the term 'dementia praecox.'[5] He thus illuminated the common roots of manifestations that had hitherto seemed disparate and confusing and indeed at times did not even receive the status of illness. By 1912, the Swiss psychiatrist Eugen Bleuler, head of the Burghölzli, renamed this group 'the schizophrenias' in order to indicate his discovery of the fundamental symptom that united it, which was the splitting of different psychic functions. The metaphor of splitting opened the way to a later consideration of the underlying mental mechanisms of the illness. The term 'schizoid' also appears in Bleuler's 1924 *Textbook of Psychiatry*[6] for the first time.

The discoveries of Kraepelin and Bleuler were separated not only by a generation gap of 29 years, but also by very different outlooks. There was undoubtedly an element of continuity in their theories, in as much as Kraepelin laid the foundations that enabled Bleuler's research, and in as much as they both contributed to the understanding of schizophrenia as a discrete syndrome with its typical pattern and range of symptomatology. However, Kraepelin's vision was rigidly organicist, equating mind with brain, whereas Bleuler was interested in the effects of experiences on mental life. This interest was itself a function of the influence of psychoanalysis on psychiatry. Bleuler was impressed by Freud and used some psychoanalytic lines of explanation in his *Textbook of Psychiatry*. However, his relationship with Freud was uneasy, and he ultimately preferred to retain his independence, allowing psychoanalysis to inform but not dominate his thinking.

As is evident from this relationship, the psychoanalytic contribution to the understanding of schizoid mechanisms was not a mere aftermath of psychiatric impetus. Since the birth of psychoanalysis had coincided with advances that revolutionized the fields of psychiatry, both disciplines were subject to fluidity and change at around the same period. This period saw the paths of psychiatry and psychoanalysis both converge and diverge, leading to mutual influences yet to the definition of differences.[7]

As discussed in Chapter 5, the Burghölzli team provided the link which connected psychiatric thinking with developments in psychoanalysis specifically via the work of Karl Abraham. He had not only explored melancholia, but like Jung, had earlier tried to grapple with the nature of dementia praecox. His response to the great enigma of the schizophrenic mind was to postulate, along Freudian lines, that it presented a regression to the most archaic level of self-sufficient auto-eroticism, later renamed 'narcissism', hence the detached nature of the schizophrenic. Unable to make satisfactory progress with such patients, Freud had already attributed their lack of engagement in the analytic endeavour to the earliest libidinal phase of mental life, the narcissistic phase that excluded objects.

These early efforts represent a nascent awareness of the possibilities that psychoanalysis held for understanding psychosis. However, the psychoanalytic work with individuals suffering from psychosis surfaced more explicitly with the Second World War. Both Fairbairn and Winnicott were able to work effectively with schizoid conditions, hence supporting their theoretical conclusions with examples from their clinical work.

KLEIN'S UNDERSTANDING OF THE SCHIZOID STATE

As already suggested, Klein partially agreed with both Fairbairn and Winnicott, ultimately assimilating into her theory facets from the thinking of both. Like them, she was attempting to unravel links between adult psychosis and infantile mental states. Above all, what both thinkers shared with Klein was a decided refusal to allow a crude equation between the former and the latter. Hence, while not implying that the infant is psychotic, Klein argued that the ingredients that go towards creating psychotic illness in adult life feature at the early stages of normal growth. Furthermore, she felt that they derive their nature from the preformed psyche with its characteristic processes.

The fact that Klein's exploration of schizoid processes was not an isolated endeavour but part of a broader professional dialogue, may account for the fact that she does not offer a definition of schizoid at any point in the 1946 'Notes on some schizoid mechanisms'. Her understanding of schizoid phenomena can none the less be surmised from a clinical case that she presents in her paper under the subheading of 'Some Schizoid Defences'. In this she provides an account of work with an adult male patient, using it to demonstrate the destructive nature of schizoid processes, and the way in which they corrode the ego's perceptive and experiencing capacities, ultimately fracturing its unified functioning.

Before providing the clinical vignette, Klein addresses the most disturbing aspect of schizoid individuals, which is the emotional deficit that they manifest. She emphasizes 'their withdrawn, unemotional attitude, the narcissistic elements in their object relations' and 'a kind of detached hostility that pervades the whole relation to the analyst.'[8] She goes on to describe how 'the patient himself feels estranged and far away', this corresponding to the analyst's impression that 'considerable parts of the patient's personality and of his emotions are not available'. Thus Klein highlights the dissociated state of schizoid individuals, the way in which they detach themselves from their responsive, emotional aspect.

This way of viewing schizoid states is in keeping with Fairbairn's understanding of their essence. He, too, counts among schizoid attributes 'an attitude of isolation and detachment', and also, crucially, emphasizes a process of a '*de-emotionalization of the object relationship*'.[9] (Original emphasis.)

However, Fairbairn was himself relying on Bleuler's understanding of schizoid as advanced in his *Textbook of Psychiatry*. In his acknowledged debt to Bleuler, Fairbairn noted: 'The adoption of the term "schizophrenia" was, of course, based in the first instance upon observation of this divorce between thought and feeling, suggestive as it is of a split within the mind.'[10]

In his own work, Bleuler had provided ample illustrations of what Fairbairn came to describe as a 'de-emotionalization' of the object relationship, specifically in the section of his textbook that deals with the schizophrenias. He, too, was powerfully struck by the fact that their 'entire conduct has the character of *indifference* ... their most vital interests, their own future, as well as the fate of the family leave the patients entirely cold.'[11] Bleuler went on to point out that appearances are sometimes deceptive, but that even in such cases, where schizophrenic individuals seem active and display 'great zeal to improve the universe or at least the health of mankind', a closer inspection still reveals 'defects in affectivity', with the consequence that to all appearances 'nothing is important to them, nothing is sacred to them. The general attitude is, "I don't care".'[12]

It is against this background that Klein's observations of the withdrawn unemotional attitude of the schizoid patient fit, as does Fairbairn's hypothesis that it originates with a de-emotionalization of the object relationship. Klein's additional observation regarding the narcissistic mode of relating typical of schizoid individuals was derived from Freud's understanding of the origins of schizoid detachment, as developed also by Abraham. While using this knowledge Klein's scope was more ambitious. She did not wish to restrict herself to describing symptoms, but wanted to unravel causes, specifically the mental mechanisms at work in schizoid states. Her clinical example thus demonstrates her attempt to capture a de-emotionalization even as it is taking place within the session. Her own experience with adults suffering from schizoid conditions was obtained from her private practice rather than a hospital setting, but it confirmed what practitioners had always noticed. Unlike psychiatry, psychoanalytic practice enabled a detailed observation of mental process, and Klein thus decided to draw from her clinical practice and trace schizoid processes as they unfold within the minutiae of the patient-analyst exchange.

The session which she has selected provides a particularly clear illustration of what is otherwise very difficult to observe: a 'de-emotionalization' in process. Klein explains how the patient began the session with latent feelings of frustration, envy and grievance towards the analyst. Klein does not suggest that this is itself an unusual clinical situation, but notes the significance of the fact that the patient is both unconscious of his feelings, and also finds them unusually threatening. In a description reminiscent of Klein's child patient Dick, her adult patient appears to be unable to tolerate even the possibility of hostile feelings in himself. When Klein interprets to him her experience of his hostility in the session, he reacts dramatically. Klein describes how he changed abruptly, and how '... the tone of his voice became flat, he spoke in a slow expressionless way, and he said that he felt detached from the whole situation. He added that my interpretation seemed correct, but that it did not matter. In fact, he no longer had any wishes, and nothing was worth bothering about.'[13]

In trying to explore the roots of this unnerving de-emotionalization, Klein suggests to her patient that her putting him in touch with his feelings of grievance seemed dangerous. This indicates that he feared the power of his negative emotions towards her, and because these seemed so extreme, could not react with a more appropriate sense of guilt or depression, as he had done on other occasions. Klein reflects that instead, on this occasion he attempted to deal with it by a particular method of splitting.

Klein then makes a point of differentiating such splitting from another kind that she had noted from the earliest time of her career, a more common one that keeps apart the good and bad aspects of the object under the threat of conflict or ambivalence. This latter kind of splitting had always been felt by her to be a normal aspect of infantile mental life, characterizing the infant's tendency to experience the object in extreme, phantastically good or phantastically bad ways. By contrast, the schizoid splitting that Klein is now witnessing in her patient consists of the patient turning 'his destructive impulses ... *towards his ego*, with the result that parts of his ego temporarily went out of existence.' (Original emphasis.) It is this that leads to an 'ensuing dispersal of emotions' and an unconscious phantasy of the 'annihilation of part of his personality'.[14]

Thus Klein spells out in clinical detail how anxiety aroused in a patient by his own aggressive intent, when intolerable, leads him to attack his own ego, to deaden those aspects of himself that experience anxiety and so annihilate his own emotional and experiencing capacities, ending up what in Fairbairn's terms would be de-emotionalized and withdrawn.

The psychotic essence of such a state is further elaborated by Klein when she stresses that what the patient achieves is far from a pleasant release from emotions. In fact, such states are not anxiety free at all:

> This lack of anxiety in schizoid patients is only apparent. For the schizoid mechanisms imply a dispersal of emotions including anxiety, but these dispersed elements still exist in the patient. Such patients have a certain form of latent anxiety; it is kept latent by the particular method of dispersal. The feeling of being disintegrated, of being unable to experience emotions, of losing one's objects, is in fact the equivalent of anxiety. This becomes clearer when advances in synthesis have been made ... At such moments it appears in retrospect that when emotions were lacking, relations were vague and uncertain and parts of the personality were felt to be lost, everything seemed to be dead.[15]

The schizoid reaction in this description amounts to an extinction of the patient's emotional reactions and hence a deadening of the vital essence of his experiencing. The patient's ego is rendered impotent, as aspects of experience that should be pieced together to create a core sense of the world evade all emotional sense. There is an alarming weakening and fragmentation of the mastering ego, with the resultant loss of control over normal reactive faculties. The ego has lost its ability to organize a coherent experience of the world. Klein's thinking thus accounts for the dementing disintegration of faculties which had been initially taken to be a 'dementia praecox', or early dementia.

Several features of Klein's interpretive approach to the case are noteworthy. First, she gives a central importance to her patient's emotional relationship with her in the session. His feelings of frustration, grievance and hate become the target of her analytic efforts, and are indeed regarded as having the power to bring about schizoid functioning. She had already developed her ideas about early object love. She was now fully in the throes of a belief that emotions dominate object relations, and that instincts operate through emotions and are actualized in object relationships. Klein's clinical case demonstrates how the patient's undue aggression surfaces and becomes mentally meaningful when it is lived out with her in the transference, hence taking on the meaning not of a generalized drive – aggression – but of a particular emotional experience – hostility. Furthermore, the patient's aggressive drive expressed through his frustration, grievance and hate threatens to become actualized in a very specific way, that is, in a hostile object relationship within the analytic situation, hence leading to extreme schizoid defences.

It is evident from Klein's technique with her patient that emotions have now become central in her thinking. The encounter between drives and an object creates meaning that is now regarded by her as emotional in essence. But this view meant that Klein could not fully agree with either Freud or Fairbairn on a crucial issue. As suggested, Freud always retained an emphasis on the biological underpinnings of psychoanalysis, and regarded the mental apparatus as coming into being in response to the urgent survival demands of the body with its drives. While the drives were regarded by him as primary motivational forces, emotions were felt to be secondary phenomena. When Fairbairn called this into question, he was already working at a different historical period. It was the 1940s, Freud was no longer alive, and there was a much larger field of knowledge with more collective experience on which to draw. It was in this context that Fairbairn wondered if it might be timely to abandon Freud's instinct theory altogether. He suggested that the libidinal urges of the infant were not pleasure seeking in a biological way, but object seeking in a social way. He pointed out that all the experience which had accumulated from the growing body of clinical work suggested that object relations were sufficient to account for development, and psychoanalysts did not need to theorize about obscure biological entities such as drives or instincts in order to obtain good results with their patients.

Klein could not altogether agree with Fairbairn. But neither could she retain a complete agreement with the traditional Freudian view of instincts. Instead, she adopted a version of libido as both pleasure-seeking and object-seeking. She argued that in her encounters with an object, the infant seeks both a quality of human attention and emotion, and also libidinal gratification or release from instinctual tension. It is the fulfilment or frustration of such needs that kindles love or hate respectively, and so creates object relationships. Freud's instinct theory was therefore indispensable to Klein. While she agreed that the infant's libido is indeed object seeking, she underscored the fact that it is the Freudian, pleasure-seeking aspect of libido which makes it possible to experience this object as fulfilling or frustrating, good or bad, loved or hated.

As well as this emphasis on the crucial role of emotions in Klein's clinical vignette, it has a further noteworthy feature, which is the assumption that the patient can somehow will an annihilation of a part of his ego. Klein tells us that the patient's emotions were not only dispersed, but that together with this he had an unconscious phantasy of an annihilation of part of his ego, and that the schizoid mechanism underlying this phantasy can actually deeply affect ego functioning. The patient's phantasy of annihilating a part of his ego seems to have accompanied an actual deadening of his responses and the divorce of his feeling from the rest of his ego functioning.

Klein not only portrays an internal mechanism that can deaden some capacities, but also suggests that the patient has some mental control over this mechanism through willing it in unconscious phantasy. This view was at one with Klein's belief that unconscious phantasy is the operative link between instinct and mental mechanisms. Now, with her formulation of schizoid processes, the patient is also shown to use phantasy as a way not only of activating mechanisms, but of relating to parts of himself, allowing or seeking to annihilate parts of his ego structure. Klein thus traced a route between self-destructive phantasies and the actual harm which a patient inflicts on his own mind.

De-emotionalization, then, was a prominent feature observed by both Klein and Fairbairn in schizoid functioning. One way in which this could relate to Klein's understanding of early infancy would be her possible belief that the infant similarly deadens his responses and annihilates parts of his ego in the face of anxiety. While Klein does not actually state this, she none the less describes the infant as using splitting processes, uses the term 'schizoid' in relation to this, and refers to schizophrenic processes in the infantile mind. In addition, Klein's account of infantile mental life now places emphasis on its immense vulnerability. The newborn psyche is easily overwhelmed and destabilized from the moment that life begins. It is not equal to the overwhelming events of the trauma of birth and the subsequent frustration of bodily needs caused by normal disruptions in the nurturing relationship. Added to these, there is the incessant pressure of internal instinctual urges which can mount rapidly in the absence of capacity for self-regulation. It would make sense to view the infant as requiring extreme defences to protect her fragile psyche, and so make it conceivable that she would resort to schizoid defences which can diminish pain by severing disturbing portions of experience from awareness and deadening ego responses.

However, thus formulated, Klein's view of early mental life carries a major flaw. A theoretical transferral of adult schizoid functioning to infants would leave a picture of infancy that does not account for ego development. It is not clear why the infant, who might wish to defend herself incessantly, would not gradually dehumanize herself instead of learning to tolerate emotions and take in increasing elements of reality. The kind of schizoid mechanism which emerges in Klein's clinical account is, as seen, a process that gradually deadens the natural responses of the psyche, eventually damaging its capacities.

Such an understanding did also form a powerful strand in her thinking on infantile defences. However, inasmuch as her adult example indicated states of mental stasis or decay, it could not be wholly applicable to the dynamic, developing psyche of the normal infant. It was necessary to do more than simply transfer to the latter ideas on adult schizoid pathology. Furthermore, Klein was already aware of the complex activity, much of it growth-promoting, that anxiety and defences generated in the inner lives of her child patients. Her thesis on infantile schizoid defences thus needed a further element, and this was provided when she formulated her concept of projective identification, which will be explored in the next chapter.

NOTES

1. Fairbairn, W. R. D. (1952) 'Schizoid factors of the personality', in *Psychoanalytic Studies of the Personality*. London: Tavistock/Routledge. (First published in 1940.) p. 8.

2. Klein, M. (1975) 'Notes on some schizoid mechanisms', in *Envy and Gratitude*, London: The Hogarth Press. (First published in 1946.) p. 3.
3. Klein, M. (1975) *The Psychoanalysis of Children*. London: The Hogarth Press. (First published in 1932.) p. 292.
4. Fine, R. (1979) *A History of Psychoanalysis*. New York: Columbia University Press. (First published in 1914.)
5. Ellenberger, H. F. (1994) *The Discovery of the Unconscious*. London: Fontana Press. (First published in 1970.)
6. Bleuler, E. (1924) *Textbook of Psychiatry*. New York: Macmillan.
7. Ellenberger, H. F. (1994) *The Discovery of the Unconscious*. London: Fontana Press. (First published in 1970.)
8. Klein, M. (1975) 'Notes on some schizoid mechanisms', in *Envy and Gratitude*. London: The Hogarth Press. (First published 1946.) p. 18.
9. Fairbairn, W. R. D. (1992) 'Schizoid factors in the personality', in *Psychoanalytic Studies of the Personality*. London: Tavistock/Routledge. (First published in 1940.) p. 14.
10. ibid., p. 20.
11. Bleuler, E. (1924) *Textbook of Psychiatry*. New York: Macmillan, p. 379.
12. ibid., p. 379.
13. Klein, M. (1975) 'Notes on some schizoid mechanisms', in *Envy and Gratitude*. London: The Hogarth Press. (First published in 1946.) p. 19.
14. ibid., p. 19.
15. ibid., p. 21.

CHAPTER 11

'Falling to pieces or splitting itself' – Projective Identification, Unintegrated States and Splitting Processes

T he description of projective identification occupies a brief space in Klein's writings, and yet, of all of her concepts, it has enjoyed the most extensive popularity. Its clinical usefulness quickly became apparent because it not only illuminated a host of pathological mechanisms, but also enabled significant advances in psychoanalytic technique. Late in Klein's life and after her death, the concept was taken up and developed in crucial ways by Bion, who used it to shed light on the earliest communication between mother and infant, as well as positing this as the model for the interaction between the patient and psychoanalyst. The implications for technique, for the understanding of normal development and for a much deeper insight into adult schizoid processes have been profound.[1]

In formulating the concept in 1946, Klein carried forward two central ideas from her earlier thinking. First, that the individual can only rid his mind of disturbing content by curtailing his own awareness, and that this happens via schizoid mechanisms that create a split in the ego. Klein had also suggested, much earlier in her career that inner turmoil, aggression or pain can be projected and displaced on to the object, thereby altering it in the infant's perception.

Klein now linked these two ideas in a new way. She suggested that splitting mechanisms do not operate in isolation, but together with processes of projection and displacement of feelings on to objects. Furthermore, these operations are underpinned by an unconscious phantasy whereby unwanted parts of the ego are ejected from the self and omnipotently forced into the object. Such phantasies derive from the relationship of the early psyche with the primitive life of the body, in the sense that those parts of the ego which register distress and pain are experienced by the infant as unwanted internal contents and equated with faeces which cause discomfort and need to be expelled aggressively. Klein's new idea that these internal contents are projected 'into' an object implied in turn that the object is gradually felt to contain the infant's internal contents or parts. The infant necessarily begins to equate the object with disowned aspects of himself, and so direct all his self-hatred on to the misrecognized object: '... this identification of the object with hated parts of the self contributes to the intensity of the hatred directed against other people.'[2]

The idea that the infant equates disturbing ego parts with unwanted faeces might have a restrictive and dulling effect on the reader's first responses to the concept of projective identification. But Klein's view quickly expanded to accommodate a much richer and more complex view of the projective process. To the infant, faeces can represent a varied array of unspecified internal contents, and in the same way, it could be different kinds of ego-states which are projected, some of them positive. But even in cases where projections are negative, the fact that they involve ego parts has immense implications both for infantile object relations, and also for a primitive underpinning of adult mental life. For a start, it makes sense of some of the most atavistic anxiety scenarios that people regularly experience: 'The phantasy of forcefully entering the object gives rise to anxieties relating to the dangers threatening the subject from within the object, that is, the fear of being controlled and persecuted inside the object.'[3]

Klein now began to understand the roots of certain irrational fears that begin in childhood but can continue into adult life, such as, for example, the claustrophobic anxiety of being trapped, and also the fear of being invaded or of having one's mind controlled. Klein could also now make sense of other phenomena, such as the way in which some individuals project positively into their objects, but through placing narcissistically valued self-aspects in others too often become prone to over-dependent relationships and to feeling denuded of their own abilities, hence lacking a healthy self-sufficiency.

It is already apparent from these ideas that, brilliantly applicable though the concept of projective identification proved to be, it also presents some theoretical difficulties. First, as formulated by Klein, it comes across as a mostly negative phenomenon, or what she described as 'the prototype of a hostile object relationship'. This restricts the most interesting possibilities which the concept opens up, including its implications for emotional communication and for the development of identity. But before further discussion, it is necessary to examine another theoretical difficulty which has an even more immediate impact on the ability to grasp the full subtleties of the concept.

Klein's formulation of projective identification resurrects, yet again, one of the typical challenges encountered in her texts, making it difficult to ascertain whether, with her concept, she is simply providing a description of phantasy contents, or whether she is actually providing a conceptual definition of a psychic process. What is more, projective identification lends itself easily to thinking in terms of phantasy contents because Klein was particularly interested in the complex phantasy scenarios bound up with it. This can lead to the error of assuming that her descriptive focus is her entire theoretical formulation.

However, Klein was well aware that parts of the self cannot actually enter another, and that a statement that they do so does not explain a mechanism. In fact, a particularly careful reading of the texts is required to establish that, dominated though the writing is by the workings of phantasy, Klein continues to maintain a flow of conceptual information that works towards defining the mental mechanism in theoretical terms, rather than only in terms of described phantasies. And while this may come across as a supplementary activity in the text, it is none the less both present and important.

For a start, Klein continues to rely on her view of phantasy as the operative link between instinct and mechanism. Particular phantasy contents thus point to the underlying mental mechanism at work: 'The processes I have described are, of course, bound up with the infant's phantasy life; and the anxieties that *stimulate* the mechanisms of splitting are also of a phantastic nature'.[4] (Original emphasis.) As is clear from the passage, Klein differentiates between mental processes and phantasy life; the former are bound up with the latter, and phantasy experiences stimulate the mental mechanisms of splitting. As well as this, there is an attempt to understand mental processes with the help of technical terms that designate phenomena rather than purely describing subjective phantasies. To the psychiatric understanding of a schizoid mechanism it was possible to add Freudian ideas that would illuminate it in a way that was specifically psychoanalytic. Such ideas would need to be technical terms that designate a psychic phenomenon, rather than descriptions of subjective mental content. Two such Freudian terms which Klein found particularly pertinent to her ideas on splitting, designated the twin phenomena of infantile hallucinatory wish-fulfilment and infantile omnipotent thinking.

Klein noted, for example, that the infant not only omnipotently conjures up an ideal object (the satisfying hallucinatory object) but simultaneously, and in a single stroke, omnipotently annihilates the painful situation which required a hallucination in the first place. The Freudian concept of omnipotent hallucinatory thinking is thus the first step to understanding the origin of splitting, because it is a moment at which the frustrating situation has been severed from awareness. In subjective terms, the infant may have a phantasy that the painful situation has been made to vanish through the sheer force of his aggressive willing: 'Omnipotent denial of the existence of the bad object and of the painful situation is in the unconscious equal to annihilation by the destructive impulse'.[5]

While it may be complicated to tease out the strand of theoretical thinking that works towards a definition in this quote, this strand is none the less present, and differentiated by Klein from unconscious phantasy contents. The magical ability to will the destruction of the actual painful situation is the content of a subjective phantasy because the infant has no actual magical control over painful situations. However, from a theoretical viewpoint, the mechanism responsible for this annihilation of pain is omnipotent denial. Klein thus provides more than phantasy descriptions, beginning with the suggestion that infantile omnipotent thinking and omnipotent denial are the processes that, psychoanalytically speaking, underlie schizoid mechanisms and the phantasy life that they engender.

The extent of Klein's reliance on the Freudian idea of omnipotence may not initially seem very striking, given that it is but one idea within the conceptual plethora that characterizes her 1946 text on schizoid mechanisms. However, this should not lead to an underestimation of the key role of this concept in her theory. She had initially absorbed the concept into her thinking partly from Ferenczi, who showed how the infant's move towards a reality sense is measured in relation to the distance travelled from the original state of omnipotence. The more mature the child, the more he is able to accept that his urgent desires do not, in themselves, conjure up satisfaction.

In this vision, Ferenczi made use of the original Freudian view of omnipotent thinking, which he developed further by examining the gradual, step-by-step emergence from omnipotence. Freud first became more deeply aware of the phenomenon not from an observation of children or infants, but from his work with an adult, the very obsessional patient known as the Rat Man. Compulsive thoughts seemed devastating to this patient not only because of their sudden, mad intrusions into his mind, but because he was convinced that the mere act of thinking them would result in a realization of their content. Being gripped by a sudden idea that his fiancée was going to die was thus more than a distressing thought. He was convinced that it would actually happen and that he would thus be punished for his thoughts. As shown, Freud had linked this adult state of mind with a more innocent scenario in infancy, suggesting that the first omnipotent, hallucinatory states enable the infant's psyche to conjure up fulfilment in response to his first keenly felt desires in life.

Both Freud and Ferenczi discussed infantile omnipotence in relation to positive infantile desires and their fulfilment, but Klein now added to this picture an aggressive omnipotence. Since Freud's Rat Man believed that his murderous thoughts would be realized, there was no reason to exclude such thinking from the mind of angry infants. On the contrary, the Rat Man's thinking must have had infantile roots. Klein thus suggested that since the first aggressions are targeted at painful situations that feel persecuting to the infant, he needs to resort to omnipotent thinking in order to deny and annihilate the pain aggressively. And now, with the new idea of projective identification, Klein added that omnipotent thinking is equally responsible for dealing with disturbing parts of the self by ejecting them into the object.

However, while the notion of omnipotent denial was illuminating in relation to splitting mechanisms, and while it could be used to account for projective identification to some extent, more was required to give it full definition. Without providing a further mental mechanism to the explanation of projective identification, the concept would amount to no more than a dual mechanism of splitting and omnipotent denial which happens to spin around itself particularly elaborate corresponding phantasies. However, Klein was aware of this, and did, in fact, add a further mechanism to her definition, which was that of identification.

It is thus that Klein's chosen terminology aptly represents her concept, because she regards the phenomenon of projective identification as a combination between processes of splitting, projection and identification. As seen, she had already thought of splitting mechanisms as severing mental faculties, such as feelings and ideation, from one another. However, if this process worked without hindrance in the mind, it would gradually obliterate all awareness. Some other process needed to prevent such deterioration. With her child patient Dick, Klein observed a situation where this was beginning to happen: his feelings were attacked and eroded through self-destructive processes so drastically that his mental life came to a virtual standstill.

Klein fully appreciated that schizoid mechanisms are self-destructive in essence, and it was this which led her to a concept that could account for the difference between the normal child, and an ill child such as Dick. Unlike Dick, normal children have a capacity for projective identification, and it is this mental process that prevents splitting mechanisms from fragmenting the mind completely. Splitting and projection, accompanied by identification, meant that whatever is severed from awareness is not lost, but rediscovered in the object. The mind thus continues a relationship, albeit an indirect one, with otherwise dispersed parts of itself, and this opens the way to an ultimate ability to reassimilate, rather than permanently lose, what has been projected. Instead of completely obliterating aspects of experience, projective identification creates a divided experience of the painful event, in which it is fully known and at the same time, only indirectly and partly known, until more of it can be tolerated.

If Klein's description of phantasy contents sometimes prevents the reader from noticing her ideas on the specific mental mechanisms at work, the opposite can also happen. There are times at which Klein's account of a mechanism is assumed to refer to the content of a particular phantasy. This error sometimes occurs with her suggestion that the infant equates the object with his projected parts, and that there is thus a confusion between self and object. However, when Klein speaks of such confusion, she is referring to a mental process, and not to the phantasy experience to which it gives rise. The object is not related to as another self, but, quite the contrary, as an extraneous source of malevolence. The confusion between self and object to which Klein refers is an objective account of a state of mind, as the infant is, by definition, not cognizant of his confusion. This is significant not least because it is extraordinarily illuminating on the nature of human aggression. Klein shows that in the origin of human cruelty, there is always a paranoid urge to blame and punish others for what has been attributed to them. In the infant, this tendency diminishes when development enhances his ability to tolerate, and so own, disturbing aspects of his self.

The relevance of this thinking to the development of a moral sense and so to Klein's concept of the depressive position, is evident, but there are other, more surprising implications. In particular, Klein offers a very unusual angle on the development of identity. She shows that it is not a question of simple and increasing self-awareness. The most intense and disturbing parts of the self are only accommodated after they have journeyed through the minds of others, and after the infant has thus externalized his ego's relationship with its most disturbing aspects.

Given the sheer amount which Klein was trying to articulate in 'Notes on some schizoid mechanisms', it is perhaps not surprising that her formulation of projective identification was rushed, and that the rich promise of the concept was never fully drawn out by her. She continued, on the whole, to sound unduly negative, regarding projective identification as the 'prototype of a hostile object relationship', and noticing mostly situations in which it failed to modify in a growing individual, leading to the overbearing and omnipotent treatment of others.

Projective identification none the less proved to be a concept replete with possibilities which Klein herself only just began to tease out, and which were left for others to develop. The most astounding ramifications of the concept thus became apparent only after Klein's death. In the early 1960s, Bion used projective identification as the springboard for groundbreaking discoveries. He suggested that since parts of the infant are only accommodated after their sojourn in the mother, it follows that she plays a crucial role in helping the infant to transform them into acceptable mental entities. With this thinking, it became apparent that the human infant never learns directly about his aggression. He only learns about it as tolerated by the mother, hence always reintrojecting his aggression together with the particular way in which it has been tolerated and handled. Such thinking was revolutionary in clarifying the nature of maternal emotional provision, and highlighted the importance of the mother's mental resilience. This was also the culmination of the line of thinking that had started with Ferenczi, and that had always stressed the shortcomings of viewing pedagogic coercion as the main means to the moral development of the child.

Projective identification was a concept that began to show how schizoid defences might operate in infancy without leading to the disintegration of the young mind. But as suggested, Klein's ideas on it and on schizoid mechanisms fit into a context where further textual obstacles are encountered. The way in which Klein understood the split-off, or fragmented, experience, was itself part of a complex vision of several kinds of fragmentation processes that characterize earliest infancy.

UNINTEGRATED STATES AND SPLITTING

While Klein was inspired by Fairbairn's view of schizoid mechanisms, it is also clear that her agreement with him did not extend beyond the idea that they were present in mental life. Fairbairn's views on splitting mechanisms fitted into a much broader vision of his own, in which he was concerned to link such mechanisms with the creation of mental structure. His elaborate model has as its starting point a Freudian view of the infant's earliest awareness. According to this, the infant does not notice very much so long as he is comfortable and unperturbed by basic needs or frustrations. Reality only begins to impinge in the form of disruptions into an otherwise undifferentiated existence, and the first introjected object is, necessarily, a disturbing one. While objectively speaking this object is bad and disturbing, it is not fully differentiated as such by the infant, who is still leading an undifferentiated, 'pre-ambivalent' existence. However, the object continues to be experienced as a vague, yet stressful, internal entity, and therefore triggers a reaction in the infant, setting in motion a splitting process. It is these which create out of the undifferentiated introjection several differentiated ego parts, and so lay the foundation for the structure of the mental apparatus.

Klein did not agree with this view. In fact, the very details of her objection to it mark out, in much bolder outline, quite how far she had travelled with her own theory. She disliked the idea that the infant initially introjects only a bad object. This appeared to imply that the world has nothing to offer the infant except a disturbing, bad object that needs to be improved upon, and hence all the credit for creating a good object should go to the human individual. Klein's position was now very far from this. In spite of the fact that her theory continued to sound sobering if not melancholic, she strongly believed that the first goodness is offered from without from the nurturing mother and the good breast. In her own vision, the infant receives both good and bad input from his human milieu and registers both as such immediately. If anything, his aggression is triggered because he has an intense experience of the goodness of the breast, and this accentuates his anger in the face of deprivation.

The other crucial aspect of Fairbairn's thinking with which Klein disagreed was connected with his view on how the first mental structure comes about. In his thinking ego parts do not exist at the beginning of life, before active processes of splitting create them, and this implies that psychic structure is the product of active mental enterprise. As far as Klein was concerned, such thinking amounted to a *tabula rasa* view of the infant psyche. While in Fairbairn's model internal structure comes into being through the activity of defence mechanisms that create internal divisions, in Klein's model splitting mechanisms do not create the first mental structure, but begin to operate within an already existing, albeit very rudimentary, structure.

Klein now needed to address more fully the nature of this presumed structure. She had already, much earlier in her career, assumed the existence of some ego activity at birth, but her new thinking on schizoid mechanisms required a much fuller account of what this might mean. And while Fairbairn influenced her thinking on schizoid mechanisms, when it came to early mental structure it was to her colleague Donald Winnicott that she turned.

As shown, Klein felt that instinctual experience, bodily sensations and apprehended 'parts and portions' of the maternal environment mingle in the primal mental substance of phantasy. She also felt that such a primal state is not in contradiction with the existence of an ego. This, however, would only be possible if the ego were not viewed as a structure that only comes into being actively, but one that has some initial archaic form by virtue of being geared to the fundamentals of survival at birth. Such fundamentals were felt by her to amount to rudimentary capacities for exchange with the environment, that is, the processes of projection and introjection. Active splitting or structuring would need to fit into this already existing setting.

In other words, quite apart from applying schizoid defences, Klein viewed the infant's original ego activity as already fragmented, enabling him to take in reality only in piecemeal fashion, to interact with only parts and portions of the object world, and to receive good or bad quality in separate, though intensely experienced, moments. As far as Klein was concerned, there is therefore a primal state that precedes the setting up of further mental structure through active splitting processes. Her theory ultimately deals with two kinds of fragmented phenomena in infantile mental life: passive, unintegrated states that characterize the original features of the primary ego activity, and active splitting processes that are superimposed on this pre-existing format. Part of the difficulty with the text of 'Notes on some schizoid mechanisms' is that these differences, though undoubtedly stated, are not emphasized. As a result, the reader is faced with an array of fragmentation phenomena not all of which are related, but which could none the less be mistakenly attributed to the single source of schizoid mechanisms. The infant apprehends only parts and portion of the object world, makes a division between good and bad, relates to part-objects, applies schizoid mechanisms that create a split in his ego and so forth. In trying to establish the sources of these various processes, it is helpful to bear in mind that while Fairbairn can be regarded as inspiring the active element in this theory, for the other, passive, element, Klein invoked the influence of Winnicott. Like Fairbairn he had clinical experience with schizoid patients, and on its basis he described, quite independently, unintegrated infantile states that were not active splitting mechanisms but that amounted in his view to a primal state of unintegration.

PRIMARY UNINTEGRATION – WINNICOTT'S INFLUENCE

Klein's conceptual challenge in her theory was to give a convincing account of an ego that exists from birth. She therefore had to preface all further thinking with a section in her 1946 paper devoted to addressing 'Certain problems of the early ego'. By the time Klein was examining this issue there was other thinking about the subject among her contemporaries. For example, she did not agree with Glover's formulations on the existence of several ego nuclei at the beginning of life, and instead noted: '... more helpful in my view is Winnicott's emphasis on the unintegration of the early ego. I would also say that the early ego largely lacks cohesion, and a tendency towards integration alternates with a tendency towards disintegration, a falling into bits.'[6]

Alluding to Winnicott's 1940 paper 'Primitive emotional states', Klein not only favoured his ideas on unintegration, but also drew on these in her formulation of the earliest ego state. The concept of unintegration, however, is problematic and difficult to trace clearly in the texts. Neither Winnicott nor Klein defined it explicitly. Both resorted to vague descriptive suggestions to the effect that the early ego lacks cohesion and reveals the tendency of falling into bits. Winnicott hypothesized a developmental process that starts very early[7] which he termed 'integration'. This process was necessary, Winnicott reasoned, because the initial state in psychical life is of a primary unintegration.

Winnicott may well have intended to leave this concept without an over-precise definition. Phillips has noted Winnicott's tendency not to over-formulate the nature of essentially mysterious entities such as the self.[8] In line with this Winnicott may have wished to underscore the fundamental mysteriousness of psychic phenomena, especially the ones most remote from adult experience or observation. Like Winnicott, Klein did not make fully specific assumptions about the unknown realm of early infancy. In her chapter she tells us 'we know little about the structure of the early ego', and then reasons that, 'we are . . . justified in assuming that some of the functions of which we know from the later ego are there at the beginning'.[9] Like Winnicott, she holds that the activities of the early ego need to be inferred from later states.

Rather than imputing precise content to the earliest mental life, Winnicott sought some of its possible traces in later experience. He felt that the nature of primary unintegration could be inferred from states of disintegration in certain adult psychiatric conditions. Winnicott was careful not to equate such states of disintegration with early psychical life. He emphasized that they were, in the first instance, the manifestation of a breakdown in adult functioning. However, such breakdown could not but reveal the undoing of developmental achievements and hence uncover earlier, more rudimentary modes of mental functioning:

> Disintegration of the personality is a well-known psychiatric condition, and its psychopathology is highly complex. Examination of these phenomena in analysis, however, shows that the primary unintegrated state provides a basis for disintegration, and that delay or failure in respect of primary integration predisposes to disintegration as a regression, or as a result of failure in other types of defence.[10]

Disintegration, the 'well-known psychiatric condition', is a failure to emerge sufficiently from primary unintegration through positive integration experiences. Winnicott took account of two aspects of psychotic disintegration when inferring the nature of primary unintegration. The first aspect was the psychotic patient's inability to locate experiences in the body and self, and the second was the patient's inability to connect temporal experience. Both amounted to the mind's difficulty with basic spatial and temporal orientation, essential for its entire functioning.

When considering the first aspect Winnicott reminds the reader that while 'localization of self in one's own body is often assumed', the experience of psychotic patients suggests that it is a developmental achievement. As an example he tells of a patient who discovered in analysis that '. . . most of the time she lived in her head, behind her eyes. She could only see out of her eyes as out of windows and so was not aware of what her feet were doing, and in consequence she tended to fall into pits and trip over things.'[11]

The psychotic anxiety and helplessness suggested in this vignette relates to the way in which the patient, though affected by the impingement of different experiences, is not easily able to locate these in her whole experiencing body. Her ego cannot sufficiently organize the relationship between her body and the world, thus impeding her ability to make sense of experiences. Deficient ego functioning is evident in Winnicott's other example: '. . . a psychotic patient in analysis came to recognize that as a baby she thought her twin at the other end of the pram was herself. She even felt surprised when her twin was picked up and yet she remained where she was.'[12]

This patient was describing a time in infancy when she had developed sufficiently to be noticing her sister and ascribing some meaning to actions such as picking up. Yet while impressions impinged on her, her ego could not apparently perform the unifying functions necessary for gathering, connecting and situating impressions appropriately in self or others.

The other aspect of disintegration that Winnicott related to primary unintegration is a failure to link temporal experience. The importance of temporal awareness figured prominently in Bleuler's descriptions of schizophrenic dissociation states. He cited examples of individuals who spoke nonsensically because they communicated fragments of experience that were not temporally connected. Winnicott's examples were drawn from more ordinary case material. He described patients who were only able to experience life in a very fragmented fashion and who were therefore striving blindly for unity within the person of the analyst: '. . . we must interpret this as the patient's need to be known in all his bits and pieces by one person, the analyst. To be known means to feel integrated at least in the person of the analyst. This is the ordinary stuff of infant life, and the infant who has had no one person to gather his bits together starts with a handicap'.[13]

The patient who needs to be linked in the mind of the analyst is not connecting his different selves as they emerge in response to consecutive events. By implication, the mother has a role in a meaningful gathering of different fragments of her infant's response that go to make up his individual history. It is this that gives the infant a sense of one self that changes over time, rather than of different selves that emerge as no more than temporal fragments.

In her own paper, Klein refers to the work of Scott who 'stressed the importance of the breaks in continuity of experience, which imply a splitting in time'. Indeed, the idea of temporal splitting fits in with Klein's notion that the infant is initially only able to relate to gratifying or hostile parts and portions of the world, that is, to the immediate events of the moment. Only later with integration does the infant learn that the world (and also his object) is a composite phenomenon made out of different parts that are connected temporally.

However, the temporal aspect of early psychical experience is not prominent in Klein's thinking in her 1946 writing. The main emphasis that she places in her understanding of Winnicott's concept of primary unintegration is summed up in her assertion that the 'early ego largely lacks cohesion', so that, 'a tendency towards integration alternates with a tendency towards disintegration'.

In his own clinical examples, Winnicott was conceiving of ego disintegration along classical Freudian lines, as signifying a failure of the ego to bind impulses and coordinate perceptions. However, what is significant as far as Klein was concerned, was that he regarded such examples as evidence that pointed to the nature of primary states. However, while he considered adult disintegration to be a disturbed, terrifying psychiatric condition, the primary unintegration which could be inferred from it is a benign, not uncomfortable, normal condition of the unformed psyche, as indeed is noted by Phillips: 'In a Winnicottian baby's life there are long periods when [the baby] is just a bundle of disparate feelings and impressions and he doesn't, as an adult would say, mind that this is the case provided, Winnicott writes, "from time to time he comes together and feels something".'[14]

What seems to be the most necessary feature of Winnicott's theory for Klein is, therefore, a way of accounting for an early ego that exists prior to the more formed and cohesive entity that emerges later. Although such an ego exists in a rudimentary, unformed fashion, it is none the less a point of origin for mental development. And while Winnicott did not account for primary unintegrated states beyond providing clinical descriptions of disintegrated psychotic states, Klein's theory went further and provided psychoanalytic concepts that could make sense of the process, and these were projection and introjection.

In 1946, it becomes clear that for Klein the most fundamental mental structure was not a stable entity in the sense that a later ego can be; rather, it is portrayed as having a mobile existence in which environment is taken in and internal content expelled continually. This kind of ego is not initially located in a fixed point, but consists, at any one moment, of what has been absorbed or expelled, that is, states of pleasure when the good object has been introjected and states of persecution when the bad object is projected or reintrojected. Klein's thinking on the depressive position accounts for how this early state of flux gradually settles into a more permanent structure, when repeated introjection and introjective identifications enable the setting up of more permanent features of the personality, optimally with the good object predominating.

Klein thus drew on Winnicott's outlook on primary unintegration not only in order to account for the earliest ego states, but also in order to depict this primary mental structure as a developmental basis from which integration processes begin. However, in thus viewing primary unintegration, she added to her vision a further complicating element. Winnicott's notion of a benign primary state immediately introduced the idea of another process that necessarily follows in its wake, which is a regressive primary disintegration. Because the infant's mind continually fluctuates between moments of integration and a return to unintegrated states, it was necessary to think of the continual joint operation of two kinds of processes in infancy: primary and regressive.

Winnicott appreciated the significance of such immediate appearances of disintegration processes. He not only believed that increasing experiences of integration were essential for the infant, but also, like Klein, conceded that disintegration processes begin immediately and are manifest as 'abandonment to impulses, uncontrolled because acting on their own.'[15] Klein was aware that for this reason, a benign primary unintegration is almost notional, for as soon as the ego has its first moments of integration, it cannot move back to a former state except destructively, through a process of undoing, or of what she called 'a falling into bits'. Even the earliest fluctuations in ego structure soon assume the significance of moves between constructive-integrating and destructive-regressive ego processes.

This further complicating strand which Klein added to her 1946 text pushes its contents to almost impossible levels of abstraction. Not only does Klein draw on Fairbairn's idea of schizoid mechanisms that create divisions in the ego, and not only does she posit a pre-existing structure that is also unintegrated, she now adds the difficult notion that in this very primary structure, and quite apart from schizoid mechanisms, there is an additional kind of disintegration process, evident in the natural regressive moves of the psyche. This dual source of fragmentation processes leads her to separate out early ego disintegrations from the issue of 'whether some *active* splitting processes within the ego may not occur even at a very early age' (emphasis added). And in case of any doubt about the fact that she is considering two, and not one, phenomena, she suggests two alternatives in the response to primary anxiety whereby the ego is either 'falling to pieces *or* splitting itself' (emphasis added).[16]

One possible way of easing the strenuous demands that such thinking places on the reader would have been the decision to class early disintegration moments as basically benign, and regarding the falling into bits as a gentle drifting apart which is no more than a kind of relaxation of psychic activity. This, at least, would mark out a Winnicottian, passive-benign dimension of early processes from a Fairbairn-inspired active-schizoid one. Such a tidy division, however, was not what Klein had in mind.

Winnicott had rightly noticed that disintegration was a secondary process, but he did not explain its origin. Klein, however, wanted to link the idea more firmly with psychoanalytic theory. She remembered Ferenczi's belief that, '... every living organism reacts to unpleasant stimuli by fragmentation. Possibly, complicated mechanisms (living organisms) are only kept as an entity through the impact of external conditions. When these conditions become unfavourable the organism falls to pieces.'[17] This led her to think about Freud's concept of the death instinct, which she had already adopted at the time of the Controversial Discussions.

Klein now suggested that the early disintegrations of the infantile psyche are triggered by the death instinct. At the beginning of life the human organism registers the impact of the death instinct as a fragmenting pressure, and it is this which accounts for the tendency to fall apart and to return, along the lines of Freud's 1920 thinking, to a former state of primary unintegration. Furthermore, Klein concluded that the death instinct triggers a primal anxiety of an acute persecutory nature which takes the form of 'the anxiety of being destroyed from within'. She added that '... in keeping with the lack of cohesiveness ... under the pressure of this threat the ego tends to fall to pieces.' Therefore Klein agreed with Winnicott that this secondary falling to pieces is also one of the underlying scenarios in adult schizophrenic states, but she added the crucial element of attributing the source of fragmentation to psychotic anxieties generated by the internally experienced death instinct.

By this stage, Klein's vision of infancy might come across as very bleak indeed, but some of the impression is a question of emphasis in her text, rather than its underlying rationale, which does assume the existence of a powerful counter-vailing force to human destructiveness. For a start, adopting Freud's death instinct was not possible without also adopting his ideas on the opposite, the life instinct, and this in turn implied immensely positive states that represent a response to life-enhancing aspects of the environment. Winnicott's thinking was of further value to Klein when he suggested that, 'The tendency to integrate is helped by two sets of experience: the technique of infant care whereby the infant is kept warm, handled and bathed and rocked and named, and also the acute instinctual experiences which tend to gather the personality together from within.'[18]

For Klein, those 'two sets of experience' were united in her concept of the primary good object and representative of the life instinct, for this implied both external nurturing and the infant's projection of libidinal and loving impulses on to the good breast. This led Klein much further. While she posited destructive fragmentation processes, and while it is fair to suggest that these create the most prominent impression in her 1946 account of infancy, it is none the less essential to note that her overall vision would mean little in the absence of a positive core to development. Klein now viewed the infantile psyche as a self-organizing entity which shows an immediate tendency towards moulding its nebulous archaic substance around whatever can provide a unifying core. And she explicitly recognized this core as the introjected good object. Libidinal pleasure-states, and feelings of love and gratitude that are projected on to the nurturing breast, are then reintrojected to form such a core. Mental states and ego-parts can then cluster around this island of security, created with the help of the human provision received by the infant, and this gradually enables integration.

From as early as 1935, Klein had suggested that the good breast is first experienced as a total situation. She now added that once introjected, it becomes a vital part of the ego, which acts as an integrating and unifying force. The Winnicott-inspired idea about the need for early integration experiences thus reinforces a positive and appreciative theory on the earliest good experiences. In Klein's thinking, it is shown to enable the infant to feel centred, and so provides a refuge from the first pains of his existence.

SPLITTING AS DIFFERENTIATION

Klein does not proceed to explain how splitting mechanisms begin to be active in what is already presumed to be an unintegrated, and also continually disintegrating, framework, and this does raise the question of how such a psychic situation, which is in the first place subjected to fragmentation processes, can be further split. One way of thinking about this issue is proposed by Kernberg, who wonders whether 'normal mechanisms of development and growth eventually become defensive operations . . .'. He suggests that one could view splitting as '. . .

first a passive consequence of the separate building up of experiences linked with very positive and very unpleasant affect states', and goes on to conclude that, 'this separate building up can eventually be used for defensive purposes.'[19]

What is suggested is that the defensive splitting described by Klein can be regarded as a reinforcement or simulation of primary unintegration processes even after they have been outgrown. Such a view would make sense in the light of Freud's death-instinct urge to cling, or return to a former state, and so fits in with essential aspects of Klein's thinking. And indeed her thinking does depict two broad moves in the infantile psyche. The life instinct, in the form of nourishing experiences, stimulates each forward psychic move, each moment of ego integration and of increased awareness. As soon as such awareness encounters the disturbance of painful situations, a regressive, death-instinct tendency defends the infant mind through a refragmenting of awareness.

However, it is also necessary to bear in mind that Klein gave substantial emphasis to schizoid mechanisms which come into being in addition to the pre-existing framework, and which are superimposed on a system that is already fluctuating in this way. The significance of this is her view of phantasy as the operative link between instinct and mental mechanism. In other words, she envisaged a degree of individual agency in the employment of schizoid defences, which she considered to be much more than either a passive drifting apart, or an involuntary disintegration under the pressure of the death instinct. However archaic the phantasy process that is implicated in schizoid mechanisms, it is driven by the adamant purpose of infantile instinctual energy.

There are other important considerations. For Klein, almost all of the earliest psychic operations were characterized by a partial, fragmentary movement, including the important moves in development and integration. For example, the natural way in which the infant introjects aspects of reality, and so grows, is initially piecemeal and partial. From a theoretical viewpoint, his first introjections are thus of part-objects. However, Klein crucially differentiated between the theoretical designation of part-objects, and what the infantile experience is like from a subjective stance. She had always noted that while infantile experience is piecemeal, and while the first introjects are part-objects, they are not experienced as such in the infant's actual phantasy. On the contrary, the good part-object is experienced as a total situation, and the power and fullness of experiencing it represents a whole to the infant. What is objectively understood as an isolated event, unintegrated into the perception of other aspects of reality, is not in fact registered as such.

This is important because of its implications for the positive aspect of Klein's theory, which is not as visible as it needs to be. It implies that when the infant begins to assimilate a broader reality, he does so from within a good experiential framework. Integration, according to Klein, leads him to relate to the 'complete person of his *loved* object' that is, an assimilation of badness and disturbance into an overall secure, nurturing framework. The concept of projective identification reinforces the idea that disturbance is only absorbed by the psyche much more indirectly, that is, after its projection into the mother. Klein did not agree with

Fairbairn's suggestion that the bad object is introjected before a good one. Her divergence from him is reinforced in her overall model, which depicts the mind as able to accommodate and address negative experiences and disturbing aspects of the self when they no longer threaten to overwhelm the good object. Klein's framework thus sites the natural existential locus of the infant with the positive experiences of pleasure, love and security, in other words, within the total situation of the good object. It is this that splitting processes seek initially to protect, by creating a firm boundary which preserves the good experience:

> To return to the splitting process, which I take to be a pre-condition for the young infant's relative stability; during the first few months he predominantly keeps the good object apart from the bad one and thus, in a fundamental way, preserves it ... At the same time, this primal division only succeeds if there is an adequate capacity for love ... My hypothesis is, therefore, that the capacity for love gives impetus both to integrating tendencies and to successful primal splitting ... This sounds paradoxical. But since, as I said, integration is based on a strongly rooted good object that forms the core of the ego, a certain amount of splitting is essential for integration; for it preserves the good object and later on enables the ego to synthesise the two aspects of it.[20]

With this thinking, the difference between adult schizoid states and the infantile schizoid mechanisms is finally clarified. The former represent a highly destructive process in a vulnerable, over-defended individual, whereas the latter express the aggressive protection of good experience that alone enables the creation of the ego's core. Accordingly, it is mistaken to view the Kleinian infant as a destructive, schizoid being, because he uses aggressive defences for a purpose, and only becomes habituated to them in the event of undue suffering and anxiety. And yet, even with this thinking, there is no complacency in Klein's vision. Her infant never becomes an ideal heroic fighter against environmental privations or ill-treatment. He remains a tragic being, and himself creates some of the worst obstacles to his own development. This becomes especially evident in Klein's last major paper, her 1957 work on primary envy.

NOTES

1. See E. B. Spillius (ed.) (1988) 'Part two: projective identification', in *Melanie Klein Today. 1: Mainly Theory.* London: Routledge. pp. 81–7.
2. Klein, M. (1975) 'Notes on some schizoid mechanisms', in *Envy and Gratitude*, London: The Hogarth Press. (First published in 1946.) p. 8.
3. ibid., p. 11.
4. ibid., p. 6.
5. ibid., p. 7.
6. ibid., p. 4.
7. Winnicott, D. W. (1975) 'Primitive emotional development', in *Through Paediatrics to Psycho-Analysis.* London: The Hogarth Press. (First published in 1945.) p. 149.

8. Phillips, A. (1990) *Winnicott*. London: Fontana Modern Masters.
9. Klein, M. (1975) 'Notes on some schizoid mechanisms', in *Envy and Gratitude*. London: The Hogarth Press. (First published in 1946.) p. 4.
10. Winnicott, D. W. (1975) 'Primitive emotional development', in *Through Paediatrics to Psycho-Analysis*. London: The Hogarth Press. (First published in 1945.) pp. 149–50.
11. ibid., pp. 149–50.
12. ibid., p. 149.
13. ibid., p. 150.
14. Phillips, A. (1990) *Winnicott*. London: Fontana Modern Masters. p. 79.
15. Winnicott, D. W. (1975) 'Primitive emotional development', in *Through Paediatrics to Psycho-Analysis*. London: The Hogarth Press. (First published in 1945.) p. 155.
16. Klein, M. (1975) 'Notes on some schizoid mechanisms', in *Envy and Gratitude*. London: The Hogarth Press. (First published in 1946.) p. 5.
17. ibid., p. 5(n).
18. Winnicott, D. W. (1975) 'Primitive emotional development', in *Through Paediatrics to Psycho-Analysis*. London: The Hogarth Press. (First published in 1945.) p. 150.
19. Kernberg, O. (1989) in T. Sandler (ed.) *Projection, Identification, Projective Identification*. London: Karnac Books. p. 83.
20. Klein, M. (1975) 'Envy and gratitude', in *Envy and Gratitude*. London: The Hogarth Press. (First published in 1957.) p. 191.

CHAPTER 12

'So unattainable' – Two Accounts of Envy

W hen Klein first presented her thinking on envy to her colleagues, Winnicott is reported to have uttered despairingly, 'Oh no, she *can't* do this!'[1] One of her most staunch adherents, Paula Heimann, already increasingly estranged from Klein, would come to regard this moment as marking an irrevocable break between the two of them. The occasion of Klein's presentation was the 1955 International Psychoanalytic Congress in Geneva, and these reactions aptly indicate the misgivings with which the concept was generally received.

A decade had elapsed since the time of the Controversial Discussions. Klein, now 73 years old, had not only survived professionally, but had also, in Ernest Jones's words, 'lived to see her work firmly established'.[2] She could also witness the developments in the growing Kleinian group which was holding its own in the British Psychoanalytic Society and making an impact with new publications.

Yet this more established status did not guarantee a universal acceptance or even a tolerance of Klein's thinking, because far from mellowing over time, her ideas seemed to have reached a new extremity. This inevitably caused disagreements even within her own circle, with some resulting rifts and defections. As against this, there was a loyal group of Kleinians who positively welcomed the new thinking presented in 1955. A sharply divided response thus greeted the Geneva paper, which was to be published two years later in 1957 as 'Envy and gratitude'. What was it about the theory of envy that created such a mixed reception, and that so outraged some of Klein's psychoanalytic colleagues?

Klein's paper on envy is not a simple case of a theory that has gone too far. In important respects it can even be regarded as an unexpected final destination into which the theory has found its way, or possibly even blundered. However, the paper's relationship with Klein's lifelong thinking is also not so simply captured. While some parts of it continue to hold with the previous body of thought, others break this link with the past. Before examining this, it is worth surveying Klein's line of reasoning in what turned out to be her last major original contribution to psychoanalysis.

Klein did not consciously intend to present any kind of revision of her thinking, since she continued to hold with the intricate picture of early mental life that she had built up so assiduously over the preceding 30-year period. But she wanted to add one more element to her thinking on the first experiences of infancy, and this was based on an insight that seemed to her to complete her vision. The element that she added was her idea of primary envy. Throughout her career, and throughout the time of elaborating her ideas on the depressive and paranoid-schizoid positions, along with the many complex defences and fragmentation processes that she unravelled, Klein did not abandon the notion of the infant's early attacks on the mother's breast and body. She now returned to this fundamental scenario of mental life for a further elaboration.

Klein's paper on envy begins with an emphasis, yet again, on the first good object and with a most evocative reminder of its unique value to the infant. She refers to the great importance of the infant's first object relation which is 'the relation to the mother's breast and to the mother'. She reiterates her conclusion that 'if this primal object, which is introjected, takes root in the ego with relative security, the basis for a satisfactory development is laid'.[3] By now, the reader might feel that Klein is endlessly repeating her descriptions of the good object, and that these are in danger of becoming something of an indoctrinating chant. It almost seems as if Klein herself is afraid to lose sight of the good object in her theory, and that each paper which studies destructive processes begins with a ritual establishment of its undying value and secure theoretical status. However, Klein's repetitions are not merely obsessive, they are also creative. Each time she contemplates the good object anew, she sees another facet of it, adding further subtle brush strokes to a deepening perspective. In her envy paper, she proceeds to spell out again, with a renewed and eloquent emphasis, further dimensions of the good object. She suggests that under the dominance of oral impulses the breast is '... instinctively felt to be the source of nourishment and therefore, in a deeper sense, of life itself'. When the infant is first plunged into the turmoil of post-natal existence, it is through a 'physical and mental closeness to the gratifying breast' that he can regain his lost sense of the secure 'prenatal unity with the mother'.[4]

Klein states again that theoretically viewed, the good breast forms the core of the ego, but now discusses this with an added depth of conviction. She points out that because of its significance, the breast is far more than a mere physical object of gratification. As far as the infant is concerned, '... the whole of his instinctual desires and unconscious phantasies imbue the breast with qualities going far beyond the actual nourishment that it affords.' This is a final confirmation that the first good object has a unique place in mental life, as it does throughout the life cycle, since the human individual continues to depend on the self- nourishing, creative core that was introjected in infancy. In the unconscious mind, the good breast remains forever the prototype of 'maternal goodness, inexhaustible patience and generosity as well as creativeness'. In a harsh world it provides the human individual with no less than the 'foundation for hope, trust, and the belief in goodness'.[5]

The descriptions of the good object in 'Envy and gratitude' are among the most poignant in Klein's writings, and also the most unequivocal. She takes obvious care to spell out in full its importance in her now-completed vision. Such descriptions are essential to the thinking that follows. It is the very importance of the good object which alerts the reader to the seriousness of any threats to it, and Klein's intense picture of its essence reflects what the infant stands to lose. An envious attack is therefore the most serious threat to mental development, because it 'contributes to the infant's difficulties in building up the good object'.

The notion of infantile attacks on the first good object were not at all new in Klein's thinking. She had already described and explained how such attacks distort the infant's relationship with the mother and turn her into a bad object, thus stirring deep anxieties and triggering early defences. She had suggested that this, in turn, undermines the ability to introject a good nurturing object into the psyche. Klein now added to her thinking more immediate, observational descriptions that are more universal in tone. It is difficult to know who Klein was addressing in her mind, but it seems to be more than simply psychoanalytic colleagues. Her observations are not delivered in technical psychoanalytic terminology, and can suitably extend her address to a broader lay community that is normally charged with infant care, such as ordinary mothers, grandmothers or nursery nurses: 'Aggression towards the mother interferes with the quality of enjoyment that the baby can experience, and therefore also impairs the baby's ability to experience new sources of gratification.'[6] It is pertinent that Klein's most immediate experience of infancy in her personal life was no longer as a professional, via child psychoanalysis, but as a grandmother, via ordinary familial contact with her grandchildren. A grand-maternal vantage point added to her writing some new, and more domestic, ways of describing infancy.

This, however, does not imply that she had stopped thinking theoretically, or indeed psychoanalytically. Thus far in her thinking, she had been assuming that the infant's sadistic attacks are triggered by an early onset of the Oedipus complex, and by added epistemophilic urges to penetrate, possess and control the maternal body. This now seemed to her over-generalized. The strange urge to attack the first source of nurture, though indeed Oedipal in the archaic sense that she had always conceived, was now seen to owe its source to more specific elements in mental life. These elements too could fit into the register of lay thinking that was less concerned with psychoanalytic constructs, and more with everyday emotions.

Klein boldly ventured the suggestion that one such trigger of early attacks is the infant's primary envy towards the first good object. This universal emotion is present at the beginning of life, and creates a major interference in the infant's struggles to take in fulfilment and goodness from the feeding breast. Envy intrudes into what should have remained a carefree relationship of pleasure and love with the breast, and preys on the infant's first emotional partnership. Instead of an unhindered ability to relish the happy relationship and absorb its essence, the infant is undermined and disturbed in his very efforts to establish a secure base in the world. Furthermore, all this comes about through the tragic circumstance of internal forces. Envy, the tragic flaw of the human species, is an anti-life force that owes its origin to the death instinct.

There is no doubt about the gravity with which Klein viewed envy. It now took the place that sadism occupied in her early thinking, but was also the specific phenomenon that expressed the essence of human destructiveness. As with all her previous thinking though, Klein continued to underscore a fundamental and conflictual duality in all mental operations, and so suggested that envy is but one side of a coin, the other of which is gratitude. While envy diminishes the quality of the infant's first pleasures, gratitude enhances it.

As suggested, the discussions of phenomena such as envy and gratitude are immediately familiar in lay terms. But as a result, they do not lend themselves easily to the kind of conceptualizing required for a convincing portrayal of archaic infantile processes in psychoanalytic terms. But before addressing this, Klein needed to spell out that envy is not unique among early triggers of sadistic attacks, and in fact fits into a context in which a number of other such processes are active. There was a significant reason for conceiving of a number of different processes. Klein had not abandoned the belief, formed at the beginning of her career, that the Oedipal scenario is the basic arena of human aggression and therefore of infantile attacks on the mother's body. She had conceived of this scenario in primitive terms, as involving the infant's phantasy urges to plunder the resources of the mother's body. While the idea of a primary envy could go some way towards making sense of such attacks, it was not in itself sufficient to account for them fully.

For a start, the Oedipal experience implied not simply envy, but jealousy, and the two needed to be differentiated. Klein suggested that jealousy is experienced in relation to a twosome or a couple, and triggered by possessive desires for a loved object when it is out of reach and seen to belong to another. Because of this triangular context, jealousy had always figured in psychoanalytic awareness. Klein now added that it figures also before the time at which the infant can clearly recognize both parents as they are, because there is a fundamental psychic ability to intuit the existence of rivals who have 'taken away the mother's breast and the mother'.

While jealousy was familiar in psychoanalysis, not so envy. Unlike jealousy, which focuses on the rivalry for a good object, envy does not place value on the object at all. On the contrary, it focuses direct aggression not on rivals for the object, but on the object itself, and represents a malign resentment of its goodness. Klein suggested that while jealousy is triggered by an outside disturbance such as awareness of a rival, envy 'stems from within', is 'insatiable', and 'always finds an object to focus on'.[7]

However, even with this differentiation between envy and jealousy, there was a need to designate one more aggressive phenomenon that was at work in the early relationship with the mother. Klein's vision of infancy had always involved the idea of acquisitive, territorial urges towards the maternal body, but jealousy and envy went only some way in accounting for these. This now led her to suggest a further element that could be identified in early sadistic attacks, and this was agreed. Klein underscored greed as the particular form of sadism implicated in human acquisitive and territorial instincts. She felt that unlike envy and jealousy, greed accounts specifically for ferocious phantasies of 'scooping out' the contents of the breast and ruthlessly extracting all the goodness from the object. As a form of aggression, greed is an exploitative tendency that underpins urges to plunder and rob. It was immediately apparent that greed, though different from envy, could be stimulated by it. One response to envy is to steal what is good from the object and so deprive it.

In her descriptions of envy, jealousy and greed, Klein does not spare the detail of the brutality of human destructiveness. However, out of all three traits, it is envy which is focal in her thinking, and which epitomizes human destructiveness. Jealousy and greed are two forms of aggression which are ultimately possessive, and which therefore hinge on the mental ability to accommodate the notion of a good object. Envy, however, is another matter because it is purely destructive. The urge that propels envy is not acquisitive or possessive, which would be more understandable, but gratuitous and spoiling. Its typical phantasy scenario is of projecting poisoning, faecal parts of the self into the breast in order to spoil its good contents. It therefore represents not aggressive acquisition, but damaging, anti-life and death-instinct tendencies.

With her thinking on envy, gratitude, jealousy and greed, Klein also shifted the focus of her theorizing away from mental mechanisms, and on to particular emotional currents that shape the course of mental life. She highlighted the way in which the emotional life of infancy underpins personality in the normal adult, and how such early emotionality is an essential ingredient in mental development. This is not to suggest that Klein decided to abandon Freud's drive theory and the belief in a pleasure-seeking infant, for an exclusive study of an object-seeking, emotional infant. In fact, throughout 'Envy and gratitude', her thinking continues to point to an underpinning drive theory, and there are frequent references to the importance of libidinal factors such as the infant's libidinal enjoyment of the breast-feeding experience. However, by this stage in her thinking, emotions, and not only instinctual gratification, are felt to be essential to such enjoyment. As is the case in adult sexual intercourse, infantile love greatly intensifies the sensual pleasure experienced with the good feeding object, therefore facilitating its introjection. In the same way, gratitude also enhances the infant's enjoyment, because it designates a sense of gain from good interactions, and so counteracts the envy of deprivation.

And yet, however interesting this focus on emotions proved to be, and however 'lay' its language, it was also, along with the other key features of Klein's paper, difficult to assimilate in psychoanalytic circles. The worst qualms about it seemed to be clustered around three main objections: that it was based on an untenable negativity; that it attributed inappropriate maturity to infantile thought processes; and that it laid too little emphasis on the role of the parenting environment as a factor in human destructiveness and pathology. It is worth examining the substance of these objections, not least because they continue to this day, and can still result in a wholesale rejection of a Kleinian text that is, characteristically, far more complex than it purports to be. This is not to deny the fact that the objections find ample confirmation in the texts. But such confirmation reflects only one of the strands in Klein's argument, and a strand, furthermore that has a complicated existence alongside other, more contradictory, thinking. But before discussing this further, it is necessary to evaluate the objections just cited.

The first of these, which concerns Klein's undue negativity, would have been met by a retort that her vision was presenting realism and not pessimism, and was for those who had the courage to face the reality of human nature as it is. However, as far as the non-Kleinian listeners to the 1955 presentation were concerned, the idea of an envious infant seemed to take Klein's thinking right back to its early gloom, and merely provide a new version of an original-sin theory. It seemed pessimistic, and not realistic, to regard the human being as starting life with the most gratuitous and anti-social of all the seven deadly sins, and yet Klein was clear that 'it is unconsciously felt to be the greatest sin of all'.[8]

Looked at in today's terms, there is no doubt that Klein's account of envy is sobering to a fault. The negativity of which she is accused is amply evident in her postulation of a particularly gratuitous form of envious sadism, which is directed at the breast even when it is available to the infant and offers pleasure, security and nourishment. This senseless aggression expresses an anti-life intolerance of the goodness that is encountered in the world, even when it is actually in the process of being enjoyed by the infant. Klein explains that the envy which gratuitously targets the available breast and is 'determined by destructive impulses ... [is triggered by] the very ease with which the milk comes ... [because] though the infant feels gratified by it ... [it none the less] also gives rise to envy because this gift seems something so unattainable ...'.[9]

The bleak outlook created through such beliefs was compounded for theoretical reasons. Klein's thinking on primary envy made use of the already unpopular concept of the death instinct, and furthermore, took it to new extremes. To attribute destructive impulses to the infant was one thing; it was quite another to propose a curious anti-life tendency which underpins attacks on the very mothering resources that are essential to mental growth. Klein's vision thus portrayed the infant as initially thwarting the good maternal provision instead of welcoming it, and this threw into question a more reassuring view that the human organism simply strives to grow, always making full use of all the nurturing that comes its way. It also depicted human destructiveness and pathology as rooted in innate rather than reactive factors. In this thinking, the infant was seen as arriving in the world with a constitutionally determined degree of envy, and it was this predisposition, rather than maternal mishandling or environmental suffering, which was supposed to explain degrees of individual destructiveness.

Such thinking led immediately to the second key objection to Klein's theory of primary envy, which was that it appeared to force her thinking into a false position on the role of external experience. Thus far her vision maintained that external mothering, and the mother's repeated reassuring appearances, are the very means whereby infantile persecutory feelings are lessened, internal distortions are finally corrected and a reality sense, along with emotional security, is established. It is the actual mother and her reassuring presence who enables the resolution of the depressive position, which alone makes healthy development possible. In this thinking the actual mother is of crucial importance, and Klein further underscored such importance when she considered external factors which affect the infant negatively. Real events such as a difficult birth, the mother's nervous inability to enjoy her infant and her general mental state, are all factors which can make the infant more prone to persecutory feelings and the corresponding defensive aggression.

With her thinking on primary envy, however, Klein now appeared to be discounting the significance of the actual parenting which the child encounters. In fact, such a false position is not altogether adopted by Klein, because parts of 'Envy and gratitude' continue to state the need for repeated good experiences by the infant during growth. However, this does not prevent some hasty conclusions, such as, for example, Klein's controversial suggestion that '... some infants are exposed to great deprivations and unfavourable circumstances, and yet do not develop excessive anxieties.'

The idea that infants who suffer 'great deprivations' can escape without a marked reaction of 'excessive anxiety' was felt to be untenable by Klein's critics. Great deprivations starve the psyche by definition, and can no more be discounted as pathogenic factors than malnourishment can be for physical growth. In any case, at the time of formulating her thoughts on envy, Klein was immersed in work with adult patients rather than with child patients, deprived or otherwise. On the other hand, Winnicott had substantial experience with deprived children, and his outlook immediately highlighted Klein's neglect of the issue of actual mothering in mental development. His perspective continues to find support in our current experience of psychoanalytic work with children. While there are, indeed, individual variations which predispose deprived children to a greater or lesser mental resilience, none who have actually suffered from 'great deprivations' can escape from some 'excessive anxiety', and the corresponding need to build defences against it.

The third, and perhaps most powerful objection to Klein's theory of envy hinges on the nature of archaic mental processes. The idea of an envious infant seemed farfetched even in terms of Klein's own thinking, and even to those who accepted the kind of early ego activity that she hypothesized. It was difficult to see how there could be a sufficient cognitive capacity in infancy to enable a clear demarcation of maternal qualities that can be envied. It is quite true that in her early thinking, Klein had already suggested an infantile awareness of the maternal body's contents. However, she had formulated the relationship to these in much more archaic terms, as propelled by instinctive oral urges to absorb the goodness offered by the mother, itself equated with a material substance such as actual nourishment or nourishing object. In her primitive phantasy life, the well-fed infant equates her satiety with a good, incorporated breast, which has become a concrete internal substance.

With the introduction of the notion of envy, these terms of reference seemed to alter, because Klein now appeared to be discussing the infant's ability to grasp the significance of abstract qualities. Envy is triggered by 'the very ease with which the milk comes', suggests Klein, because 'this gift seems something so unattainable'. The breast is now envied its gifts, something that Klein also describes as its creative powers. However, this implies the infant's ability to employ abstract thinking which can designate nonmaterial qualities in differentiated others. It seems to go well beyond Klein's much more careful phrasing, used earlier in the very same paper on envy, when she explains that 'the whole of [the infant's] instinctual desires and unconscious phantasies imbue the breast with qualities going far beyond the actual nourishment that it affords.' It is legitimate to suggest that the breast is imbued with qualities, because this does not imply that the qualities are recognized intellectually. While qualities can certainly be experienced along with the feeding, the infant can continue to experience both as an undifferentiated oneness – a material substance that is being incorporated. This more careful phrasing does not seem to extend to all of Klein descriptions of primary envy. There are times at which she appears to be suggesting an envy that emerges from sophisticated comparative assessments which seem well beyond an infant, let alone a newborn.

Bearing in mind such reactions, it is not surprising that Klein's paper was experienced as provocative. However, it is also significant that the objections just cited are not altogether psychoanalytic. The complaints that the envy theory is negative, solipsistic in its exclusion of environmental influence, and attributes unlikely maturity to infantile processes are all commonsense complaints, based on prevailing cultural views of the limits of an infantile mind. And since psychoanalytic theory often flies in the face of ordinary expectations, any legitimate critique of Klein's envy theory would need to go beyond commonsense, and be based on psychoanalytic terms of reference.

And yet, when Klein's envy paper is examined in psychoanalytic terms, it continues to raise, rather than resolve, contentious issues. One of the difficulties with 'Envy and gratitude' is that the commonsense objections to it find further substance when it is examined from a metapsychological perspective. To suggest that the infant envies the available breast and the 'very ease with which the milk comes' because it seems 'unattainable', flies in the face of a fundamental psychoanalytic tenet, which is Freud's conception of omnipotent processes in early life. According to this, hallucinatory processes in early life act precisely to prevent a sense that the 'ease with which the milk comes' is not within the orbit of omnipotent control, and so 'unattainable'. What is more, the Kleinian concept of phantasy which was so focal, and defended at such length in the Controversial Discussions, relied for its very sense on the Freudian idea of hallucinatory wish-fulfilment, made possible through omnipotent processes. Only a radical revision of this thinking and a decision to dispense with the idea of omnipotence in infancy, could justify the notion that the infant at birth can appreciate the fact that the milk which comes with ease is not omnipotently manufactured by her desires. And since Klein continued to hold with the beliefs about infantile omnipotent mechanisms, it is hard to know how she intended to fit her ideas on envy into the rest of her framework.

This, added to all the commonsense objections, might seem to seal the fate of Klein's concept of primary envy, and confirm the many reservations expressed about it since the time when it was first presented. However, to do so would be premature, and also to miss the essence of Klein's vision at this stage of her thinking. Her theory of envy undoubtedly has flaws, and is often couched in deceptively naive and unlikely descriptions. It is also, characteristically, much more complex upon a closer scrutiny. 'Envy and gratitude' is not a single hypothesis that stirs a particular set of objections. It is, in important ways, a text that is having an argument with itself, and that puts forward both sides of this argument. As suggested earlier, one strand of this argument is more in keeping with Klein's earlier thinking, while the other strand seems at odds with it.

There is a counter-argument to Klein's complicated notion of the destructive envy triggered by the 'ease with which the milk comes'. What is often not sufficiently emphasized, and may seem of little consequence, is that Klein discusses not one, but two forms of primary envy, and that each of these provide alternative final destinations for her theory. The first form of envy, which is the gratuitous aggression towards the good, available breast, seems to confirm the melancholic view of a death-instinct-dominated human nature that undoubtedly forms a powerful strand in Klein's overall theory. If it is taken as the main message of her paper, it seems to confirm it as the fitting conclusion to a treatise on human negativity. However, with a second form of envy, Klein presents an alternative to this senseless, death-instinct envy of the available breast, and so offers a different conclusion which suggests a different kind of treatise. This is a much more forgiving one, about infantile fragility and the consequences of early deprivation.

It is significant, and largely overlooked, that Klein also suggests a second form of envy that is triggered by the *unavailable* breast, and by the pains and suffering of deprivation. This second form immediately depicts a more justified envious aggression in the infant. Klein describes how it is experienced when the baby is inadequately fed, so that his greed and persecutory anxiety are increased, leading to the sense that 'when the breast deprives him, it becomes bad'. The implications of this line of thinking are substantial. By putting it forward, Klein necessarily brings into the picture the role of the external environment in determining infantile aggression. In this alternative, it is the deprived infant who understandably becomes aggressive, and to this is added the idea that such aggression can also take the form of envy.

The counter-argument, though offering a much less negative outlook, might not initially appear to resolve the difficulties raised by Klein's primary envy theory, particularly since it continues to beg questions about the nature of infantile mental processes. Can the infant really know that she is deprived, and if so, is envy the most likely response? Such doubts are reinforced by Klein's apparent attribution of adult ideation to the infant, when she suggests, for example, that '... when the breast deprives him, it becomes bad because it keeps the milk, love and care associated with the good breast all to itself.' And yet in spite of such an unlikely sounding early scenario, Klein's ideas on deprivation do fit into her view of primitive psychic life in a much more logical way, and represent the strand of 'Envy and gratitude' that is in continuity with a central aspect of Klein's lifelong work that portrays early life as a struggle to establish a core of goodness and security in the personality. According to this, early deprivation amounts to more than vague experiences of disturbance or pain.

For a start, Klein now believes that the newborn psyche already anticipates an encounter with a good object. Natural survival urges, stamped with oral characteristics, activate an instinctive quest for nurture, and are, in this sense, inscribed with an intuition of what is sought. Even the infant who has not encountered a good object experiences a specific state of tension that points to what is missing, because '... there is in the infant's mind a phantasy of an inexhaustible breast which is his greatest desire'. This has implications towards the way in which frustration is experienced.

As discussed, Freud suggested that the infant's psyche copes with the tension of frustration through a process of hallucinatory wish-fulfilment, which temporarily fends off a painful awareness of what is missing. Freud argued, however, that if satisfaction is unduly delayed, the capacity for hallucinating becomes exhausted and breaks down. Yet when this happens it also serves a function, because the infant, no longer hallucinating, is able to take in a portion of reality. Klein's understanding of the envy of the depriving breast concerns precisely the moment at which the capacity for hallucination breaks down. Unlike Freud, she did not believe that it was simply the occasion for accommodating some reality. She had already spelled out her belief that it is only later in development, at the time of integration, that the infant is actually able to recognize a whole reality and accept the idea of the object's unavailability. Therefore, before this level of recognition is reached, the very young psyche responds to a breakdown in hallucination in a more primitive manner, by replacing one phantasy with another. The phantasy of the good feeding breast gives way to the experience of an obstructive, withholding force that assumes the phantasy form of a bad breast. Therefore, when hallucination becomes exhausted, the infant, now exposed to his painful need, feels assailed by a bad object.

The complicated notion that this object is felt to hold on to itself the desired satisfaction is also in keeping with Klein's earlier conclusions and overall vision. She had already suggested that infants are born with an intuition of rivals who can monopolize life supplies. As well as this, she had formulated ideas on the mental processes of projection and displacement. These earlier formulations account for her suggestion that the infant, when frustrated, attributes to the object his own aggressive intent to monopolize the source of goodness. When hallucination breaks down, the desired satisfaction so recently conjured by the mind does not simply fade without trace: its comforting essence is now imagined to have been transferred elsewhere. Alongside this experience, the frustrated, desiring part of the infant has been projected and displaced on to the object. It is thus that the object is felt to withhold, possess and enjoy the good breast.

One of the revealing elements in this vision is the link between paranoid processes and envy. Klein could now see that the earlier the deprivation suffered, the more likely the individual to resort to paranoid interpretations that depict deprivation as a deliberate malevolence inflicted by others. In such conclusions, she was also, at this stage of her life, relying on substantial experience with adult patients, which enabled her to note evident links between extended childhood deprivation and the emergence of a chronic, paranoid resentment towards others in later life.

Out of the two forms of envy that Klein describes in her chapter, it is evident that she attaches far more importance to the first one, the gratuitous envy of the available breast, while the second is almost added as an afterthought. And yet, as suggested, it is the first kind, the envy of the available breast and its creative powers, which is difficult to fit into her psychoanalytic theory on archaic mental processes. What is more, when Klein comes to illustrate envy with clinical vignettes, it is the second form of envy, experienced towards the depriving breast, which regularly surfaces in her examples.

KLEIN'S CLINICAL EXAMPLES OF ENVY

The adult patients whom Klein describes experience envy when they feel deprived, because this always leads them to imagine that someone else is withholding and enjoying the satisfaction owing to them. For example, Klein gives the illustration of a female patient who missed two sessions because of a pain in her shoulder. Klein describes how upon her return to therapy, the patient was full of grievance because she felt that while she had been unwell, no one cared about her or bothered to enquire after her health. The patient then related a dream in which she is in a restaurant awaiting service, but no one comes. She decides to join a queue and help herself. In front of her is a determined woman who is helping herself to two or three little cakes. The patient decides to do the same.

The patient's associations to this dream reveal a connection between the woman in the queue and Klein, as well as connecting the little cakes with the person of Klein. Klein interprets the dream as showing the patient's feeling that she had missed out on two sessions, the two or three little cakes, and that while she was away ill, the analyst not only withheld nurture, but fed herself. In this situation, the analyst is regarded as a depriving object who withholds solicitude and sessions from the patient, neither enquiring after her when she is ill, nor finding ways of providing sessions that cannot be attended. Moreover, the analyst is not only seen as withholding emotional resources, but as keeping these for herself, so that she can 'have her cake and eat it'. Such envy is underpinned by more infantile phantasies which depict the analyst as the possessor of an infinite feeding resource on which the patient depends. They thus fit in with Klein's suggestion that the infant envies the breast the very ease with which it can produce milk. However, it is also significant that in this example, the breast is envied for being unavailable, and in this sense depriving, while the patient was unwell.

In other clinical examples, deprivation similarly surfaces as a cause of envy. Klein describes another female patient who, upon enjoying a measure of professional success, needs to feel that she has completely triumphed over the analyst. In the patient's dream, the analyst appears as a cow chewing a woolly carpet, while the patient sits on a magic carpet which is hovering at the top of a tree. Klein is all too aware of the rivalrous envy in this dream. The patient imagines that, professionally speaking, she has reached the 'top of the tree', leaving behind an old cow of an analyst whose words are woolly and worthless. Klein suggests that this is a full devaluation of the analyst out of envy. However, she yet again enlists a sense of deprivation as an explanatory cause, describing how in infancy this particular patient suffered 'a grievance against the mother who had not fed her satisfactorily'.

In a further example, Klein describes a male patient who dreams about trying, without success, to help a delinquent boy, and then accepts a lift from the boy's father. However, instead of driving him in the right direction, the father drives him further and further away from his destination. Klein interprets this as a transference criticism of herself, for taking him in the wrong direction. The patient thus expresses an envious devaluation of her work and the resulting mistrust in her ability to provide help. Having isolated himself from the analyst and lost faith in the direction suggested by her, he is left feeling unable to deal with the delinquent boy in himself. From his viewpoint, he is alone and deprived of a trustworthy analyst.

Before examining further the link between deprivation and envy, another, more urgent issue claims attention and begs an immediate question. How could Klein tell that her patients' attacks stemmed from envy, as opposed to, say, anger, or indeed justified criticism? For example, the aggression expressed in their dreams might equally represent veiled complaints about her analytic misjudgements or failures. And indeed Klein was preoccupied with this very conundrum. At first she felt that she could address it satisfactorily by enlisting for evidence contextual factors. She assumed that it would be possible to determine if envy was in question by taking into account the broader clinical context within which the session material and the dreams were understood. She therefore underscored the fact that the issue of envy had already been recognized by the patients whose material she cites. However, Klein was not satisfied with this. Psychoanalytic technique could not be based on what the patient is able to acknowledge consciously. And while the broader clinical context certainly provides more useful details, further material does not, in itself, constitute evidence.

It was this awareness that led Klein to examine very closely situations in which she believed she was witnessing envy in the clinical situation, and she gradually found that she was able to offer a much more substantiated mode of detecting it. She realized that destructive attacks on the analyst can be considered as envious if they follow on from positive analytic work from which the patient benefited. This thinking immediately led her to appreciate a very important link: that between her theory of envy and a phenomenon that had been troubling psychoanalysts throughout their history, which was the negative therapeutic reaction.

THE NEGATIVE THERAPEUTIC REACTION

It is already widely appreciated that Freud encountered obstacles to clinical work as soon as he established his method of free association. Far from associating freely and easily, his patients' minds would become blank at crucial moments, and he came to view this as a manifestation of the resistive force of repression. It was repression, Freud reasoned, that was preventing ideation from emerging into the patient's consciousness, and so creating a resistance to the flow of material. This thinking developed and found a much fuller expression in increasingly sophisticated understandings of repression and of the mind that activated it. It was then that Freud realized that there is a much more formidable obstacle to psychoanalytic progress, which is the negative therapeutic reaction. He noted situations in which the patient's resistance had been interpreted satisfactorily and led to visible relief. And yet instead of the expected further improvement, there was an inexplicable worsening of the patient's condition. In the face of this strange phenomenon, Freud was obliged to conclude that the patient's deterioration denoted a masochistic reaction against personal gain, itself rooted in an unconscious sense of guilt which led the patient to feel undeserving.

Klein now shed new light on a factor that could equally be at root when a patient begins to make progress and inexplicably reacts badly to this. An envy of the analyst's ability to help could be such a factor. To receive actual help and experience change taking place is also alarming to that part of the patient which can suddenly feel inferior by comparison with what is offered. The very means of getting better is beyond his control and lies with the analyst, to be dispensed at the latter's discretion. This can arouse a deep sense of dependence and inadequacy, thus contributing to envy. Within the analytic situation envy is therefore most likely to be manifest in inappropriate criticisms of the analyst, or doubts about the value of analytic work when it has already proved to offer relief.

In other words, the typical negative therapeutic reaction which Freud had attributed to unconscious guilt, was now not only seen to have a further cause in envy, but also to be a good prognostic tool for establishing its presence. When patients react badly to progress, they are not necessarily depriving themselves through feeling guilty and unworthy, and could equally be attacking the analyst in order to spoil her good work. In one of Klein's examples such spoiling surfaces clearly: she describes a male patient who dreams that he is smoking a pipe which contains the shredded pages of one of Klein's books. She understands this as his envious tearing up and destroying of her work. Klein's suggestion that envy can explain a negative therapeutic reaction proved of lasting value for psychoanalytic technique. However, this insight did not address the issue of the source of envy, and the controversy provoked by Klein's suggestion of a primary envy of the available breast.

ENVY AND DEPRIVATION

As suggested, in spite of her theoretical emphasis on the unwarranted envy of the available breast, nowhere do Klein's clinical examples demonstrate envy other than as linked with deprivation, even though this becomes apparent only on a close examination of the text. On the face of it, it is obvious that Klein does not focus on deprivation as the single, or even the main source of an envious disposition. On the contrary, as suggested, she allots a more important place in her theory to the gratuitous envy of the available good object. As well as this, she does not discuss, but only refers briefly to, the source of envy that she notes in her clinical examples. What is more, the text makes it clear that even the second form of envy, that stirred by deprivation, is not simply defined. A patient's experience of deprivation can be relative and subjectively determined. The analyst may not in reality be depriving, but can be none the less perceived as such for various reasons. By the same token, there are infants who receive adequate mothering and yet remain frustrated. As far as they are concerned, the object is depriving. Above all, there is the strange case of those who are responsible for creating their own deprivation. For example, the female patient who misses two sessions might be shunning the analyst deliberately, and so is herself the cause of the deprivation which then stirs her envious grievance.

With this thinking Klein soon ran into an intractable problem of origins. Was it primary envy which initially led the patient to disable the analyst (by not coming to the sessions) hence creating a vicious cycle of self-deprivation and further envy, or was it an initial sense of deprivation, however subjectively perceived, which led to an aggrieved avoidance of the analyst and so triggered a secondary reaction of envy? In grappling with this circular, chicken-and-egg problem, Klein noted further complications. People may not experience envy in simple, conscious ways, but quite the contrary. In the unconscious, primitive levels of the mind, envy is accompanied by destructive phantasies that lead to an archaic sense of having omnipotently attacked and damaged the object. To acknowledge it would lead to guilt and self-criticism, and such feelings need to be evaded through the use of defences. What is more, the typical defences against envy aim at diminishing the object in order to lessen envy; in other words, the object is made out to be worthless, and the subject is thereby deprived.

Klein listed a range of such defences against envy. She suggested 'confusion', 'flight from the mother to other people', 'devaluation of the object', 'devaluation of the self', stirring up envy in others, greed, the stifling of love and intensifying of hatred. While these are described as defences by her, they do not denote mechanisms, nor are they designated with existing psychoanalytic concepts and fitted to a metapsychological framework. Unlike splitting mechanisms, for example, they do not alter the structure of the mind or change the functioning of the ego. They are more in the nature of emotional and cognitive stratagems that are employed to deny or evade an experience of envy. So that, for example, confusion muddles the individual about whether the object is good or bad, hence blurring the actual value of the object of envy. A flight from the mother to other objects results in an abandonment of the envied object and a restless search for new and presumed better ones, and a devaluation of the object obviously implies that it need no longer be envied.

Since, as suggested, Klein is not describing complex mental mechanisms but everyday behaviours accessible to ordinary observation, it is relatively easy to identify the kinds of defences that she is describing. The idea of a secret envy can indeed make sense of those who confuse good and bad, who do not trust easily and hence do not have to inhabit a world in which others are trustworthy, valued and hence enviable. A flight from the mother makes sense of those who are always abandoning their existing relationships as worthless, and endlessly discovering new and supposedly better people. A devaluation of the object is perhaps the most illuminating of Klein's suggestions. A person who is critical and contemptuous is probably hiding envy, rather than merely exhibiting an over-confident personality. Klein's thinking underscored, for the first time, that arrogance and contempt are hallmark narcissistic responses to envy, and thus denote a secret insecurity and not an over-confidence, as might first appear to be the case.

An understanding of the defences against envy also led Klein to appreciate the importance of gratitude, and the disadvantages of insufficient gratitude. An individual who is enviably unable to acknowledge the good that is received is also prevented from enjoying it. He or she chooses to forgo the experience of receiving something worthwhile from others, and is thus deprived of pleasure and personal enrichment. Since envy sabotages the capacity to introject much that is so beneficial, it strikes at the root of object relations, preventing the subject's ability to benefit from them. A contemptuous devaluation of the object is thus underpinned by a deep envy, an inability to enjoy what is offered, a secret desire to destroy it and a resulting sense of deprivation.

This line of reasoning appears to confirm that for Klein envy does indeed come first, that it is primary and that it derives from a constitutionally determined degree of death instinct with which the infant is born. This primary envy is responsible for defensive devaluations of the object which amount to a self-deprivation, and it is only thus that the second form of envy, that triggered by deprivation, comes into the picture. A conclusion which puts envy first, has indeed influenced the way in which 'Envy and gratitude' has been understood in psychoanalytic circles. And while it does indeed figure in the paper, it is also, as suggested, only one of the strands in Klein's reasoning. However, it is possible to appreciate an alternative strand by noting a further significant factor. Klein's clinical examples are particularly illuminating in a specific respect. They illustrate that, clinically speaking, it is meaningless to propose two kinds of envy, because both forms are necessarily experienced as arising from deprivation. Even if deprivation arises because the patient has devalued the analyst, it is not possible to experience this envy in the first place other than from a disadvantaged frame of mind, since envy implies a sense that something is lacking. By the same token, the infant who can perceive the breast as possessing milk that flows with ease, only envies this if it seems unavailable, not under his omnipotent control, or what

Klein herself described as 'so unattainable'. In an opposite situation and when an infant feels that the milk is within his omnipotent control, it is experienced as a mere extension of his desiring self, to be conjured at will. There is nothing to envy when this is the case. Indeed when Klein was describing the gratuitous, death-instinct envy of the available breast, she crucially justified it precisely on the grounds that the gift of the milk coming with ease seems 'so unattainable'.

This creates some theoretical difficulties for the reader. Had Klein decided to place an explicit emphasis on deprivation in its broadest sense, a significant shift would result in the view of how envy develops. According to such a version, excessive envy would depend on an unusual sense of helplessness or deprivation in infancy, perhaps in cases where feeding and nurture are felt to be faulty, out of control or unreliable. There would be an unusual and premature breakdown in hallucination, leading to a torturing sense that goodness is never within easy reach. This would, in turn, trigger a sense of persecution and grievance, as well as give rise to envy.

And yet Klein would not have agreed with such an emphasis. Was it perhaps, as some believe, that in her old age she was expressing her full extremity of outlook and showing her true colours? Yet to conclude this is also to overlook a significant factor in Klein's emphasis on an envy of the available breast. She needed to postulate such an envy for theoretical, and not only clinical, reasons. Hers had never been a theory that placed all the developmental agents with outside influences and environmental factors. On the contrary, her intention in 'Envy and gratitude' was to focus on internal obstacles to development, and on internally derived destructive forces. What Klein wished to underscore in her paper is that the individual's particular expression of envy is a personal template of self-destructive predispositions which are innate. Each individual brings a different degree of death instinct or destructiveness into the world, and Klein's overall project in her theory of envy was to provide a key to solving internal, constitutional differences between people. An over-emphasis on deprivation and on the importance of actual maternal provision, would simply reinforce the natural desire to blame others, and so leave the individual without insight. Klein thus reasoned that: 'No doubt, in every individual, frustration and unhappy circumstances rouse some envy and hate throughout life, but the strength of these emotions and the way in which the individual copes with them varies considerably.'[10]

She was thus trying to isolate her object of study, which was the internal setting of individual dispositions, from the many external events that impact upon, and complicate it. She was keen to shed light on the painful mystery of individual variations, and on the largely inexplicable fact that some seem better able to handle life's hardships than others. Klein noted that at times of particular stress and anxiety, it is inevitable that for all individuals 'the belief and trust in good objects is shaken'. However, 'it is the *intensity* and the *duration* of such states of doubts, despondency and persecution that determine whether the ego is capable of reintegrating itself and of reinstating its good objects securely.'[11] Individual variations which predispose some individuals to a less resilient response were thus the target of Klein's explorations.

A theory of primary envy was intended to offer more analytical access to self-destructive tendencies which weaken the ability to cope with life's hardships. Individuals who are prone to excessive intolerance suffer more, and could be helped to understand the root of their resentment. And because envy is relatively accessible to observation and self-examination, Klein believed that it is the best way to approach internal obstacles which prevent a fuller enjoyment of life. As regards envy that is stirred by deprivation, she was aware that this too can be explored analytically. However, it is necessarily a secondary, reactive phenomenon and therefore contains no clues about the origin of internal and primary destructive factors.

Since Klein wished to account for innate factors that underpin individual variations in people's responses, she suggested a pure form of primary envy that expresses the death instinct directly, and that is not complicated by the turbulence of external events. Primary envy was thus important theoretically, for designating our worst internal obstacle – the innate factor that predisposes us to lesser or greater degrees of destructiveness. And yet this is notional in practice, because an essential aspect of the experience of envy described by Klein is that someone else is enjoying what is not available to the subject. The fact that Klein overlooked the inevitable deprivation implied in this, indicates her possible belief that she could not manage theoretically without the notion of an innately determined primary envy. To her mind, only this could provide a satisfactory explanation for destructive and self-destructive tendencies which have innate roots.

However, as suggested, 'Envy and gratitude' is a text that offers two alternative versions of infancy and two possible stories about human nature. Envy is not the only agent that is invoked to account for innate destructiveness and, in fact, the text contains another version of infancy, in which Klein considers another kind of constitutional agent that predisposes individuals to different degrees of destructiveness. This other agent is almost added to her paper as an afterthought, and indeed remains so marginal as to have escaped widespread notice. And yet its theoretical significance far outweighs this scant attention. The other constitutional agent is what Klein comes to describe as a 'fragile ego'. With it Klein depicts another possibility: that there is no difference in the amount of death instinct, destructiveness or envy with which different infants arrive in the world. Instead, there are innately determined variations in the way that infants experience life's normal flaws, or ordinary daily deprivation. What, in adult terms, seems like good enough provision may come across as insufficient to some infants. Such infants, born with a 'weak ego', are fragile for a variety of reasons and so require more comforting and nurture. They are more easily disturbed when care is temporarily interrupted and are altogether more persecuted by life's ordinary flaws. Such infants may grow up to be individuals who are easily outraged by small omissions in environmental attention, and who are also easily stirred to envy. The implications of postulating a weak ego are substantial for Klein's theory of envy, because she realizes that what she describes as the strength or weakness of the ego is a constitutional determinant responsible for a number of personal characteristics, among them the degree of envy to which an individual will succumb. Klein goes on to explain that: 'Difficulties in bearing anxiety, tension and frustration are an expression of an ego which, from the beginning of postnatal life, is weak in proportion to the intense destructive impulses and persecutory feelings it experiences.'

The thinking in this passage does not permit a quantification of individual destructive impulses in general terms. They are only excessive or moderate in relation to the ego's capacity to handle them, and within a context of two interacting mental phenomena – the ego and the impulses. Klein concludes that '... a constitutionally strong ego does not easily become a prey to envy'. Such thinking is not, as it might first seem, at odds with her view that the early ego is unintegrated and largely lacks cohesion. The early ego-state should not be confused with mere weakness, because it is equipped from the beginning to interact with the world through projections and introjections. However, not all infants are uniformly able to engage in this developmental dialogue with the world. Individual variations at birth mean that some infants are able to tolerate worldly impingements more easily or even welcome them with instinctive curiosity. To other infants, worldly impingements are more disturbing and persecuting. Their primitive aggression is easily mobilized and their psyche gets into the habit of deflecting, rather than accommodating, worldly impressions, thus resorting overmuch to splitting mechanisms.

Klein's thinking on the question of a constitutionally fragile ego was already in evidence twelve years earlier, in her 1945 paper on the Oedipus complex. It is noteworthy that in her account of the two child patients that she selected to illustrate her ideas, she ascribed innate weaknesses to both. Furthermore, she took trouble to show that constitutional factors interacted with adverse environmental conditions. Klein understood the internal state of the ten-year-old Richard in terms of its interaction with 'constitutional as well as environmental factors'.[12] An innately weak ego meant that he found it difficult to cope with early anxieties so that his 'oral, urethral and anal-sadistic anxieties were excessive' and, in turn, his 'fixation to these levels was very strong.' Added to such initial fragility, there was a host of environmental difficulties. Richard's breast-feeding relationship had been short and unsatisfactory. He had been a delicate infant who suffered from illnesses. The home atmosphere was 'not altogether happy' because of 'a lack of warmth' between his parents. Added to this, his mother, though not outright ill, was none the less 'a depressive type'. She thus worried excessively about her delicate, illness-prone son, and this poor beginning led to Richard becoming 'rather a disappointment to her'. At the same time, she favoured his successful older brother.

With Rita, similar interactions between constitutional and environmental factors are noted by Klein. Constitutional factors meant that Rita's 'oral sadistic impulses were very strong'. In the face of these, her ego was weak so that 'her capacity to tolerate tension of any kind was unusually low'.[13] Klein describes these difficulties as 'the constitutional characteristics that determined her reaction to the early frustrations that she suffered'. Klein also notes these frustrations. Weaning had caused Rita distress from which she did not fully recover by the time she came to see Klein, so that she was still a poor eater. Rita's mother then became anxious about her toilet training, and this caused further difficulties between mother and daughter. Klein concludes that 'Rita's obsessional neurosis proved to be clearly connected with her early habit of training.'[14] Klein's account of pathology in both of these child patients thus depicts complex interactions between a constitutional ego-strength that the infant brings into the world, and environmental deficits that this constitution encounters. A weak ego is defined in this exchange between constitution and the environment, its weakness determined in relation to various degrees of deficiency in the interaction.

By the time of the 1957 envy theory, although Klein is not explicit on this, a fragile ego is sufficient to count as an innate indicator of individual envy, and dispenses with the theoretical need to postulate an innately determined quantity of it derived from the death instinct. The notion of a fragile ego is also entirely in keeping with important currents in the rest of Klein's thinking. A strong ego withstands anxiety better, is not easily assaulted by ordinary disturbances and hitches, and enables the subject to feel less deprived of goodness and have less need to envy. Klein reinforces the point about the fragile ego in her discussion of technique, where she repeatedly states the need for patients to internalize good experiences and so strengthen themselves until they no longer need to envy.

The result in 'Envy and gratitude' is two different stories about human nature. The first depicts the human individual as coming into the world with a certain constitutionally determined quantity of death instinct, expressed as envy. This is the story of a human being who bears the destruction of death in his instinctual equipment. The second version depicts a human being as arriving in the world with greater or lesser degrees of ego strength, and hence more or less prone to react with persecution and aggression. This is the story of a human being who is born unequal to life's challenges and who struggles with his own instinctual turmoil in the face of deep survival anxieties. These two narratives contain an age-old dilemma of whether human aggression is innate or reactive, and whether the human individual starts out life as a perpetrator or a victim. And while the second possibility is less emphasized by Klein at this stage in her career, it none the less fits better with some of her central lifelong beliefs, such as her conviction that the ego is at first fragile and liable to 'fall into bits', and that development is the painstaking struggle to establish within the psyche a core of goodness which unites and strengthens it.

NOTES

1. Grosskurth, P. (1985) *Melanie Klein*. Attributed to Clare Winnicott. London: Maresfield Library. p. 414.
2. Jones, E. (1955) Preface to *New Directions in Psycho-Analysis*. London: The Hogarth Press.

3. Klein, M. (1975) 'Envy and gratitude', in *Envy and Gratitude*. London: The Hogarth Press. (First published in 1957.) p. 178.

4. ibid., p. 179.

5. ibid., p. 180.

6. ibid., p. 182.

7. ibid., p. 182.

8. ibid., p. 189.

9. ibid., p. 183.

10. ibid., p. 190.

11. ibid., p. 194.

12. Klein, M. (1975) 'The Oedipus complex in the light of early anxieties', in *Love, Guilt and Reparation*. London: The Hogarth Press. (First published in 1945.) p. 372.

13. ibid., p. 399.

14. ibid., p. 399.

CHAPTER 13

'An unsatisfied longing for an understanding without words' – Loneliness

K lein's last paper, published posthumously in 1963, has little trace of the grim conclusions that emerged in parts of the 1957 envy theory, particularly as implied in the notion of a gratuitous envy of the good, fulfilling object. In this last work, devoted to the subject of loneliness, Klein's outlook returns to a more compassionate, poignant appraisal of the human psyche. She gives further emphasis to the constitutional misfortune of the infant born with a weak ego, and shows how someone who is thus disadvantaged by nature, is ill-equipped from the beginning to cope with the considerable hardships and pains of the world. In a much more mellow tone, Klein's last paper leaves us more with sympathy than disapproval for humankind. She vividly conjures a state of fundamental human weakness in the face of turbulent instincts and internal conflict, and shows this to be inherent in the condition of living. She also traces the origin of such painful conflict to the realities of life and death that necessarily loom over every struggle for survival. At the same time, less is made in Klein's last paper of the wanton savagery, envy and destructiveness that she had always ascribed to the instinctual motivational system of the developing individual.

The subject of the last paper befits its mellow tone. Loneliness, defined as the 'yearning for an unattainable perfect internal state' is a human inevitability in a mind that is shaped by object relations from birth, and that depends on them thereafter.[1] In this last paper, life is seen as a quest to allay loneliness, and much of what motivates us is regarded as our yearning to have a sense of being mentally accompanied on our life's journey. We long to develop a mind that is understood and recognised, both by others and by ourselves.

The theory of loneliness is brief, but none the less lucidly fitted by Klein into her lifelong thinking. Her mature beliefs are succinctly and eloquently articulated, with an undoubted empathy for the conflicted human individual. She reminds the reader with a renewed clarity how the earliest ego is initially 'lacking in cohesion and dominated by splitting mechanisms', thus confirming two kinds of fragmentation processes. She also discusses the use of splitting defences for the positive purpose of growth, so that '. . . the good part of the ego and the good object are in some measure protected, since aggression is directed away from them'.[2] She reiterates how such necessary splitting alternates with a drive towards integration, and how this becomes essential for the secure introjection of the good object into the psyche to form the core of the developing ego. Klein also now re-emphasizes her view that these early events are far more than sensual, libidinal experiences. She is not merely discussing a pleasurable breast-feeding relationship, but a crucial psychical contact with the first good object. Most importantly, a good relationship with the maternal object 'implies a close contact between the unconscious of the mother and of the child'. This first psychic intimacy is '. . . the foundation for the most complete experience of being understood and is essentially linked with the pre-verbal state'.[3] Klein is now able to add that since the pre-verbal understanding of earliest infancy is never recaptured in quite the same way again, its loss is one of the early sources of loneliness. By implication, the later quest for intimacy is never fully satisfied, so that '. . . however gratifying it is . . . to express thoughts and feelings to a congenial person, there remains an unsatisfied longing for an understanding without words.'

The experience of loneliness does not end with this. At every stage, the object-seeking human infant is bound to re-experience the spurn and disappointment of loneliness. In the paranoid-schizoid position, 'paranoid insecurity is one of the roots of loneliness'. The infant feels alone in a hostile world, and, furthermore, needs to struggle with the process of psychical integration. Since this never feels completed, the individual never reaches a state of experiencing 'a complete understanding and acceptance' of his emotions. And it is not only others who are felt to be incapable of offering such a whole understanding. The individual remains with a permanent sense that aspects of the self, though intensely experienced within, continue to elude self-understanding. This partial self-alienation creates a sense of incompleteness, a yearning for unavailable aspects of the self and a resulting inner loneliness. In the depressive position, ambivalence and grief may leave the individual isolated with, and threatened by, the degree of his own hatred. The individual feels unworthy and deserted by a good object which keeps eluding his secure grasp, externally through absences, and internally through aggressive destructions.

It is noteworthy that in these descriptions Klein uses the word 'painful' repeatedly, and also generally portrays the conflicts of development as a suffering. For example she describes the process of integration as 'extremely painful', and when discussing the plight of the schizophrenic talks about how he feels 'hopelessly in bits' and alone with his 'misery'. There is no evidence that Klein wishes her last word to the world to indicate a moral disapproval of paranoid-schizoid states, as has sometimes been mistakenly assumed. The individual who exemplifies such states in extreme form, that is, the schizophrenic, is pitied and not judged; 'it is important', Klein tells us, 'not to underrate the schizophrenic's pain and suffering'. This is certainly the language of compassion and not of condemnation. In keeping with it, Klein warns against adopting a judgemental, super-ego outlook. She suggests that the individual's loneliness is exacerbated when a 'harsh super-ego has engendered a very strong repression of destructive impulses'. Just as her own super-ego does not condemn humanity harshly in this last work, she advises that a judgemental super-ego does not promote a healthy development in the child. She thus advocates a tolerance towards children's destructiveness, even though she does not mean by this that parents must be submissive. She suggests that '... the parents, by accepting the child's destructive impulses and showing that they can protect themselves against his aggressiveness, can diminish his anxiety'.[4] She also warns that a harsh super-ego in the child is undesirable because it 'can never be felt to forgive destructive impulses', and so encourages the denial of aggressive emotions instead of an appropriate processing of them.

This note of tolerance infuses also Klein's theoretical conclusions, and is accompanied by an added emphasis not on the malevolence of an envious disposition, but on a constitutionally tragic predicament – the weak ego at birth:

> If, however, the ego is very weak, which I consider to be an innate feature, and if there have been difficulties at birth and the beginning of life, the capacity to integrate – to bring together the split-off parts of the ego – is also weak, and there is in addition a greater tendency to split in order to avoid anxiety aroused by the destructive impulses.[5]

Such fundamental disadvantages are of crucial consequences. They lead to 'an incapacity to bear anxiety' which is of 'far-reaching importance'. They result in a lesser ability to integrate experiences and work through early anxieties. By comparison, the ability to introject the good breast with some security is now described as a 'characteristic of some innate strength in the ego'.[6] It immediately sets in motion a benign cycle, since 'a strong ego is less liable to fragmentation', and more capable of 'achieving a measure of integration and a good early relation to the primal object'. Therefore, destructive impulses are mitigated, which lessens the harshness of the super-ego. The growing child has a greater tolerance of deficiencies in the object and the world, which, in turn, ensures a 'happy relation to the loved object', as well as a valuation of the mother's 'presence and affection'.[7] Within such a propitious early situation, introjective and projective processes are likely to function well and reinforce feelings of closeness and of understanding and being understood, all of which mitigate loneliness.

Klein is clear on how this optimal early scenario, which mostly depends on a munificent fate, mitigates destructiveness and envy. She hardly refers to envy in her last paper, and when she does, it is always in the context of adversity. She concludes that the best natural insurance against envy is the strong ego's greater capacity for enjoyment. This capacity enables pleasure to be experienced securely and without 'too much greed for inaccessible gratifications', or indeed 'excessive resentment about frustration.' Ultimately this means that '... a child who, in spite of some envy and jealousy can identify with the pleasures and the gratifications of members of his family circle, will be able to do so in relation to other people in later life.'[8]

In this last work Klein depicts a human individual who is lonely from infancy onwards, in the sense of battling firstly to integrate himself, and then to keep his good object. And while loneliness is viewed by her as a lifelong reality, she realizes also the special plight of old age. She was herself writing in old age, and obviously with some of her own loneliness in mind. Grosskurth describes her last days as physically difficult. Klein complained about progressive osteoarthritis and excessive tiredness, but otherwise noted that 'the children give me much joy'. This joy was specifically due to her beloved son Erich, who had been so important at the start of her career, and who now also enabled her to experience the pleasures of grandmotherhood. When shortly after this Klein's extreme fatigue was discovered to be partly caused by a cancer of the colon, she was obliged to go into hospital. She was visited there by her colleagues, and Grosskurth notes that 'Hanna Segal, Esther Bick and Betty Joseph came to see her regularly'.[9] Betty Joseph was also aware how much Klein was still able to relish her remaining days. At the same time, Klein retained her strong-willed, impetuous aspect, stubbornly rejecting the hospital night nurse, whom she disliked. Judging this behaviour in the light of her own theory, it seems that by this stage she understandably projected a death-bearing, bad internal object on to the night nurse. Klein died in hospital, but does indeed appear to have been both lucid and emotionally engaged with others to the last.

Perhaps the secret for her ability to accept her life's ending can be glimpsed in some of the thinking in the loneliness paper, which was actually completed for presentation a year before her death. When reflecting on the predicament of old age, Klein suggests that the optimal way to endure it is through 'gratitude for past pleasures without too much resentment because they are no longer available'.[10] Just before death, as immediately after birth, the human individual needs to cherish the good in order to counter a primal grievance against an unfair world. However, Klein does not leave us with an idealized picture of a grateful old age. She notes pragmatically that sometimes 'preoccupation with the past' is a defence adopted 'in order to avoid the frustrations of the present'.[11] Sometimes old-age nostalgia represents gratitude for good memories, but at other times, boring ruminations about the past represent a defence against acknowledging present lacks and frustrations.

Klein's writing thus ends with a lonely human being, rather than an envious destroyer driven by original sin. This is not to suggest that she disowned her earlier insights into human aggression. But her outlook now intimated that we are the victims of the worst part of our nature. This is why loneliness is partly tragic, since some of it is brought on the individual by himself, and by the destructive processes that have made it impossible to keep within a safe good object. Because of this, loneliness gives added impetus to our search for social ties. It creates a 'great need to turn to external objects', and so drives some of our quest for object relations.[12]

It is indeed fitting that a theory of object relations should end with a study of loneliness. Klein concludes with a statement on the human need for others. The loneliness paper, though, has other, more complex implications. The lonely states depicted by Klein are ultimately traced to a lifelong conflict between love and destructiveness. However, this conflict is also seen as rooted in our very sociability as a species. It is the extent of our need for others and our ceaseless quest for kindred spirits in the world, that are partly responsible for the intensity of our disappointments. Others are never as fully available to us as we wish them to be, nor indeed are we as available to them as we would like to think. In Klein's mature thinking, our destructiveness is triggered when we are unable to tolerate such disappointments, rather than out of a selfish need to obliterate others in order to remain alone. Klein's work on loneliness thus conveys to us her meaningful last thoughts. And while there is no evidence that she intended to revise the content of her earlier theoretical framework, nor amend her sober vision of human cruelty and destructiveness, she concludes by advocating a scientific, morally neutral appraisal of these.

This has substantial implications towards how Klein would have viewed clinical technique. There is little indication that she would have favoured a punitive or suspicious approach, the kind in which the patient's supposedly perverse and destructive motivations are foremost in the analyst's mind. For some reason, such harshness did creep into the technique of some psychoanalysts, mistaken by them for an essentially Kleinian feature. Yet there were others who noted this distortion and objected to it. Already in 1936, Riviere complained that 'The very great importance of analysing aggressive tendencies has perhaps carried some analysts off their feet, and in some quarters is defeating its own ends.'[13] In a similar vein, Spillius noted in 1988, when discussing Kleinian technique, that '. . . most of the papers of the 1950s and 1960s, especially those by young and inexperienced analysts, tend to emphasize the patient's destructiveness.'[14] Spillius rightly emphasizes that this tendency represented 'a step backward from the work of Klein herself'. It is possible that a harsh technique resulted in part from some of the typical insecurities that have always beset professional psychoanalysts. In their struggle to work in depth and to retain a properly neutral stance, some young analysts may have adopted clinical harshness as a form of rigour, as if rigour should reside in the severity of the analyst's outlook, rather than in the degree of awareness that is created for the patient. Whether or not this has indeed been the case, it is also possible to understand why it was Klein's rather austere vision that sometimes fuelled such anxious approaches to the patient's psychic life.

There is, indeed, no denying that a melancholy element casts a shadow on many of Klein's formulations. However, it never reaches the status of a conclusion on human nature. Klein certainly spells out the savagery of human destructiveness forcefully, but in the end, sees it as poised in battle against life instincts. She also sees it as dependent on factors that are beyond individual control, among them the constitutional capacity of the ego to withstand the pains and frustrations of life. To this is added the importance of external factors, which may aid or exacerbate initial weaknesses. There is no general message in this about whether humanity is destructive or benign, only the idea that it needs to battle with destructive and loving tendencies. Klein's contribution to our thinking was to point out how this battle might begin and evolve, and suggest factors, both internal and external, that contribute to its outcome.

NOTES

1. Klein, M. (1975) 'On the sense of loneliness', in *Envy and Gratitude*. London: The Hogarth Press. (First published in 1963.) p. 300.
2. ibid., p. 300.
3. ibid., p. 301.
4. ibid., p. 312.
5. ibid., p. 303.
6. ibid., p. 309.
7. ibid., p. 310.
8. ibid., p. 310.
9. Grosskurth, P. (1985) *Melanie Klein*. London: Maresfield Library. p. 461.
10. Klein, M. (1975) 'On the sense of loneliness', in *Envy and Gratitude*. London: The Hogarth Press. (First published in 1963.) p. 311.
11. ibid., p. 311.
12. ibid., p. 312.
13. Riviere, J. (1991) 'A contribution to the analysis of a negative therapeutic reaction', in M. A. Hughes (ed.) *The Inner World and Joan Riviere*. London: Karnak Books. (First published 1936.) p. 142.
14. Spillius, E. B. (1988) *Melanie Klein Today, Vol I.: Mainly Theory*. London: Routledge/Tavistock. p. 6.

Index